Dog-Friendly Europe

CONWAY

Bloomsbury Publishing Plc
50 Bedford Square, London, WC1B 3DP, UK
Bloomsbury Publishing Ireland Limited,
29 Earlsfort Terrace, Dublin 2, D02 AY28, Ireland

BLOOMSBURY, CONWAY and the Conway logo are trademarks of Bloomsbury Publishing Plc

First published in Great Britain, 2026

Copyright © Lottie Gross, 2026

Illustrations © Richard Thomson (rt-imagery.com)

Lottie Gross has asserted her right under the Copyright, Designs and Patents Act, 1988, to be identified as Author of this work

This book is a guide for when you spend time outdoors. Undertaking any activity outdoors carries with it some risks that cannot be entirely eliminated. For example, you might get lost on a route or caught in bad weather. Before you spend time outdoors, we therefore advise that you always take the necessary precautions, such as checking weather forecasts and ensuring that you have all the equipment you need. Any walking routes that are described in this book should not be relied upon as a sole means of navigation, so we recommend that you refer to an Ordnance Survey map or authoritative equivalent.

This book may also reference businesses and venues. Whilst every effort is made by the author and the publisher to ensure the accuracy of the business and venue information contained in our books before they go to print, changes to such information can occur during the production and lifetime of a publication. Therefore, we also advise that you check with businesses or venues for the latest information before setting out.

All internet addresses given in this book were correct at the time of going to press. Bloomsbury Publishing Plc does not have any control over, or responsibility for, any third-party websites referred to or in this book. The author and the publisher regret any inconvenience caused if some facts have changed or sites have ceased to exist, but can accept no responsibility for any such changes.

All rights reserved. No part of this publication may be: i) reproduced or transmitted in any form, electronic or mechanical, including photocopying, recording or by means of any information storage or retrieval system without prior permission in writing from the publishers; or ii) used or reproduced in any way for the training, development or operation of artificial intelligence (AI) technologies, including generative AI technologies. The rights holders expressly reserve this publication from the text and data mining exception as per Article 4(3) of the Digital Single Market Directive (EU) 2019/790

A catalogue record for this book is available from the British Library

Library of Congress Cataloguing-in-Publication data has been applied for

ISBN: PB: 978-1-84486-704-2; ePub: 978-1-84486-705-9; ePDF: 978-1-84486-703-5

2 4 6 8 10 9 7 5 3 1

Typeset in Aestetico Formal by Phil Beresford

Printed in UAE by Oriental Press

To find out more about our authors and books visit www.bloomsbury.com and sign up for our newsletters
For product safety related questions contact productsafety@bloomsbury.com

Dog-Friendly Europe

EPIC HOLIDAYS FOR YOU AND YOUR HOUND

LOTTIE GROSS

Conway

LONDON • OXFORD • NEW YORK • NEW DELHI • SYDNEY

↓ Arty overlooks the the Oderteich reservoir in Germany's Harz Mountains

CONTENTS

1
FIND BLISS ON THE BEACHES OF NORTHERN FRANCE
24

2
ADVENTURE ON THE ISLANDS AND BEACHES OF BRITTANY
36

3
CYCLING, SEA AND SAND IN THE NETHERLANDS
46

4
EAT YOUR WAY AROUND THE PINTXOS BARS OF SAN SEBASTIÁN
54

5
LIVE LIKE FRENCH KINGS AND QUEENS IN THE LOIRE VALLEY
64

6
TAKE IN CITY AND SCENERY IN WALLONIA
76

7
RIDE STEAM TRAINS AND HIT THE MOUNTAIN TRAILS IN GERMANY
86

8
WATCH THE HUMAN TOWERS OF CATALUNYA
98

9
CRUISE THE CANALS FOR COASTAL FUN IN THE SOUTH OF FRANCE
108

10
GO URBAN HIKING IN THE GERMAN CAPITAL
118

11
CITIES, SWIMMING AND SPECTACULAR
SCENERY IN EASTERN GERMANY
128

12
EXPLORE RAILS AND TRAILS IN THE ALENTEJO
140

13
TOUR THE TERRACED VINEYARDS OF THE DOURO
150

14
SEE SPECTACULAR ARCHITECTURE
IN THE CATALAN CAPITAL
160

15
SUN YOURSELF ON THE BEACHES OF THE COSTA BRAVA
170

16
TAKE A BALTIC BEACH BREAK IN NORTHERN GERMANY
180

17
EXPLORE THE CHRISTMAS MARKETS
OF LAKE GENEVA
190

↓ Morzine, France

18
GO SNOWSHOEING IN THE FRENCH ALPS
202

19
TAKE THE TRAIN TO THE TOP OF EUROPE
210

20
HIKE OTHERWORLDLY LANDSCAPES IN THE SOUTH OF FRANCE
220

21
SEE CITY AND SUMMITS IN THE STRIKING DOLOMITES
232

22
SUN, SAND AND A SIDE OF CULTURE IN ITALY
242

23
TAKE A TOUR OF QUINTESSENTIAL ENGLISH COUNTRYSIDE
252

24
WALK IN THE FOOTSTEPS OF GIANTS ON
THE NORTHERN IRISH COAST
262

25
GO BEACH HOPPING IN THE SCOTTISH ISLANDS
272

INDEX
285

PHOTO CREDITS
288

INTRODUCTION

When I signed the contract for this book, I had the creeping realisation that I may have made an enormous mistake. I was quite intimidated by the prospect of researching and writing each of these chapters. You see, my secondary school French language skills are basic at best, my GCSE German non-existent these days, and those few Spanish lessons I took in my early twenties did little more than teach me to order gin and tonics at a bar (*'gin tonic, por favor?'*, if you're wondering). With very few language skills and a dog by my side, I felt that this time I might be somewhat out of my depth. How would I communicate and advocate for my slightly anxious, sensitive little dog? How would I know whether he's allowed inside a restaurant or cafe?

I needn't have worried. Over the months I spent touring the Continent with Arty, my Manchester Terrier, I learned that we dog owners have an unwritten, universal language. We don't need words, for there are glances, wry smiles and sympathetic head tilts that communicate everything we need to know and understand about one another. There's a secret camaraderie among people who care for or have cared for a four-legged creature, and on our adventures we discovered a deep respect for those of us who are brave enough to travel far and wide with our best friends at our side.

I didn't need to ask if my dog was allowed inside, because half the time on my approach to a cafe or restaurant or sun-kissed terrace in a city square I could see delight spread across the faces of the staff, who readied themselves to greet Arty before they had even asked where I wanted to sit. When he wasn't greeted with open arms and treats from behind

↑ A dog park in Barcelona, Spain
← The Viking longship on Unst, Shetland, Scotland

the bar, he was entirely ignored – as if it was a fact of life that a woman and her small dog should be allowed to share a croissant in the morning.

On my two-month-long trip across France, Spain and Portugal, which was spent mostly in a tiny 28-year-old caravan that dutifully followed my car along motorways and mountain roads, we had countless conversations that transcended the language barrier. I somehow had entire discussions about my dog's breed (or 'race', as it translates in many countries) without speaking a word of the local dialect, purely through mutually understood gestures. I was able to explain that yes, my dog wears a GPS on his back because he's a much faster runner than I am and he has a penchant for literally anything that moves. And I was able to advocate for him – a sometimes nervous, reactive boy – among other dog owners, who understood what was required when I used my body to block his sight and threw treats down on to the floor as another dog passed us on a trail.

Thanks to this, and the ease of travelling around the European continent, our road trips around the Netherlands, Belgium, Germany and Switzerland were a resounding success – except for the time we got kicked off the train in Leipzig for the dog not wearing a muzzle (a mistake

I won't make again after we had to walk the entire length of the city for an hour in the dark to get back to our hotel). And our epic train journey from Oxfordshire to Venice was as much a joy as it was a learning curve – the biggest lesson being that the dog's bladder is made of steel, after he held it for over 24 hours because Venice didn't have a suitable patch of grass to pee on after our sleeper train arrived. (Fear not, he found a lovely rose bush to let it all out on in the gardens of the JW Marriott while we were enjoying a tour from the general manager.)

The only real disaster we experienced during our entire research period was a car breakdown on the motorway in France, but even then, we were able to cruise to the parking lot at the nearest toll plaza where, while we waited to be rescued, I made lunch in the caravan and the dog sunbathed on the tarmac, making eyes at the lorry driver in the space next to ours who was cooking meatballs on a small stove during his break.

Travelling the European continent with a dog is real pleasure, but be warned: it doesn't come without dangers. In showing my dog the European way of life – the French baguettes and rotisserie chickens for lunch, the pintxos bars in San

↓ Arty in the Dolomites, Italy

↑ Belgian beer in a bar in La-Roche-en-Ardenne, Belgium
→ The Château de Valmer, Loire Valley, France

Sebastián, the sunny vineyards of Portugal and Catalunya – I have created a multicultural monster on four legs. Arty, an already entitled and frankly overly demanding Manchester Terrier, has seen a better way of living and now he spends his days back in the UK no doubt dreaming of becoming a winery dog, who can snooze among the vines of the Douro before pottering around between picnicking tourists who, with the generosity of the inebriated, dispense pieces of tangy cheese at will. He now has aspirations beyond my means and I'm quite sure he looks at me with a new kind of disdain on our soggy, wintry walks back in Britain. So explore this world at your peril – or at least at the peril of your credit card, which is best kept well away from your dog should they somehow learn to use it.

I had long thought our home country of England couldn't be matched for dog-friendliness. In the five years since I've owned dogs and travelled with my pets, I've been astonished at the breadth of experiences available to us dog owners, from hotels offering dog-friendly afternoon teas to the museums that let you learn with your pet by your side. 'The UK is surely the world's most dog-friendly destination', I thought. Until I wrote this book.

Now I know you can visit the châteaux of the Loire, sip cava in the vineyards of the Catalan hills, and ride the rails to Europe's highest train station for epic views across glaciers in Switzerland, all with your dog by your side. There are dog-mad hotels that serve tapas for pets and will provide spa gowns with their initials on should you book the most luxurious pet package. And there are beaches reserved specifically for our animals to have their own sun, sea and sand holidays.

The 11 countries I have travelled to research this guide are not representative of the whole European continent, of course. I couldn't include everywhere, not least because it would take years to do so. But here in these pages lies a good start, and what's missing is no doubt a good excuse to return and write more – after all, I know that's what Arty wants.

How to use this book

This book is a holidaying guide to a hand-picked selection of European destinations. It features 11 different countries across its 25 chapters, and each of those chapters focuses on a specific region or city. Some destinations are closer together than others, meaning you can plan a multi-destination adventure with your dog, and many of them are so jam-packed with activities and hikes, you'll want to reserve a good week or two just for that one place.

Chapters are ordered by driving time (shortest to longest) from the nearest port of entry when arriving on to the Continent from the UK. The only exception to this is the UK-centric chapters that are located towards the end of the book for adventures closer to home for British readers, or adventures further afield for those coming from the Continent.

You should be able to search for any specific attractions or places listed in this book on your chosen maps app (I use Google Maps, for example, on which I can save my desired places to visit for ease), but where a location might be difficult to find – such as a remote beach or a specific dog-friendly area of a beach, I have used the what3words address to identify the location. what3words addresses look like this: ///travel.with. dogs (incidentally, that address points to a suburb of Beijing, which is most definitely not included in this guide). You can find a what3words location by going to what3words.com and typing the address in as it is listed in the guide; this will point you to the specific three-metre-squared area on the map.

Each chapter has all the essential information you need, but I've used symbols in the accommodation listings to denote specific features. Here's what they mean...

 This is a campsite.

 This is a hotel or B&B.

 This is a self-catering property.

 This accommodation has beaches nearby.

 The number of dogs allowed per room or property.

 The number of people in a self-catering property.

 This property has grassy gardens.

 This property has an enclosed garden.

 This is a luxurious property.

 This is the author's pick as an accommodation that stood out beyond the rest.

Dogs on tour: what you need to know before you go

If you've travelled around your home country with your dog, you're already set in good stead for adventures across Europe. But there are some things certain nations do differently. Here are a few things to consider before you travel:

Dog culture

Local attitudes to dogs vary across the European continent – not every country mollycoddles their pets like we do in the UK (dog-friendly spa day, anyone?). In my experiences with Arty, the Swiss, French and Italians are generally the most dog-loving peoples, the latter even allowing dogs to sit up at the table in some restaurants and inside the trolleys in certain supermarkets (Migross and Despar have been known to allow them). In Belgium and the Netherlands, dogs are generally accepted as part of the family, and while you might find fewer places to dine with them indoors, you'll still find they are a welcome presence when allowed.

Conversely, places like Spain and Portugal have a more reserved relationship with their pets, and you may well find lots of dogs are still outdoor dwellers, living in garden kennels and sometimes chained up outside properties as guard dogs. As such, it pays to be mindful of the local culture around dog ownership: if you're somewhere where people might not be used to mingling with dogs in museums or on boat trips, be respectful of their space and ensure your dog doesn't become an irritation or a nuisance.

Rules around dogs vary throughout the Continent too, but wherever you go, dogs aren't usually allowed inside shops selling food, though outdoor markets are fair game and Europe has plenty of those to keep your fridge stocked.

Dangers to dogs in Europe

With new and exciting places come new dangers, too. Ticks and fleas are the biggest worry for dogs in Europe. April to September is the main season for ticks,

↑ Arty at the Nobu Hotel, Barcelona, Spain

though they can still be active in winter in some places, so always carry a tick removal tool. But there are other dangers you may not have come across at home, such as the pesky pine processionary caterpillar, whose long hairs carry a protein that can be toxic for dogs. The caterpillars lie dormant in nests in pine trees over winter and tend to come out in spring in warmer climates, such as southern France, Spain and Portugal. Keep an eye out on the ground from March throughout summer, as one sniff or snaffle of one of these could cause a severe reaction in your dog, which can sometimes be fatal.

Sand flies also present a danger for dogs: they carry the leishmania parasite, which can cause leishmaniasis – a sometimes-fatal disease that causes skin lesions and, occasionally, kidney failure. The flies are usually only found in southern Europe and the European Centre for Disease Prevention and Control (ecdc.europa.eu) has a useful map of affected areas; consult your vet regarding vaccination if you're travelling to impacted regions.

Muzzle culture

In some countries, you might be expected to muzzle your dog in certain places, like on public transport, in busy museums or on ferries. Spain, France and Italy have rules around muzzling dogs on public transport, and you might find you're asked to muzzle your dog in other places, too. Carry one with you at all times, just in case. A box muzzle that allows your dog space to pant and drink is essential in warmer climates.

Closing time

This final point is less about dogs and more of a Continental quirk. You might find in some places, such as France,

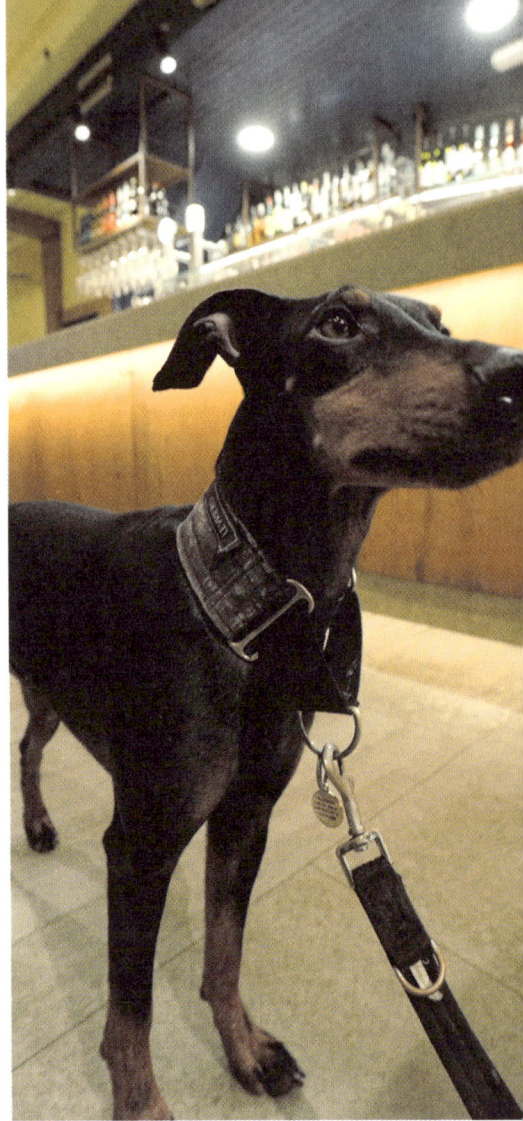

↑ Sampling the pintxos bars of San Sebastián, Spain

Portugal and Spain, that many shops and attractions close during lunchtime hours, so do plan ahead for any visits you're hoping to make. Across many countries in Europe, you'll also find that most museums and attractions are closed on Mondays and Tuesdays to allow for weekend opening hours. In Germany, don't get caught short without supplies on a Sunday, as the vast majority of shops will be shut, too.

INTRODUCTION

Getting onto the Continent from the UK

There are myriad options for travelling between the UK and Europe, but not all of them are dog-friendly, and those that are may not be suitable for some dogs (especially nervous pets or those with separation anxiety). My preferred option for getting across the English Channel is always LeShuttle (leshuttle.com), the car train that whizzes vehicles and their passengers across the stretch of sea between Kent and Calais. It takes 35 minutes and you needn't leave your dog alone at any point during the journey; they're even allowed inside the departure terminal, and there's an enclosed area for exercise and toileting before you travel.

Even if you're without your own vehicle, you can still travel on LeShuttle thanks to Le Pet Express (lepetexpress.com), a minibus service that operates from Ashford International train station and boards the LeShuttle trains with both humans and their pets inside (dogs travel in built-in crates next to their owners). Of course, the alternative way to reach Europe – whether driving or taking public transport – is by ferry, and there are several operators serving lots of destinations, including Amsterdam, the Hook of Holland, Calais, Roscoff, Santander and Bilbao. Discover Ferries has a helpful breakdown of the different pet accommodations on all ferry operators (discoverferries.com/travel-information/ferry-pet-facilities), but below are my favoured and recommended routes.

LeShuttle Folkestone–Calais (France)
Crossing time: 35 mins
Dog accommodation: in car together with owners
Foot passengers allowed with pets: no
Pet toileting: exercise area at terminal prior to boarding
leshuttle.com

P&O Ferries Dover–Calais (France)
Crossing time: 90 mins
Dog accommodation: in car; pet lounge
Foot passengers allowed with pets: no
Pet toileting: outside pet deck
poferries.com

Stena Line Harwich–Hook of Holland (Netherlands)
Crossing time: 6 hrs 30 mins
Dog accommodation: pet cabins; kennels
Foot passengers allowed with pets: yes
Pet toileting: outside pet deck
stenaline.co.uk

DFDS Newcastle–Amsterdam (Netherlands)
Crossing time: 15 hrs 45 mins
Dog accommodation: pet cabins; kennels
Foot passengers allowed with pets: yes
Pet toileting: outside pet deck
dfds.com

Brittany Ferries Plymouth–Santander (Spain)
Crossing time: 20 hrs 15 mins
Dog accommodation: pet cabins; kennels
Foot passengers allowed with pets: no
Pet toileting: outside pet deck
brittany-ferries.co.uk

Stena Line Liverpool–Belfast (Northern Ireland)
Crossing time: 8 hrs 30 mins
Dog accommodation: pet cabins; kennels
Foot passengers allowed with pets: yes
Pet toileting: outside pet deck
stenaline.co.uk

Driving vs public transport

The easiest way to travel with a dog is almost always by driving. If you're travelling to the Continent from the UK or Ireland, you'll no doubt have some long journeys ahead of you to reach the likes of Germany, Spain, Portugal and Italy. Long drives should be broken up so dogs can enjoy some exercise, and realistically you shouldn't spend more than six hours in the car on a given day. This means you'll need some strategic stop-overs in dog-friendly hotels along the route. This guide doesn't have an exhaustive list of dog-friendly properties throughout Europe, but brands like Moxy (moxy-hotels.marriott.com), B&B Hotels (hotel-bb.com), Holiday Inn (ihg.com) and NH Hotels (nh-hotels.com) are reliable and prolific chains with plenty of conveniently placed properties across the Continent.

If you don't drive, getting around Europe by train can be a joyously relaxing experience – providing you know the rules of the rails when it comes to dogs. Generally, dogs are allowed on most trains throughout the destinations in this book, but some operators have restrictions (such as Renfe in Spain, which only allows dogs of certain sizes) and many will ask that you muzzle your dog, or place them in a carrier that can sit on the floor beside your feet. If you're travelling by public transport, follow these tips for a smooth journey:

- **Try it at home first** – acclimatise your dog to travelling by train. Start with short stints watching the trains pass on the platforms before boarding, and take short journeys.
- **Bring water and a bowl** – make sure your dog stays hydrated. Some trains might be hot, while others might have dry air conditioning.
- **Consider packing a settle mat** – your dog will then have their own space to lie down on and relax. Do a little training with your settle mat at home before you travel so they recognise it as their space when they're travelling.
- **A long-lasting chew** – a pizzle or braided animal skin will keep them entertained on longer journeys.
- **Pack a muzzle** – some countries (such as Germany) require this by law, while many operators have their own rules and will enforce them with fines if necessary.
- **Keep them leashed** – dogs should always be on a lead on public transport and should never be allowed to bother other passengers.

↑ Arty on a train in Saint Valery-sur-Somme, France

Accommodation etiquette for dogs

Exploring and sleeping in new places can be both exciting and daunting for dogs, but there are several ways you can ensure they keep calm and carry on:

- **On arrival, do a sniff about** – while on the lead, let them follow their nose and have a sniff in the gardens of the property so they can familiarise themselves with their new surroundings. This will also ensure they have time for a toilet break before heading inside.
- **Bring their bed** – if you have space in the car or your case, bringing their own bed from home is a brilliant way to ensure they have their own familiar, safe space to retreat to in your cottage or hotel room.
- **Bring bedding** – generally, dogs aren't allowed on the beds in hotels or self-catering accommodations, so keeping them on the floor is essential. If you've got a dog that sleeps with you at home, it might be worth asking in advance if you can bring your own bedding so as not to make a mess on their linens.
- **Bring a throw for the bed or sofa** – many dogs won't understand why the sofa at home is OK, but the one in your hotel room is off-limits. Bringing a throw to cover it so they can relax with you is the best way to ensure everyone remains happy and comfortable.
- **Take a walk before breakfast** – even if you only do 15–20 minutes around the hotel gardens, a light stroll before you take the dog down to breakfast will ensure they've had a little exercise and stimulation – and a chance to toilet – before you settle down for your morning croissant, keeping them calm and collected while you dine.
- **Don't leave them alone unless allowed** – most properties will ask you not to leave your dog alone in the room while you're out – this is to stop the dog becoming distressed in its unfamiliar surroundings and becoming a nuisance to other guests through howling and barking. If you need dog-free time on your trip, consider booking a dog sitter or walker through the various platforms available. In Italy, use Bau Advisor (bauadvisor.it), which can be booked in conjunction with museum tickets in some cities. For France, PatchGuard (patch-guard.fr) is a reliable service. And across the Continent you will find sitters and walkers on rover.com, too.

↑ Arty partaking in a postlunch snooze at Hotel Antines, Italy

Camping with dogs

Europe is a brilliant place for camping with dogs. Whether you're bringing canvas, your own camper or motorhome, or you've a caravan to tow behind the car, there are campsites and motorhome stops aplenty, many in beautiful rural locations or right by the sea. The Caravan and Motorhome Club has hundreds of sites throughout Europe, the vast majority of which are dog-friendly (and many are listed in this guide), and sites like pitchup.com and acsi.eu have even more.

Camping with dogs does come with some extra challenges, though, so here are a few tips for those:

- **Get yourselves a tie-out tether** – these corkscrew-shaped metal sticks are an essential for any camper, as they offer a way to tether your dog safely by your tent or van, meaning you don't need to be leashed to your pet the entire time. Simply clip your dog's lead on to the tether, or loop it around the top, and they'll have relative free rein within the confines of their lead or longline. These are best used in conjunction with a harness to ensure any livelier dogs don't accidentally hurt their necks when running or lunging at the end of their lead.
- **Create your own garden** – if the tether system doesn't work for you, you can create your own enclosed garden around your camp with the use of an awning on your caravan or camper, along with wind breaks. This will mean they can roam within your camp safely without bothering others, though it still pays to pop a lead on the dog in case of a rogue escape.
- **Pick it up** – dogs should never be allowed to toilet on other people's pitches, and most campsites won't take kindly to your dog leaving mess on your own pitch, either. Be sure to take the dog for regular wee walks so they can toilet in the appropriate places. Most campsites will have a dog walk on site, or an enclosed dog area where they can run free.
- **Don't leave your dog in hot weather** – we all know dogs die in hot cars, and hot caravans and campers can be equally dangerous. Never leave your dog alone in the tent, caravan or campervan if the weather is hot. Or at all, for that matter, in case they whine or bark and disturb others.

→ Arty and Mabel wearing ear-protecting hats in Roscoff Botanical Gardens, France
↓ Arty and the author take some time out on Minn Beach, Shetland, Scotland

How to pack like a pro for your dog

Having spent several years travelling with my dogs, I've amassed a vast collection of occasionally useful but often utterly pointless dog-travel garb. There's an entire cupboard dedicated to 'Dog Things' in my house, most of which don't get to see the light of day. But there are a handful of select items I will never leave for a trip without. Here's what we're packing:

- A Ruffwear Webmaster three-point harness, to avoid Houdini moments (ruffwear.co.uk)
- A Halti double-ended training lead, handy for clipping around a table leg or allowing for shorter/longer lead when necessary (companyofanimals.com)
- A waterproof, wipe-clean settle mat for public transport and pubs (skinnydogcollective.com)
- A water bottle with in-built bowl for on-demand hydration without waste (amazon.co.uk)
- A waterproof longline (loveyourfurbabiesltd.co.uk)
- A non-slip dog bowl with a lid for dinner on the go (pupandkit.com)
- A Pawfit GPS tracker for peace of mind away from home (pawfit.com)
- An Equafleece for the chilly days (equafleece.co.uk)
- A dog raincoat for downpours (skinnydogcollective.com)

INTRODUCTION

Being responsible abroad

While it's wonderful we can bring our dogs on holiday with us almost anywhere, it's important to understand that sometimes they can have a negative impact on the environment. Being a responsible dog owner will mean we can all continue to travel with our dogs safely and with as little restriction as possible. Follow these rules and you won't go wrong:

- **Protect wildlife & livestock** – dogs should never be allowed to chase wildlife or livestock. This means keeping them on a lead around other animals, such as sheep, seals, deer, shoreline birds and ground-nesting birds. The only exception to this rule is cows – if you find yourselves in a field of over-curious cows, the safest thing to do is drop the lead and head for the nearest exit, then call your dog to follow.
- **Pick up poo** – even if you think nobody will step on it, you need to clean up your dog's mess and dispose of it correctly. This is because dog faeces has chemicals in it that can kill some plants and encourage growth of other, more invasive species. Picking up your dog's poo will mean healthier ecosystems for all.
- **Keep your dog on a lead in new places** – for much of your travels, you'll most likely be exploring new places. This means you're likely unaware of potential dangers, from steep cliff edges on coast paths to deep lakes, quicksand or boggy ground. By keeping your dog on a lead, you'll ensure they don't end up in dangerous situations.
- **Never leave them alone in hot cars** – the rate at which a car can heat up in the sun is exponential and it really doesn't take long for it to become dangerous for a dog. Never, ever leave your dog alone in the car – even with the windows cracked – for any length of time in the warm sun. When a dog's body temperature gets above 40°C it can trigger fatal heatstroke, which is very difficult to treat.

↓ Lido Beach, Italy

The dog-friendly phrasebook

ENGLISH	FRENCH	DUTCH	SPANISH	BASQUE	CATALAN	GERMAN	PORTUGUESE	ITALIAN
Is my dog allowed inside?	Mon chien est-il autorisé à entrer?	Is mijn hond binnen toegestaan?	¿Puedo dejar entrar a mi perro?	Nire txakurra barrura sartzea baimenduta al dago?	Es permet l'entrada del meu gos?	Ist mein Hund drinnen erlaubt?	O meu cão é permitido entrar?	Posso entrare col cane?
My dog is friendly.	Mon chien est amical.	Mijn hond is vriendelijk.	Mi perro/perra es amigable.	Nire txakurra lagunkoia da.	El meu gos és amigable.	Mein Hund ist freundlich.	O meu cão é amigável.	Il mio cane é dolce.
My dog is not friendly.	Mon chien n'est pas amical.	Mijn hond is niet vriendelijk.	Mi perro/perra no es amigable.	Nire txakurra ez da lagunkoia.	El meu gos no és amigable.	Mein Hund ist nicht freundlich.	O meu cão não é amigável.	Il mio cane non è molto amichevole.
My dog is nervous.	Mon chien est nerveux.	Mijn hond is nerveus.	Mi perro/perra es nervioso/a.	Nire txakurra urduri dago.	El meu gos està nerviós.	Mein Hund ist nervös.	O meu cão está nervoso.	Il mio cane è timido.
Can I let my dog off the lead?	Puis-je lâcher mon chien sans laisse?	Mag ik mijn hond loslaten?	¿Puedo soltar a mi perro/a de la correa?	Nire txakurra askatu dezaket?	Puc deixar el meu gos sense corretja?	Darf ich meinen Hund von der Leine lassen?	Posso soltar o meu cão da trela?	Posso lasciare il mio cane senza guinzaglio?

Where: Coastal Hauts-de-France, France

When: Year-round

Best port of entry: Calais

Driving time from port of entry: 10 mins

1
FIND BLISS ON THE BEACHES OF NORTHERN FRANCE

For Brits, Pas-de-Calais has often been somewhere you pass through on your pilgrimages to warmer climes – perhaps southern France where the summers swelter, or up to the Alps where winters contain adrenaline-fuelled fun. But this department in the Hauts-de-France region very much deserves your attention, not least because it's one of the most dog-friendly areas in the whole of France.

While many of this country's beaches are made off-limits to dogs in the height of summer, Pas-de-Calais and its neighbouring department, Somme, have a healthy smattering of exceptionally lovely stretches where your pets can enjoy the sun, sea and sand, too – even in August. And what's more, several of the local tourist offices have **dog goody bags** for visiting pets – pop into the likes of Le Touquet and Berck tourist offices and they'll get a pack of treats, map for walks and details on the beach rules, too.

This coastline is loftily named the Côte d'Opale (Opal Coast), and on a warm day when the sun is illuminating the ocean, it's easy to see why: this is a glistening, glittering stretch of coast, characterised by white cliffs like those it faces in Dover and grassy, undulating dunes backing its white- and yellow-sand beaches. It spans over 80km, all the way from Calais in the north down to Berck in the south, where just across the departmental border the **Baie de Somme** offers yet more seaside temptation.

Here you'll find everything, from bijou towns built for well-heeled Parisians to tiny, quaint villages where small family-run restaurants make the most of the locally caught seafood. There are purpose-built seaside resorts, natural reserves for fantastic walking, a **coastal path** with magnificent views of England, and several WWI and WWII sites for those with a keen interest in military history. From north to south, these are the highlights of coastal Hauts-de-France.

Calais

This seaside town has long had something of a bad rap. Often seen as a drive-through destination rather than somewhere to stick around, Calais has been overlooked,

↑ A common sign on the coast of Hauts-de-France
→ Sunset on the beach in Calais

FIND BLISS ON THE BEACHES OF NORTHERN FRANCE

ignored and sometimes even disparaged – issues around migration and refugee camps have painted a negative picture of it. But Calais is on the up. Significant investment in recent years has buoyed the town's economy and its tourism offering, and now a couple of days in Calais is most certainly a weekend well spent, not least because Brits can bag bargains on wine and beer before heading back across the Channel.

Beyond the booze outlets – and there are many – lies a town with a magnificent yellow-sand beach (open to dogs from mid-October to mid-May), a smattering of World War history and a creative community making the streets their own gallery.

Familiarise yourself with the lay of the land on a **walking tour** of the town's technicolour street art – a legacy of the annual street art festival that takes place each summer. You can follow a route past some of the highlights on gpsmycity. com or join one of the tourist office's tours throughout summer – ask at the tourist information on Boulevard Georges Clemenceau. Expect to see flamboyant parrots, colourful optical illusions and a surrealist, cartoon-like work of a seagull riding an octopus.

While the dog won't be allowed on the town beach in the height of summer, they can stroll with you on the seafront – just beware of the dragon. Each day in summer, and most days in winter, an enormous **mechanical dragon** emerges from its housing on Avenue Winston Churchill and roams the seafront, occasionally with humans riding on its back. Dogs can't hitch a lift on the dragon, but you can watch it menacingly prowl by the beach; keep clear of its nostrils – you don't want any singed whiskers when it blows fire from its nose.

For dogs that simply need to be on the sand, there's an unsupervised stretch of beach around 1.5km from the Compagnie du Dragon called **Blériot-Plage** where they're welcomed year-round. For greener walks, head to **Parc Saint-Pierre**, **Parc Richelieu** or wander around the **Citadelle de Calais**, a 16th-century fortress with origins as a medieval castle.

Calais has a strong fishing industry, so don't miss trying the freshest fish at one of the many restaurants on Rue Jean Pierre Avron opposite the fish market; Le Grand Bleu (legrandbleu-calais.com) is a dog-friendly favourite.

Boulogne-sur-Mer

Look past the deeply unfortunate new town in Boulogne and beeline straight for its **charming walled centre**, an inland enclave of stone houses, cobbled streets

↑ The beach at Berck

and floral gardens. This major fishing port sits a 35-minute drive from Calais and offers a chance to explore a fortified old town with a handsome château at its centre. This is the perfect place for a *flâner*, the French practice of simply having a stroll with no particular aim or destination. Start out at the 13th-century **Château de Boulogne-sur-Mer** and then follow the footpaths of the fortress's ramparts along its walls and through Jardin Valentine Hugo. At your will, turn off the ramparts and into the old town's centre to wander through its quaint streets and stop in pretty cafes for a coffee or crêpe.

Outside of this walled haven sits the newer town, a slightly ugly but on-the-up kind of place where yet more **street art** awaits. There are guided tours and self-guided visits via an app (streetart.boulogne-sur-mer.fr), and works include a scowling lion by French artist Scaf Oner and a pair of gates cleverly painted on to a staircase by Spanish artist Gonzalo Borondo.

Le Touquet

Another 40 minutes' drive south of Boulogne-sur-Mer and you'll pass through the small town of Étaples and into luxurious Le Touquet. What was once a coastal hunting forest has now become a bougie seaside escape, where well-heeled Parisians have been holidaying since it was developed by its owner, Alphonse Daloz, in 1882 (hence its other moniker, Paris Plage). Today, Le Touquet is packed with **elegant seaside mansions**, high-end art galleries, leafy parks and is fronted by a vast sandy beach that stretches all the way to the Canche estuary.

Your first port of call here should be the tourist office, where dog welcome packs are handed out to all with furry companions, containing treats, poo bags and leaflets on the best dog-friendly places to eat and drink. An amble through the town centre will take you past boutiques, designer stores, galleries and cafes (many let dogs in, just ask before you enter), and keep heading northwest and you'll finally reach that **beach**.

The main supervised section is off-limits for dogs in summer, but year-round they can run off-lead at the northern end of the beach, which is backed by a **vast dune system** that harbours songful common linnets and swathes of sea buckthorn. Walk through the dunes to climb a wooden observatory for views over the seascape, and if you head all the way to the Canche estuary, you can round the corner and follow the river to the sailing club where Restaurant La Base Nord (labellehistoiregroupe.com) is the perfect pit stop for a wine in the sun and an upscale fish supper. On hot days, walk the dog in **Bois d'Artois** woodland or **Parc des Pins**.

Berck-sur-Mer

Perhaps the most striking thing about Berck-sur-Mer is its white-sand beach – a vast, flat expanse that seemingly goes on forever at low tide and, possibly in a bid to create some sort of Wes Anderson aesthetic, has **pastel-coloured beach huts** scattered randomly across its central section. This thriving beach community is a 20-minute drive south of Le Touquet and makes a brilliant base for anyone seeking sandy fun. Dogs are welcome on the northern and southern ends of its beach year-round (stay outside of the blue flags in the central section and you'll be fine; in winter it's more flexible), and there's plenty of space for them to race around after a ball or frisbee.

If you've a dog with a prey drive, note that there's a sand yachting school here and their little wheeled vehicles really pick up some speed when there's a good breeze. Keep the dog on a longline if they're liable to chase, and if you've a penchant for adrenaline then book in for your own lesson (eoleclub.fr). Wind is well used in Berck, as this town is also home to an **international kite festival** each April that sees thousands of people descend to fly their own, as well as a host of creative fabric creatures that fill with air when launched into the sky.

For a lovely walk, head to the southern end of the beach to the **Sentier Dunaire**, where trails lead through the dunes overlooking the Baie d'Authie. Look out for the seals that flop on to the sand and

↓ A beagle rides the train in Saint-Valery-sur-Somme

FIND BLISS ON THE BEACHES OF NORTHERN FRANCE

around the groynes at the end of the beach (keep dogs on leads here).

The Berck tourist office hands out dog welcome packs and will give your dog plenty of love if you pop in to collect one. Around town there are plenty of dog-friendly dining options with indoor and outdoor seating (Rue Carnon has the best).

OTHER ADVENTURES NEARBY

If you're not all beached out yet, there are yet more brilliant stretches of sand to enjoy with the dog. Outside of the official bathing areas (usually well signposted), dogs can enjoy the beaches at **Stella Plage**, **Fort Mahon Plage**, **Saint-Cécile Plage** and **Merlimont Plage** throughout the year. In winter, there are no restrictions even in the central areas of these beaches.

Along with a handsome coastline comes plenty of excellent coastal walks, and Pas-de-Calais has several. One of the most spectacular is around **Le Cap Gris-Nez**, an area of 49-metre-high cliffs and a working lighthouse with wonderful views along the coast; on a clear day you can even see the cliffs of Dover 28km away. Start out at Tardinghen and take a 7.5km trail west along the coast to the lighthouse and back inland via Framezelle. Allow two hours and stop for lunch at the lovely Restaurant la Sirène (lasirene-capgrisnez.com) en route. Directions can be found on alltrails.com, though note that the beginning of the trail takes you along a beach off-limits to dogs in summer, but there's an alternative track inland you can take instead.

↑ Views over wetlands between Le Crotoy and Saint-Valery-sur-Somme

FIND BLISS ON THE BEACHES OF NORTHERN FRANCE

Shorter walks with more endless coastal views can be had around **Cap Nez Blanc**, where you'll find the towering Dover Patrol Monument dedicated to the Royal Navy command of the same name from WWI. For a stroll across dunes, park up on the road and head into the thick shrubs to follow the loop around **Dune de Sainte-Cécile** (parking and access at /// perkily.bluffed.sensuality). Dogs must be on a lead.

For something a little different – and more sedate – take a **steam train** around the Baie de Somme. Hop on to the vintage carriages of the **Baie de Somme Railway** at Le Crotoy and take the hour-long journey to Saint-Valery, a small town that sits on the *Canal maritime* d'Abbeville à Saint-Valery and the mouth of the River Somme. You'll have a little time in town to grab a crêpe and a drink before boarding and returning the same way; the journey passes a vast salt marsh where birds of prey hover in the sky seeking snacks and swans and egrets swim, while sheep graze on the grasslands.

There are inland adventures to be had, too – **Montreuil** is a lovely little town for a diversion away from the coast, where you can walk the town ramparts, enjoy a drink on a terrace in the main square and visit the 16th-century citadel with your dog (musees-montreuilsurmer.fr).

WHAT'S FOR DINNER?

Whether it's a casual *moules frites* paired with local cider or a fine-dining fish dish with a zingy French wine to accompany, there's no denying that Pas-de-Calais is a champion of **exceptional seafood**. With myriad fishing vessels going out to sea daily and fresh seafood markets in Boulogne (daily on Quai Gambetta) and Calais (six days a week on Quai de la Colonne), you're never going to be too far away from an Atlantic prawn or meaty piece of seabass.

↑ Enjoying steamed mussels with onion in France

But this region also has a few specialities not of the sea that might surprise you, the most moreish being the *Welsh complet* – a French take on a Welsh rarebit. Supposedly, it was introduced in the region in the 16th century by Welsh soldiers. Another unusual menu item is *potjevleesch*, or 'potted meat', which is made with four different types of meat and served topped with chips to melt the jelly that holds it all together.

If cheese is your thing, don't miss a dalliance with what's said to be the world's smelliest cheese, the Vieux-Boulogne. Drinks-wise, blonde beer is the ale of choice here, while wines made in Pas-de-Calais are gaining popularity – look out for the jokily named Charbonnay by Olivier Pucek, which has been cultivated on a former slag heap.

FIND BLISS ON THE BEACHES OF NORTHERN FRANCE

WHERE TO SLEEP

Les Secrets des Loges

From £80 per night
les-secrets-des-loges.com

Located in Calais town centre, this lovely, homely B&B is small but welcoming, furnished with upcycled antiques. Quirk abounds here, in the headboard made from rowing boat oars and the strong nautical theme in some rooms, and hosts Natalie and Laurent are kind and dog-loving – they'll even share dinner with you if you don't fancy going out into town. Breakfast of fresh croissants and juice is included. Note that there may be cats staying as well, so it's best to book elsewhere if your dog isn't cat-compatible. There's a small patio for sitting out in the sun, but no garden for toilet trips; it's a 10-minute walk from Parc Saint-Pierre.

Evancy Boulogne-sur-Mer La Marina

From £90 per night
evancy.com

If you choose to stay in Boulogne, this Evancy apartment block is a great base; it's just a 15-minute walk into the old town. Your apartment may come with serene views over the marina with the Château de Boulogne-sur-Mer in the distance, and inside you'll find fresh, clean decor with modern amenities and furniture, and a fully equipped kitchen for making your own meals. Breakfast can be included for an additional cost, and there's underground parking for a fee, too.

Evancy Trésors d'Opale

from £80 per night
evancy.com

This excellent serviced apartment block is an easy five-minute walk down the road and across the dunes from the wonderfully vast Sainte-Cécile Plage. The property has parking, a swimming pool and garden, and you can even book a breakfast of croissants, jam and cheese to be collected from the reception each morning. The apartments are swish, all modern furniture and balconies with tables and chairs, and you'll have a fully equipped kitchen in which to cook your own meals should you prefer.

Hôtel Barrière Le Westminster

From £200 per night
hotelsbarriere.com

Live like a posh Parisian and embrace the finer things in life with your dog at this four-star property in the centre of Le Touquet. Just a 10-minute walk from the beach and sitting across the road from a large leafy park with ample shade for hot days, it's an ideal base for being bougie about town. Dogs can't dine with you indoors here, so you'll have to rely on the terrace for eating and drinking opportunities, or head into the town's many lovely cafes and restaurants that allow dogs inside. Humans will love the indoor pool, while dogs will love the attention they get as well as the bowls provided in the room. Bedrooms are decorated with colourful modern artworks, and the larger rooms have

↓ The author and her dog at Fort d'Ambleteuse

living areas as well as large king beds. If you don't mind leaving the dog alone while you dine, don't miss dinner in the exceptional restaurant.

ESSENTIALS

Getting there: Calais has its own train station (connecting to Calais-Fréthun for those arriving via Le Pet Express Channel crossing) and is well connected to the UK via several ferry routes as well as the swift and easy LeShuttle.

What to pack: A longline offers your dog more freedom where they need to be leashed on the sands; don't forget a parasol or beach tent for summer days – there's very little shade on this coastline.

The dog rules: Generally, dogs are allowed on the 'unsupervised' areas of Pas-de-Calais beaches year-round. This means if there's no signage suggesting otherwise and no lifeguard, they are free to roam. Out of peak season, usually from October to March, dogs are allowed on almost all the beaches in the region, though it's often a good idea to check with the local tourism office to confirm, as these rules can change.

Getting around: There is a good – and most importantly, free – public bus network with Calais town and its surrounding areas (sitac-calais-opale-bus.fr). There are also trains between Calais and Boulogne and Etaples (for Le Touquet), but connections to the rest of the coast are hit and miss. Driving around is the most flexible option.

More information: Tourist offices can be found in Calais, Le Touquet and Berck. visitpasdecalais.com

↑ The Saint-Valery-sur-Somme steam train.
→ A tower at the edge of the 16th-century citadel at Montreuil.

MAKE IT A ROAD TRIP
This part of France is the perfect appetiser to an exploration of Belgium – head to Wallonia, the country's lesser-known region where Dinant makes a glorious base for beer-centric adventures amid dramatic riverside scenery (see page 86). Alternatively, track down the coast to Brittany, where you can explore several enchanting islands (see page 36).

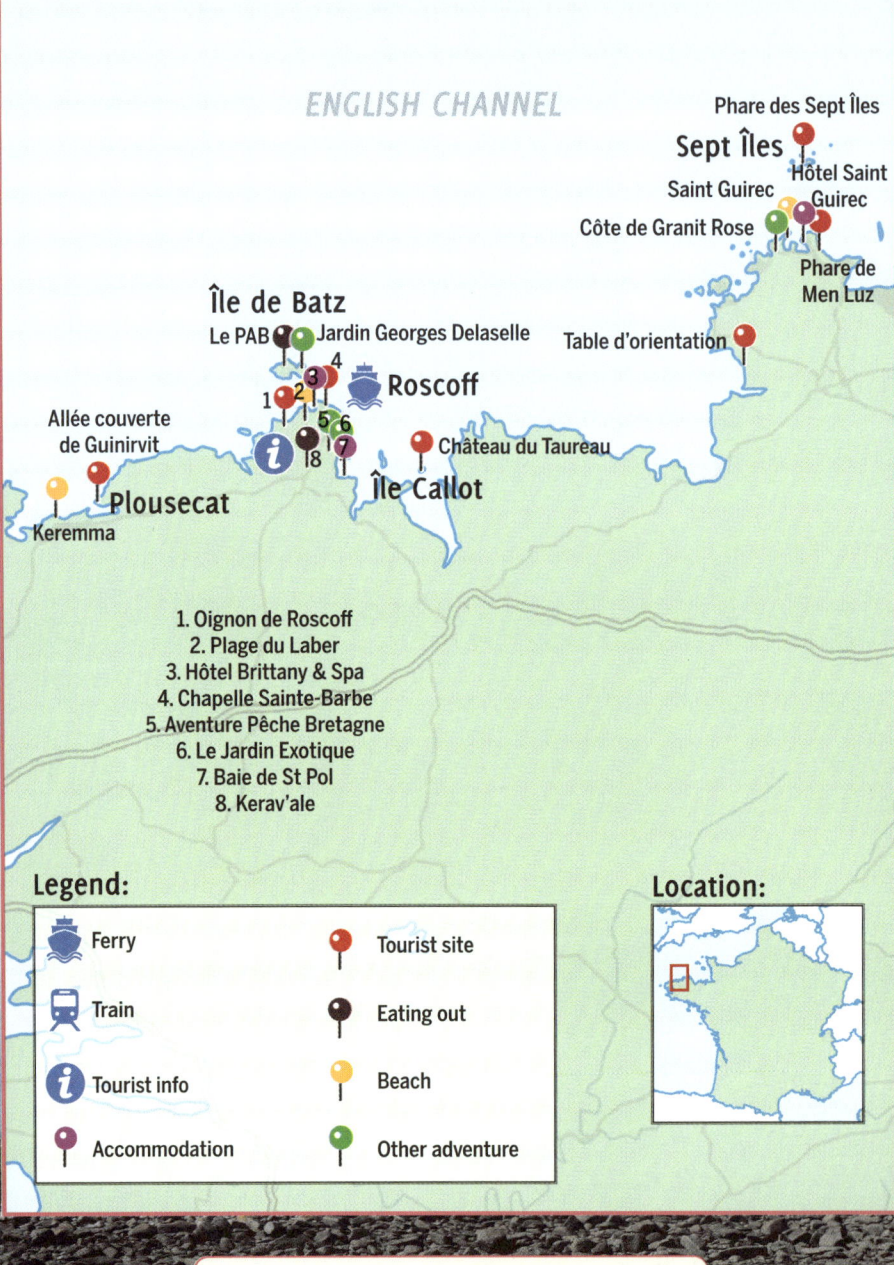

1. Oignon de Roscoff
2. Plage du Laber
3. Hôtel Brittany & Spa
4. Chapelle Sainte-Barbe
5. Aventure Pêche Bretagne
6. Le Jardin Exotique
7. Baie de St Pol
8. Kerav'ale

Legend:
- Ferry
- Train
- Tourist info
- Accommodation
- Tourist site
- Eating out
- Beach
- Other adventure

Location:

Where: Northern Brittany, France
When: March–October
Best port of entry: Roscoff
Driving time from port of entry: 15 mins

2
ADVENTURE ON THE ISLANDS AND BEACHES OF BRITTANY

Sitting on France's westernmost peninsula, Brittany is a rugged coastal region with a long, varied history. Inhabited since prehistoric times – evident in its many standing stones and ancient tombs that are still present today – it has seen Romans, Normans, the Spanish and Germans occupy its shores. And why wouldn't they? This part of France is as bountiful as it is beautiful, with a strong agricultural heritage and fantastic sea fishing that provides a veritable **cornucopia of comestibles**.

These days, the only invasions come from tourists: each summer thousands of visitors – both from France and often the UK – come to embrace the Breton pace of life. The region's appeal lies largely along its coastline, which is home to some of the **oldest geology in France** dating back as far as 2 million years. On the mainland, sweeping white sands and remote coves offer idyllic spots to spend a day by the sea, and dramatic cliffs and chunky, weather-beaten rocks craft a breathtaking coastline that's best enjoyed on the footpaths that track the fringes of its land. Beyond the mainland, amid the bracing sea that sparkles in sunshine and broods beneath cloud cover, a sprinkling of **small islands** can be discovered just a short hop by boat or via causeways that connect at low tides.

There are islands all along the coastline of Brittany, but it's in the northern reaches of this region where you'll find the wildest and most dog-friendly, with beaches, birdwatching and **botanical gardens** to enjoy with your companion by your side. Take in these three for starters, then head south for more island adventures if you haven't yet got your fix of the Breton coastline.

↑ Unusual rock formations on the Breton coast

ADVENTURE ON THE ISLANDS AND BEACHES OF BRITTANY

Île de Batz

Just 15 minutes by boat from the jaunty coastal town of Roscoff, Île de Batz is one of the most accessible and beguiling of Brittany's islands. Less than 4km from end to end and only 1.5km north to south at its widest point, this tiny island is inhabited by just a few hundred people and, despite its relative proximity to the mainland, it feels gloriously remote as a result.

Boats land on its southern edge throughout the day, depositing passengers on the edge of the village centre where you're greeted by a bustling cafe on the seafront serving **Batz'tate** (Batz baked potato) served fresh out of their outdoor oven, sweet crêpes and savoury **galettes**. Fuel up here – dogs welcome inside and out – as you'll need the energy to tackle this island's main event: the 12km coastal path that passes more than ten beaches where dogs are welcome year-round on leads.

The **coastal path** is an easy walk with relatively gentle terrain; the east of the island is a patchwork of farmland and grassy cliffs, while the western end is full of drama, with rocky outcrops and the occasional 18th-century military battery. It will take a few hours to complete in one go, but it's better to take a day – bring a picnic, swimwear and something to sit on and you can take breaks on its soft-sand beaches, letting the dog run after a ball or frisbee, or frolic in the surf.

Take the trail clockwise around the island and you can finish with a stroll around the handsome **Jardin Georges Delaselle**, which has a positively tropical feel with palms, enormous agave and cacti, and some truly otherworldly floral displays from the southern hemisphere. Your final reward for a circumnavigation of Batz can be found in the village centre, where **Le Pab brewpub** pulls pints of strong beer and serves magnificent seafood in its suntrap garden.

↑ The causeway to île Callot revealed by low tide

Île Callot

Just 2km long, Île Callot is yet another **idyllic island** off the coast of Brittany. Fringed by white-sand beaches and home to just a handful of houses used as holiday homes for visitors, this low-lying isle has no ferry service but instead is connected to the mainland town of Carantec by a **kilometre-long causeway** that's revealed by low tide for several hours a day.

Wander over with the dog as soon as the causeway becomes accessible and you'll find yourself joined by tractors pulling oyster nets, and if the tide's particularly low, don't be surprised if there are wetsuit-clad individuals trudging alongside with buckets in hand: this is **clam-digging country**, and you'll see them wading up to their necks to reach the tinier isles around Callot where tasty morsels hide beneath the sandy sea floor.

Being so small, you needn't spend an entire day in Callot, but you'll certainly want a few hours at least to relax on its beaches (dogs allowed all year; must be on leads from May to September) and tackle its short but spectacular trail that runs from the southernmost to the northernmost point. The island has few trees but abounds with colour

ADVENTURE ON THE ISLANDS AND BEACHES OF BRITTANY

and greenery thanks to flourishing pennywort, flowering currant, sea campion and gorse, and views of Roscoff are excellent from its northern reaches. At the very northern tip, head up to the **table d'orientation**, a helpful viewpoint diagram marked with other islands and sights on the mainland visible on a clear day. Just be sure to check the tidal times so you don't become Robinson Crusoed on the island.

Sept Îles

You'll get several islands for the price of one on the **boat trips** that depart the town of Perros-Guirec, just over an hour's drive from Roscoff. Armor Navigation (armor-navigation.bzh) takes passengers on its sturdy vessels out to the blustery Sept Îles, an archipelago of several islands and many more rocky outcrops sitting just under 5km from the Breton mainland.

The islands have remained largely uninhabited throughout history, aside from the 15th-century monks who came to pray on the Île-aux-Moines. Today, the only residents here are a pair of lighthouse keepers who now take turns to oversee the island's singular **working lighthouse**, a few seals and over 20,000 pairs of migratory seabirds that settle here from spring to September.

Due to the breeding seabirds, dogs can't set foot on the islands themselves, but this is of little consequence when the best views of its residents are from the water. Watch **squawking gannets** perched on the rocks from the comfort of the boat, which has indoor and outdoor seating, and look out for **puffins** bobbing about in the water. You might spot **dolphins** as you drift around the islands and see **grey seals** lolling about on the beach, and see cute little **kittiwakes** take graceful flight around

↑ Arty watches seabirds from the Sept-Îles cruise

→ One of the many beaches along the Breton coast

you – a stark contrast to the guillemots whose wings flap frantically after take-off, as if they're unsure of their own ability for flight.

There's a commentary on board, largely in French, though some of the staff speak English and will translate should you need it. There's also an English-language handout that adds more context as you sail. As you cruise back to the mainland, look out for the **former home of Gustave Eiffel**, the engineer behind the Parisian tower, and enjoy views of the Côte de Granit Rose, a rocky landscape around Saint-Guirec where boulders by the sea have a curious pinkish hue.

OTHER ADVENTURES NEARBY

While Brittany's islands are enchanting, the mainland has equally exciting opportunities for dog-friendly fun. Between your island adventures on the north coast, you'll pass through historic seaside towns, skirt by vast sandy beaches and happen upon coastal walks with spectacular scenery. If travelling over from the UK, you're most likely to arrive into the **port of Roscoff**, an historic trading town whose handsome architecture is a hangover from its heyday when wealthy shipowners built their homes here.

Get to know the town on its **heritage trail walk** (maps are available in the tourist office or at roscoff-tourisme.com; there are information boards at each stop) and you'll pass by its unique Gothic church with its ornate belfry and visit the **Chapelle Sainte-Barbe**, perched atop a bluff with wonderful views across the town port – it's particularly lovely at sunset. As you wander, you'll find Roscoff is packed with fine patisseries, dog-friendly cafes and

restaurants and seafront bars with terraces ideal for sundowners. The town is also home to an intriguing little **onion museum (instagram.com/maisondesjohnnies)**, which charts the history and production of the *oignon de Roscoff* – the region's most famous export – and the so-called 'Onion Johnnies' who travelled to Britain to sell their braided pink onions. The information boards are largely in French but are easily translated with the Google Lens or Translate apps on your phone.

Just south of the ferry port in Roscoff is an out-of-the-way gem: **Le Jardin Exotique** (jardinexotiqueroscoff.com). This botanical garden is small – it'll take just 45 minutes to wander its expanse – but is a beautiful spot for a short stroll with the dog and has some remarkable plants from South America, Australasia and southern Africa. Southwest of the town lies its only dog-friendly beach: **Plage du Laber**.

Beyond Roscoff lies a mainland coastline well worth exploring, with footpaths that track the cliff edges and enormous beaches to let the dog run free on. For coast path walks, head to **Plouescat** (a 30-minute drive from Roscoff) to see chunky rock formations and the gigantic ancient standing stone, **Menhir de Cam-louis**. Nearby is the Baie de Kernic where you'll find more prehistory: On the shingle and sand beach just south of **Porz Meur** sits the fascinating **allée couverte de Guinirvit**, a Neolithic gravesite with several stones arranged to create an alleyway (visible at low tide only).

Not far from here you'll find one of the region's best **beaches at Keremma**, a more than 5km stretch of white sugary sand. A vast dune system at its western end is brimming with wildlife, and at low tide the beach seemingly stretches out towards the ocean forever. Dogs should be kept on a lead in the dunes and the local tourist office states that they must be on a lead on the beach, too, though locals seem to get around this by bringing a longline.

Another excellent coastal walk is on the **Côte de Granit Rose**, a section of the Breton coastline that has curvaceous pink granite boulders, battered by wind, rain and ocean into unusual shapes. In the village of Saint-Guirec, head for the coastal path that tracks north from La Plage Saint-Guirec. Those confident on their feet will enjoy scrambling on the rocks around **Phare de Men Ruz**, a pink granite lighthouse, and down on to the small sandy coves along the coast. See more of the region's gorgeous granite in a nearby **sculpture park** – a few minutes' drive from Saint-Guirec's centre – where works have been carved from the stone by artists from all over the world.

Finally, if planning a visit to Île Callot, don't miss a wander along the coast path on the eastern side of the Carantec peninsula for excellent views out to the lighthouse on Île Louët and the neighbouring **Château du Taureau**, home to a private 16th-century castle.

↓ The reddish rocks on the Côte de Granit Rose

WHAT'S FOR DINNER?

Food is central to Breton life and this region of France really knows how to indulge. Expect to find cakes and biscuits made with rich, salted butter – try a *kouign-amann*, a southern-Breton cake packed with the stuff, or Breton biscuits – and exceptionally velvety fondant perfectly prepared in patisseries across the region. Brittany is the home of the crêpe and the *galette*, both thin pancake dishes, the former usually sweet (order it with some Breton salted caramel) and the latter savoury, often served with cheese, mushrooms and a fried egg.

Of course, seafood wins out in restaurants here thanks to the thriving fishing industry, and you must try some of those pink onions. If you're feeling adventurous, local Roscoff brewery Kerav'ale makes an onion beer called 1828, though a better drink to imbibe is the local cider.

WHERE TO SLEEP

Baie de St Pol

From £20 per night
caravanclub.co.uk

Listen to the sound of the waves hit the shore at this lovely campsite in Saint-Pol-de-Léon, a little town just 10 minutes' drive south of Roscoff. If it weren't for the coastal road that allows access to the campsite's entrance, you'd be almost camped on the pebble beach here. The site has a small pool and will take orders the night before for your morning bread and pastries to be delivered to their reception. There's a restaurant that operates in summer, and pitches for motorhomes, campers and caravans are both hard-standing and grass, plus there's a small field for tents, too. The nearby town of Saint-Pol-de-Léon has a handsome Gothic cathedral and plenty of lovely restaurants.

Hôtel Saint Guirec

From £100 per night
hotelsaint-guirec.com

Expect simple rooms in a spectacular location at this beachfront property in Saint-Guirec, the ideal base for exploring the Côte de Granit Rose and boat trips to the Sept Îles. While the bedrooms won't wow, the views over the beach from your balcony will and breakfasts and dinners in the seafront restaurant (dogs allowed) are wonderful – the food is local-centric and ultra-fresh. Note that dogs are allowed on this beach from 1 November to March only.

↑ Arty poses on the rocks at Plage de Keremma
→ The polytunnel at the Roscoff Botanical Gardens

Hôtel Brittany & Spa

From £100 per night
hotel-brittany.com

Book one of the suites or deluxe bedrooms at this four-star hotel and you'll get magnificent sea views out towards Batz. Rooms are all contemporary with comforting touches like tartan cushions and bedspreads, and those with balconies have outdoor furniture for lounging in the sun. Dogs are allowed in the rooms only here, which means they can't join you for breakfast, lunch or dinner. Don't let that put you off dining here, though – let the dog snooze in the room if they're happy to and head down to the restaurant whose head chef, Loïc Le Bail, has a Michelin star. Expect stunning presentation of local ingredients crafted into divine morsels, and a few off-piste additions like an artichoke for dessert. The on-site spa is a welcome retreat when the weather's not on your side, too.

ESSENTIALS

Getting there: Driving is the easiest way to reach this region of France, especially if you're coming over from the UK on the Plymouth–Roscoff ferry route.

What to pack: A longline is essential for beaches where dogs must be on a lead. If travelling in summer, consider a parasol to create shade on the beaches when it's hot.

The dog rules: Where they're allowed, dogs generally have to be on a lead on most beaches throughout Brittany and it's best to keep them on a lead on the coast path. Always check the signage on beaches.

Getting around: Driving is the best way to get about in this part of Brittany, though if you can cycle with your dog there's a decent cycle route along the coast (the EuroVelo 4). Bring your own bikes with a dog trailer or hire one from Aventure Pêche Bretagne (aventurepechebretagne.com) in Roscoff Marina.

More information: For more information on arrival, the Roscoff tourism office is on Quai d'Auxerre; for up-to-date events listings head to brittanytourism.com or roscoff-tourisme.com.

MAKE IT A ROAD TRIP
You can extend your dog-friendly French adventure in the Loire Valley (see page 64) for vineyards and châteaux – a five-hour drive from Roscoff – or head northwards along the coast to the Cote d'Opale (see page 26) for more dog-friendly beaches and boat trips.

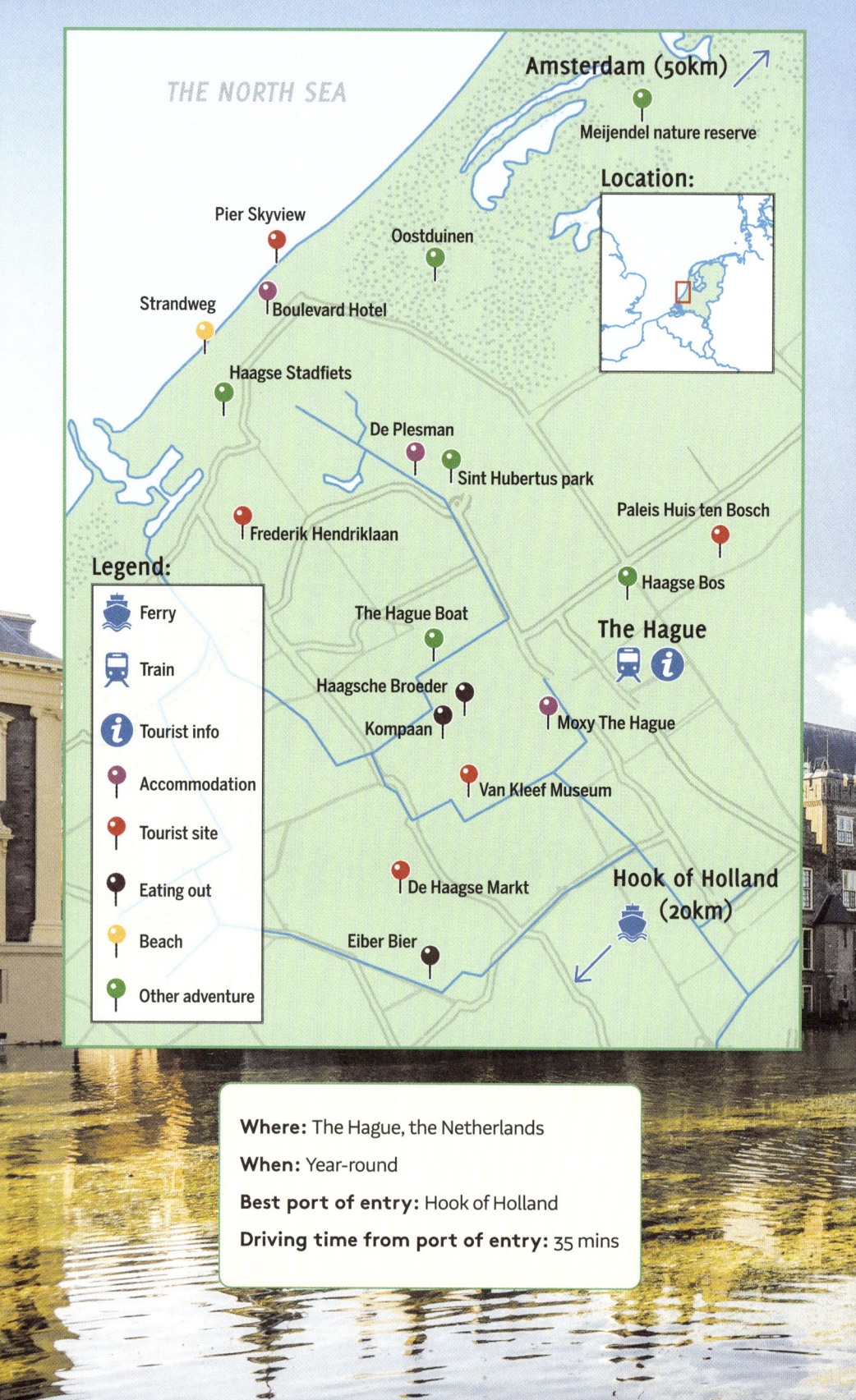

3
CYCLING, SEA AND SAND IN THE NETHERLANDS

The Hague

The Hague, or Den Haag as it's known in Dutch, has something of a staid reputation. Home of the International Court of Justice, the European Commission and Europol – and several more important organisations designed to bring European and world nations together – it's perhaps got a rather less sexy reputation when compared with gritty port city Rotterdam or lively Amsterdam. But offer this city, the third largest in the Netherlands, your open mind and it will return the favour with fine food and – to the surprise of many – fun on the sand.

The Hague is indeed a coastal city, sitting just 20km north of Rotterdam and 60km south of Amsterdam on the edge of the North Sea. Its core city centre is set back from the coastline, making way for the cheerful seaside resort of **Scheveningen** to spread along the seafront. This oceanfront neighbourhood is likely to be your dog's favourite spot, as a **miles-long beach** yawns in both directions along the coast, offering a vast stretch of soft yellow sand for them to sink their paws into. Over summer, the main section of the beach is reserved for humans only, but the southernmost and northernmost sections both welcome dogs year-round.

This is a place for promenading along the lengthy **Strandweg** that backs the sand. Wander along it, either north or south, and you'll pass several beach clubs with outdoor loungers, sofas and deck chairs that beckon when the sun is shining. Stop in for a drink or bite to eat with the dog (the majority will allow dogs inside and out) before heading down on to the sand, where hundreds of families come to set up their picnic blankets and beach tents in summertime. Hours could be spent languishing on the sand in the sunshine, or playing in the surf

that rolls off the sea. But there are a few dog-friendly highlights along this stretch coast you won't want to miss if you've young people in your party.

The first is the **unmissable pier** that stretches 300 metres out towards the sea from the end of Zwolsestraat. Dogs are welcome to join you inside and out, where you'll find arcades with video games, souvenir shops, food vendors and, on the terrace above, rooftop bars with brilliant views of the coastline. At its very tip lies the Pier Skyview (skyviewdepier.nl), a **50-metre-high Ferris wheel** that you can board with the dog by your side for even more spectacular aerial views. Sit in your gondola and watch as the people on the beach beneath you become specks on the sand.

For more wonderful coastal walking beyond the Strandweg, Scheveningen sits right next door to the Oostduinen, a **natural dune system** to the north of the main resort, where a network of trails connects around small lakes and ponds behind the beach. It's part of the **Meijendel nature reserve**, which becomes ever more wild as you head further north. Here you can see up to 250 different species of birds and you might even spot the free-roaming **Konik horses**. Hiking trails abound and you could walk for well beyond 20km here if you so wish (dogs should be on leads to protect wildlife and livestock), but another pleasant way to explore the reserve is by bicycle.

You can hire **electric cargo bikes** from Haagse Stadfiets (haagschestadsfiets.nl), which have a box with a leash attachment on the front so your canine companion needn't trot breathless behind you. The long-distance LF1 cycle route passes through the nature reserve, but there are circular routes to follow that loop through the urban centre, too – an idyllic way to enjoy this city of cycling enthusiasts.

↓ Families enjoy a summer's day on the beach at The Hague

OTHER ADVENTURES NEARBY

The Hague is a city brimming with culture, but much of this is off-limits to dogs whose presence is not welcome in its galleries and museums. Still, there are a few highlights in the city centre that shouldn't be passed up – not least because this is one of the greenest cities in the Netherlands with plenty of beautiful parkland to enjoy with the dog.

Haagse Bos is a **hundred-acre forest** with a pond at its centre and a deer park at its southwestern end. Look out for the regal Paleis Huis ten Bosch, a 17th-century palace built as the summer residence for Prince Frederik Hendrik, which now serves as the **royal home** of the Dutch king and queen. A little closer to the coast, Scheveningse Bosjes is another city-centre woodland where towering old oaks sway in the breeze and come January and February, snowdrops carpet the forest floor. Both parks have **off-lead walking areas** for dogs, so look out for signage that indicates where it's safe for them to roam free.

For more urban mutts, the city is a warren of fascinating smells and sights. Let the dog embrace it all on a **self-guided walking tour** – the tourism board has designed several themed walks, from those that focus on royal residences to tours for kids and winter wonders (see them all at denhaag.com/en/walking). Alternatively, save your legs and board **The Hague Boat** (thehagueboat.com), which allows dogs on its guided tours of the city's canals. For an indoor endeavour, the modest **Van Kleef Museum** (museumvankleef.nl) is a curious little place to learn about Dutch jenever and enjoy a tasting of the historic distillery's liqueurs and bitters. The dog won't be allowed to taste the samples, but the distillery can provide a bowl of the Hague's finest tap water instead.

To enjoy a little **dog-friendly retail therapy**, head to the pavements of Prinsestraat for bougie bars and cafes, or Frederik Hendriklaan (known locally as De Fred), a handsome 1km street packed with cafes, independent boutiques, delis and bookshops – most of which will allow your dog to peruse alongside. Alternatively,

↓ Dried fruit for sale at De Haagse Markt

throw yourselves into the action at **De Haagse Markt** (open Mon, Wed, Fri and Sat; dehaagsemarkt.nl), one of the largest multicultural markets in Europe where you'll find everything from washer-dryers to fresh fish, flowers and jewellery for sale, as well as plenty of tempting Dutch cheese.

Speaking of cheese, a day trip to Gouda is a delicious diversion just 20 minutes by train from the main station. The charming little town has an attractive historic centre, and if you time it right you can attend the weekly **Gouda cheese market** (Thursdays) where the dog might just get some fuss from a 'Gouda girl', or a smooch from one of the horses pulling wagons of cheesy wheels. If you are here in spring, from late March to early May you can take the dog for a stroll around the **Keukenhof tulip fields** (Keukenhof. nl). Take the 40-minute train to Hillegom and then hop on the Keukenhof Express (small dogs only), which deposits you at the Keukenhof Gardens for the most vibrant dog walk you'll ever have (there's also a canal tour dogs can board).

WHAT'S FOR DINNER?

In such an international, multicultural city, it's well worth trying a variety of cuisines – not just Dutch. Catering to its well-heeled residents and visitors, there are myriad upscale modern European restaurants offering excellent tasting menus here, many of which are dog-friendly (call ahead to check). You'll also find a vast number of restaurants focusing on Middle Eastern cuisine, with falafel featuring on many a menu – Sababa (sababa.nu) on Prinsestraat is a popular venue.

If you want to go full Dutch, though, don't miss tasting a *kroket* (a deep-fried, breaded roll filled with meat) or a cheesy *kaassouflé* (a deep-fried, breaded wrap filled with cheese). Those with a sweet tooth will want to try a *Haagse kakker*,

a currant bread filled with almond and cinnamon paste, and the city's traditional coffee-flavoured candy: a *hopje*. The city is home to the historic 19th-century Van Kleef distillery, so look out for its liqueurs in cocktails and don't miss sampling its jenever – the Dutch precursor to gin. There are several breweries in the city, too, including Haagsche Broeder, Kompaan and Eiber Bier.

WHERE TO SLEEP

Moxy The Hague

From £75 per night
marriott.com

This reliable chain is a handy central base if you want to be in the thick of the action in the city. It's a short tram or bus ride from Scheveningen, and it's just a five-minute walk to the vast Haagse Bos park. Bedrooms are modern and simple, decorated in the typical grey and purple Moxy design, with plenty of hanging hooks and lovely high-pressure showers. The only snag here is the sensor-activated light under the bed – useful for night-time bathroom trips but often annoying if you've got a dog prone to fidgeting; a plaster over the sensor will do the trick, though. Dogs are allowed in the restaurant and bar area for breakfast, lunch and dinner, and there's underground parking for those who drive.

De Plesman

From £85 per night
deplesman.com

If want to base yourself in one of the greener areas of The Hague, this design-led hotel is the perfect retreat. It sits right

CYCLING, SEA AND SAND IN THE NETHERLANDS

MAKE IT A ROAD TRIP

If you fancy venturing further on to the Continent, you could head to Belgium's little-known Wallonia region for a scenic riverside adventure (see page 76), or it's a six-hour drive to Germany's Harz Mountains (see page 86) from The Hague. You're also just a four-hour drive from Calais and the Opal Coast (see page 26).

next door to Sint Hubertuspark, offering leafy morning walks on your doorstep, and is just a 10-minute tram ride from the beach. If you're put out by not being allowed to bring the dog into the city's art galleries, it needn't matter here: the hotel is part hospitality venue and part exhibition space, with photography of The Hague by artist Soo Burnell throughout its halls. Expect art deco touches in the decor and design, and a little aviation history – this building is the former headquarters of Dutch national carrier KLM. Dogs can join you on the outdoor terrace for breakfast, or they can stay in the room while you dine. There's private parking on site.

Boulevard Hotel

£70 per night
boulevardhotel.nl

For beach-centric adventures, this property is your best bet. Set right on the promenade next to the beach, it's in prime position for morning surf-chasing and wanders up and down the beach-side boulevard. Bedrooms are simple and perhaps a little dated, but always clean and, most importantly, plenty have sea views. There's also an apartment in the hotel with its own kitchen for self-catering stays. Dogs can join you in the restaurant, but if you prefer to dine without them they can be left in the room. There's a parking elevator and street parking just outside the hotel for a charge, but it's also just a few minutes' walk from the Badhuiskade tram stop.

ESSENTIALS

Getting there: The Hague is a well-connected city by train, and public transport is the best way to get here; the main station has direct services connecting with Amsterdam, Brussels, Paris and Rotterdam. It takes just an hour by metro and train from the Hook of Holland port where the ferries from Harwich dock, and it's only a few hours by train from the Le Pet Express drop-off at Calais-Fréthun train station. Driving here is also possible and there's plenty of underground parking throughout the city.

What to pack: You'll definitely need dog beach towels for this trip, as the sand gets everywhere here. A parasol or beach tent for shade is also a good idea in summer.

The dog rules: Dogs must be kept on a lead on the beachfront boulevard and in the dunes behind the beach. On the beach, dogs are welcome year-round on the section north of the Zwarte Pad car park (///video.length.nitrate), otherwise they can enjoy access to the whole beach from 1 October to 15 May. Note that there are rarely but occasionally seals on the beach – put your dog on a lead immediately if you spot one and move away.

Getting around: Trams and buses are all dog-friendly here and there's no requirement for a muzzle.

More information: There's a tourist information point in Den Haag Centraal railway station; online, head to thehague.com for more detail.

← Arty relaxes on the dog-friendly beach in The Hague

Where: San Sebastián, Spain
When: October–May
Best port of entry: Bilbao/Santander
Driving time from port of entry: 1–2 hrs

4

EAT YOUR WAY AROUND THE PINTXOS BARS OF SAN SEBASTIÁN

San Sebastián

A city hemmed in by mountains on one side and an oft-wild, frothing Atlantic on the other, San Sebastián has an enviable location on the northern Spanish coastline. With a trio of sweeping sandy beaches right at the city's doorstep and undulating foothills within easy reach, it's a fantastic location for adventuring outdoors with dogs. But Donostia, as it is known by its Basque residents, also has one major draw that brings in millions of visitors each year: its food.

The Basque region has always had a healthy relationship with food – its proximity to **mountains and seas** has meant a diverse palate of ingredients feature across its typical plates. French influences made their way across the nearby border in the 1800s and tiny supper club-style gastronomic societies began popping up throughout the region, where largely men would gather to cook and converse and share their culinary skill.

Then, in the 1970s, after years of suppression and attempted erasure of the Basque culture by dictator Francisco Franco, whose government rule lasted until 1973, **New Basque Cuisine** was born. A revival of creativity across Spain took place – the Movida movement – and in the Basque region it happened at the stove. What came from it was an elevated version of traditional **Basque cooking** and it put the region firmly on the culinary map – not just in Spain, but the world.

Today, San Sebastián is home to a healthy smattering of **Michelin-starred restaurants** – the highest accolade for any establishment making meals – as well as the Basque Culinary Centre, which turns out some of the best chefs in the country, many of whom cut their teeth working in the **pintxos bars** of the city's old town. And that's where the dog comes in – you may not get them into the finest dining places in the city, but they're almost always welcome at your feet while you indulge on a cornucopia of pintxos.

Essentially the Basque version of tapas, pintxos are small snacks often served on crusty bread or on the end of a toothpick. Hot pintxos come direct from the kitchen on small plates, and it's all best accompanied by a glass of Basque wine or a glug of local vermouth. A delightfully casual affair, they're often eaten standing up at the bar, and fortunately, some of San Sebastián's best spots will let the dog in, too.

↑ The pintxos counter at Casa Vergara
→ A view of the Basílica de Santa María del Coro from Calle Mayor

One of the best streets for finding great pintxos is 31 de Agosto Kalea, which has some firm favourites for both locals and visitors. Here are a few of the best dog-friendly pintxos bars, all within walking distance of one another, and what to order in them:

Borda Berri for the ribs
virtualtxoko.com/project/borda-berri

A tiny, no-frills bar on Fermín Calbeton Kalea with only a couple of tables and a ledge to stand at, it doesn't take much for Borda Berri to get busy. And, boy, does it get busy – this place is famous for its moreish sticky, smoky pork rib (*kebab de costilla de cerdo*). It specialises in meats and you can also sample pig's ears and roast duck.

Jose Mari for the artichoke
josemaritaberna.com

Handily across the road from Borda Berri, Jose Mari has an immensely tempting spread of pintxos on the counter. There's a menu for freshly made hot food too, though, and the globe artichokes are the one to watch for – they come with blue cheese and walnuts, and go wonderfully with *txakoli*, the local lightly sparkling white wine.

↑ The meat plate at La Cepa de Bernardo

Casa Vergara for sea urchins
grupogarrancho.com

The bar at Casa Vergara is a tantalising proposition: rows and rows of pintxos are lined up, skewered with toothpicks or delicately balanced atop chunky white bread. Order a selection of whatever looks good here, but don't miss out on the hot stuff – there's a traditional Basque stew (*sukalki*) and some seriously zingy sea urchins (*itsas triku arrunta*).

↑ Sea urchins and sangria at Casa Vergara

EAT YOUR WAY AROUND THE PINTXOS BARS OF SAN SEBASTIÁN

La Taberna del Pícaro for octopus and steak
facebook.com/latabernadelpicaro

This chic little bar is a short wander across the bridges over the Urumea river and into the city's 'new' town (it's not that new), where the Victorian ocean front gives it serious seaside town vibes. The grilled octopus (*pulpo*) is a highlight here, and meat eaters will want to pair their surf with some turf and order the sirloin (*solomillo*), which also comes with freshly fried crisps.

La Cepa de Bernardo for the meat plate
barlacepa.com

An old-timey bar where legs of ham hang from the ceiling, this place will set the dog's nose on fire. The main highlight here is, of course, the meat – thin slices of silky, salty cured ham (*jamón de Jabugo*), cuts of marbled pork tenderloin (*lomo*), and chunky rounds of sausage from pigs fed only on acorns. Wash it down with a *caña* of the local lager or a red wine from the region and you've got a perfect pairing.

La Viña for cheesecake
lavinarestaurante.com

Every good pintxos tour must finish with the region's top dessert: a Basque cheesecake. Made with a soft cheese and baked in the oven, it's got a burnt exterior that adds a satisfying bitterness to cut through the creamy vanilla centre. Think crème caramel, but far more substantial. Order it here and you'll be rubbing elbows with the locals, who flock here on weekends to drink vermouth and catch up with friends.

↓ Arty watches waiters pass at Casa Vergara

OTHER ADVENTURES NEARBY

The absolute best way to get to know San Sebastián as a city is on the dog-friendly **free walking tour** by Go Local (golocalsansebastian.com). Its English-speaking guides will show you the city's main sights, exploring its history and connections to food, and the tour is largely outdoors except for a visit to a church, where dogs are welcome.

From October to May, outside of the main summer season, dogs are allowed to run free on the city's **three beautiful sandy beaches**, Ondarreta and La Concha near the old town and Zurriola on the new town side. Come here in wintertime and it's like a dog park, with breeds of all kinds mingling and leaping in the surf like some sort of Darwinian nightmare.

For some more sedate dog walks, a pair of striking hills ensconce the city – to the west and overlooking the ocean is **Monte Urgull**, which has a ruined fortress at the top and several viewpoints along the trails to its 123-metre summit, while to the east lies the 243-metre-high **Monte Ulia**. Both hikes offer plenty of shade and excellent views over the city and coastline. A little further afield is **Monte Igueldo**, where you can take a cog railway up to the summit for views over La Concha Bay and a visit to a **vintage fairground**.

Beyond the city itself lies a rugged and wind-buffeted coastline, fringed by sandy beaches and pockmarked by tiny fishing villages. **Getaria** is a charming little fishing port west of San Sebastián, where you'll find a Gothic church, a small beach and plenty of places to sample the fish and seafood caught locally. A little further along the coast, utterly spellbinding cliffs jut upwards from the ocean and beach at **Zumaia's Itzurun beach**, part of the Basque Coast Geopark. You can take a circular or there-and-back walk along the clifftops from the San Telmo Ermita chapel, and then head down on to the beach for a closer look at the striking Flysch Rocks on the beach (*Game of Thrones* fans might recognise them from its seventh season).

WHERE TO SLEEP

Nobu Hotel

From £350 per night
sansebastian.nobuhotels.com

Part of the US-based chain, this luxurious property is finished in the same chic, minimalist style you'd expect from any Nobu. Sitting right on the seafront at La Concha, some rooms have dreamy views, but the outdoor terrace is the place to be for fine food, great cocktails and sea views. Dogs under 15kg are welcome, and while they won't be allowed in the restaurant, you can leave them in the room or order breakfast in bed.

Hotel Catalonia Donosti

From £80 per night
cataloniahotels.com

With a rooftop pool and a chic spa, this hotel is a real gem in San Sebastián's old town. Bedrooms are contemporary with seductive dark colour palettes and bold printed wallpaper. There's no size restriction for dogs, but you will be required to pay a refundable deposit on arrival and they won't be allowed in common areas – including the restaurant. But with so many great pintxos bars on your doorstep, you certainly won't be stuck for places nearby to dine with the dog.

↓ A view over San Sebastián from Monte Urgull

↑ The cliffs around Itzurun Beach in Zumaia
→ A dog trots along the wet sand on one of San Sebastián's beaches

Camping Zumaia

From £16 per night
campingzumaia.com

The drive into Camping Zumaia isn't exactly scenic – you head off the motorway and find yourself on the town's industrial estate – but once up here on the hill overlooking the town, it's a far more attractive prospect. There are verdant hilltop views, level pitches terraced on the side of a slope, and it's in easy walking distance of the town centre. The on-site restaurant does decent comfort food and there's a dog walk at the top of the hill. It's somewhat exposed here, so if the weather's not on your side, prepare to batten down the hatches.

ESSENTIALS

Getting there: San Sebastián is a 1–2-hour drive along the toll road from either Bilbao or Santander, both ports for the Brittany Ferries crossings from Plymouth and Portsmouth. It's possible to get here by train, too, with a line running along the coast connecting to Madrid in Spain and the town of Hendaye in France.

What to pack: Beach towels (for both you and the dog) are essential, and some sort of cooling mat for summer breaks might be helpful.

The dog rules: Dogs are only allowed on the beaches in town from October to May. They need to be kept under control when in public off lead, and mess must be cleaned up.

Getting around: Dogs are generally allowed on most public transport (you may need to muzzle them) around San Sebastián, though buses may only admit smaller pets that can be carried. The city is relatively small, though, so on-foot adventures are much more fun.

More information: There's more information on the highlights in San Sebastián on sansebastianturismoa.eus.

MAKE IT A ROAD TRIP
Whether it's your first port of call or your final stop before home, San Sebastián is a brilliant city break to pair with Barcelona (a seven-hour drive; see page 160) or the canals of the Camargue (a six-hour drive; see page 108).

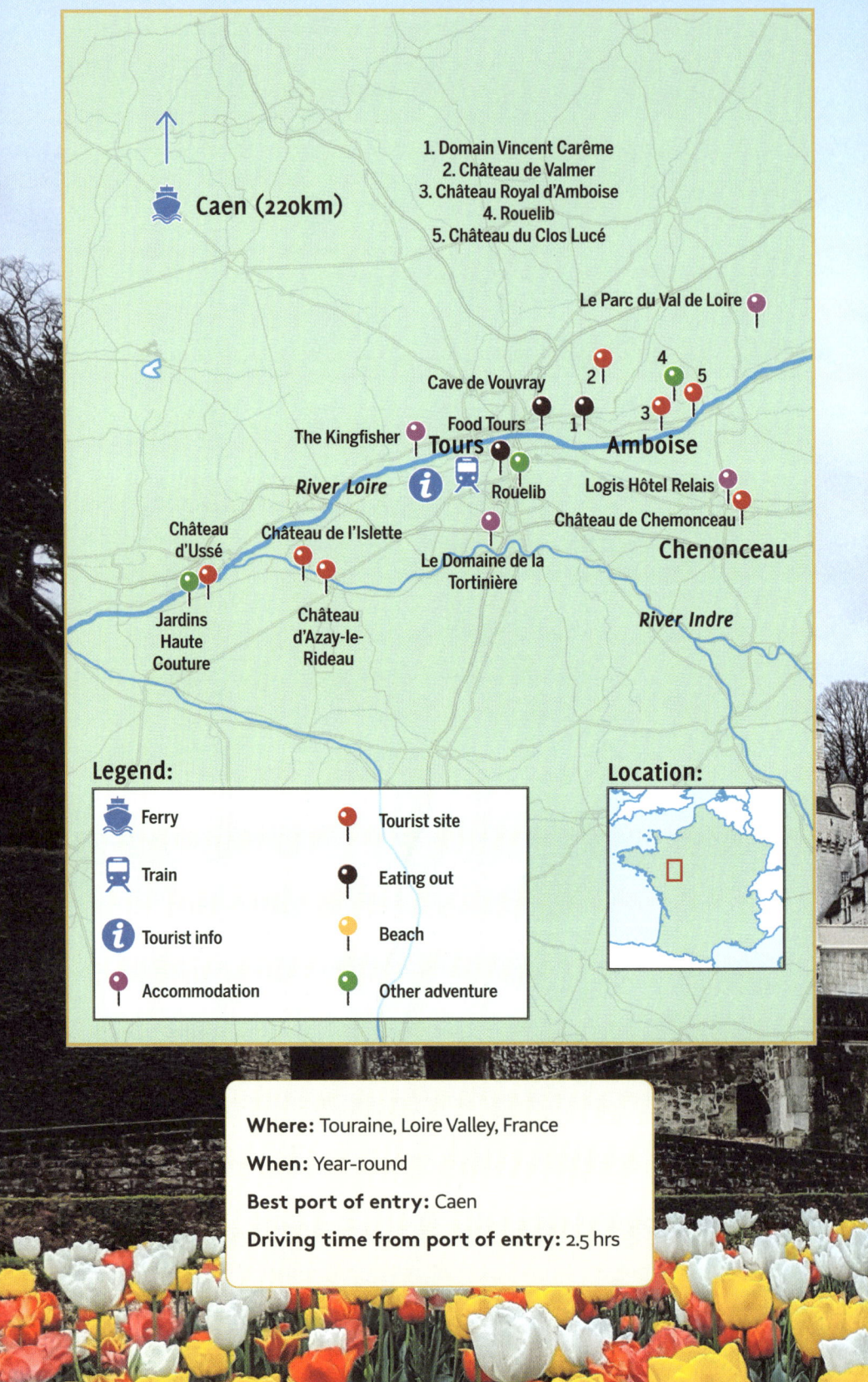

5
LIVE LIKE FRENCH KINGS AND QUEENS IN THE LOIRE VALLEY

The longest river in France begins somewhere deep in the southern Massif Central and trickles its way down through the mountains northwards, eventually leaning west to empty at Saint-Nazaire on the Atlantic coast 1,000km later. It wends its way through myriad thriving cities, bucolic landscapes and quaint French villages, but no section of this river and its wide valley is quite as enchanting for dog owners as the Touraine region, centred around the city of Tours.

Decadence is the name of the game here. Just a couple of hours from Paris, it has long been the summer getaway for the capital's high society, from the aristocracy to actual royals. This is why, on the banks of the Touraine Loire, you'll find a staggering number of frankly **outrageous châteaux**, and a handful of marginally more modest castles.

Fortunately, the French aristocracy have had a romance with their own dogs for centuries, which means our pets today are often welcomed into these magnificent constructions, or at least within the oft-**manicured gardens** that surround them. Of course, where the French gentry go, fine food and wine follows, and many of the châteaux produce their own, harbouring vast dark cellars housing fortresses of ageing bottles.

↓ The Château d'Azay-le-Rideau surrounded by the swollen waters of the Indre River

The Loire produces many notable varieties, but the Touraine region is famous for its bubbles in the form of Vouvray. This **sparkling wine** is made in the same manner as Champagne, but with 100 per cent chenin blanc grapes giving it a fruity freshness on the palate – and it often sells for half the price of its Champagne rivals. The ideal summertime aperitif, it's best consumed in the shade of a French oak, overlooking the fairy-tale turrets of a limestone castle or on the banks of the mighty Loire river.

Time it right and you'll find even more magic along the Loire. A once-lost 18th-century tradition has won its way back into the Touraine region in recent decades: come here in summer and you'll find hundreds of *guinguettes* popping up on the banks of the Loire and Indre. A *guinguette* is essentially a makeshift bar, often by the riverside, where music and merriment go on into the early hours of those balmy summer evenings. Today, they pop up all over the region, from the riverside in Amboise and Tours to the gardens of Chenonceau and beyond. Thanks to their outdoors set-up, they are almost always dog-friendly, and they're a fantastic place to sample plenty of those local wines.

↑ Inside the Château de Chenonceau

DOG-FRIENDLY CHÂTEAUX

Château de Chenonceau
chenonceau.com

Perhaps the most famous château in the region, Chenonceau sits a 40-minute drive east of Tours on the banks of the Cher. This tributary of the Loire surrounds the silvery stone castle on all sides, as a sturdy network of arches raise the building elegantly above the water like a ballerina standing on the tips of her slippers. When the flow is sedate enough and the sky bright, the castle is reflected like a watercolour on the surface of the river, giving a dream-like quality to the entire picture.

The house itself is vast inside, with turrets and round towers to explore and long galleries with pleasingly tiled chequerboard flooring. The floral displays here are the highlight. The estate has its own master florist, Jean-François Boucher, and his ostentatious arrangements follow ever-changing themes throughout the seasons. Outside, the gardens and surrounding estate make beautiful walking ground.

Pets are a big part of life at Chenonceau (there are several resident cats and plenty of staff bring their own pets into work with them) and dogs are allowed everywhere here, including into the house. They must be carried when indoors and there are no size restrictions – the rule is, if you can haul it, you can bring it in. Staff have seen keen visitors carrying dogs as big as German Shepherds on their shoulders – just beware, there is no elevator and very little seating.

Château du Clos Lucé, Amboise
vinci-closluce.com

A 35-minute drive east of Tours, or a 20-minute drive north of Chenonceau, Clos Lucé is a markedly different kind of château. Built from pink bricks, it stands regal above a sweep of sloping lawns and formal gardens. During the 15th century it became the royal summerhouse for the kings of France, but its most famous residence by

LIVE LIKE FRENCH KINGS AND QUEENS IN THE LOIRE VALLEY

far was Leonardo da Vinci. Invited to the region by King Francis I and his mother, Louise de Savoie, the artist spent the final three years of his life here working on various projects with his students.

Today, the gardens are a real tribute to his artistry and engineering. You'll find installations reminiscent of his technical designs, such as the water wheel, and sculptures inspired by his most famous artworks. Dogs are welcome throughout but must be carried inside the house. There's a dog-friendly cafe at the top of the gardens, but the highlight here is Auberge du Prieuré, a Renaissance-inspired restaurant where you're served by staff in period dress and the menu uses ingredients and cooking styles from the 15th and 16th centuries.

Château Royal d'Amboise

chateau-amboise.com

Following again in the footsteps of Leonardo da Vinci, you'll find his final resting place in the recently restored chapel at Amboise's royal castle. He's not the only attraction here, though: despite its town-centre location, there are 90 species of birds flitting within its gardens, whose fortress-like walls offer serene views over the Loire. Inside, following a digital guide on an iPad offered with your entry ticket, you can explore the bedrooms and dining halls where French kings and queens once lived. Note, dogs must be carried indoors, which can make grappling with an iPad a little tricky.

Come in summer to make the most of a roster of events, from outdoor opera performances to sunset picnics, all of which are dog-friendly. Some of the best views of this castle can be had from across the river, so once you've visited, head out of town over Pont du Maréchal Leclerc and wander down by the river for a truly special sight across the water.

Château de l'Islette

chateaudelislette.fr

Around 30 minutes by car west of Tours, set on another Loire tributary, L'Indre, this charming castle is a classic Renaissance construction: made from silvery tufa stone, with steep dark grey rooftops and turrets on every corner. Set within a beautiful garden and a wider estate with several waterways, it's an idyllic setting for an afternoon picnic. Pick up a basket in the on-site boutique and fill it with their French goodies – from terrine to soft baguettes and perhaps a little local wine – and then find a table or bench to set yourselves down at within the gardens.

If you venture indoors (no dogs allowed inside), you'll find it's part family home (with a modernised kitchen and all), and part museum to its most famous former guest: Auguste Rodin. It was here that he spent time with the lesser-known but still wildly talented Camille Claudel, a sculptor who, over the years of working together became his lover. In summer, there are garden concerts and dogs are welcome at those, too.

↑ Tulips in flower in the gardens of Château d'Ussé

↑ The world-renowned florists hard at work at Château de Chenonceau

Château d'Azay-le-Rideau
azay-le-rideau.fr

If you've seen any image of Château d'Azay-le-Rideau, it's likely taken from the southern lawn, where L'Indre river slows just enough to create a near-perfect mirror of the castle in its surface. A marvellous sight that was created in the 20th century by widening the waterway, it's now the most sought-after photograph on the grounds of this magnificent castle, which is a 30-minute drive southwest of Tours. The estate dates back to the medieval period, but the castle was built in the 1500s, when it was acquired by the then king's financier, Gilles Berthelot. It has some of the best examples of Italianate architecture within the Loire region, with ornate sculptural decorations on its facade.

Dogs are allowed in the parkland and gardens here, where the best vantage points for that mirror image are, and in the house, though they must be carried in a bag, so indoors is only suitable for smaller dogs.

Château d'Ussé
chateaudusse.fr

Almost every single château in the Loire could be fit for a fairy tale, but Château d'Ussé wins out for its true fairy-tale connections: this is the place that inspired Charles Perrault's classic *Sleeping Beauty*. Just a 15-minute drive from Azay-le-Rideau and l'Islette, it's an exciting option for families. Follow signage to the turrets where the Sleeping Beauty exhibition is laid out across several rooms with some admittedly disconcerting mannequins, and then head into the main living quarters where you'll see handsome trompe l'oeil ceilings pretending to be fine marble and 17th-century tapestries draped on the walls.

Unusually for most Loire châteaux, dogs are allowed to walk with you around the castle itself, as well as within the grounds and gardens – no back ache from carrying them around here.

LIVE LIKE FRENCH KINGS AND QUEENS IN THE LOIRE VALLEY

DOG-FRIENDLY WINE EXPERIENCES

Château de Valmer
chateaudevalmer.com

Few sights in the Loire combine the Touraine region's two main highlights – wine and châteaux – but Valmer is a triumph on both fronts. The main house is relatively modest, mainly due to a fire caused by an electric iron in the 20th century that ravaged much of the building. But the terraced gardens are truly wonderful, with a rose garden and kitchen garden, and two of the most witchy, gnarled weeping pagoda trees you'll ever see. There are tours of the grounds led by the gardeners and trained guides – often encompassing tastings of edible flowers and herbs – and you shouldn't miss the fascinating cave chapel.

The real treat, though, is the wine tasting and cave tour. The wider estate has 35 hectares of vineyards and has been used for growing vines for well over 1,000 years, and its bottles are stored in the ever-cool tunnels bored into the rocky ground around the main house. Today, it produces Vouvray in all its forms – white and rosé, still and sparkling, brut, sec and demi-sec. Sample it at the shop – and pick up a bottle to take home.

The château is open to visitors from April–September and dogs are welcome throughout the grounds and wine caves. It even has its own friendly springer spaniel who'll greet you with plenty of wag in her tail if she spots you.

Cave de Vouvray
cavedevouvray.com

All those limestone châteaux and the myriad cathedrals and churches throughout the Loire had to get their stone from somewhere, and most of it was quarried from the hills around the valley. They were gutted in such dramatic fashion that it has left behind hundreds of vast cave networks throughout the Touraine region, and Cave de Vouvray is one of the most extensive with 3km of tunnels.

↓ A wall of wine bottles within the Vouvray caves

Naturally, the French put these tunnels to good use and today the Cave de Vouvray, which is a 20-minute drive east of Tours, stores around 6 million bottles of wine within its alcoves. Dogs can join you on the guided visit, which explains the winemaking process for Vouvray and other wines, and involves a tasting of various local wines in the shop afterwards (the dog only gets water, obviously).

Domaine Vincent Carême
vincentcareme.fr

A little further east from Cave de Vouvray, lifelong winemaker Vincent Carême hosts tastings at his own cellar in Vernou-sur-Brenne, sometimes accompanied by his beagle. All organic, his wines vary from a classic Vouvray to a rare pet nat rosé, which is a kind of sparkling wine made with almost no intervention.

As he's chief winemaker and tends to his vines most days, tastings are best booked in advance. The cellar door is open Tues–Fri 9.30am–12.30pm and 2pm–6pm, plus 2pm–5.30pm on Saturdays.

OTHER ADVENTURES NEARBY

If you find yourself all châteaux-ed out, there's plenty more to do in Touraine beyond the castles and wine cellars. The attractions in the city of Tours are museum heavy and largely not dog-friendly, but you can enjoy a walking tour of the city with a foodie bent with **Food Tours in Tours** (foodtoursintours.com), whose guides have been eating everything the creative cheffing community here has to offer for decades. They'll start you off with a glass of Vouvray (or a local beer if you prefer) and introduce you to some of the region's best cooks while dispensing nuggets of history (and occasional morsels of cheese to the dog).

If it's the gardens that really interest you here, you'll love **Jardins Haute Couture** (www.jardinshautecouture.fr), just a 10-minute drive from Château d'Ussé. A mix of French and English styles, this beautiful garden is set around a quaint family home where you can stop for tea or cocktails. Expect to see lots of roses, lavender, rosemary and Mediterranean plants, all thriving with

↓ Arty enjoys fuss from the guide on the Food Tours in Tours excursion

↑ Arty poses on the bridge at Château d'Azay-le-Rideau

pollinators in spring and summer, and events with live music and theatre.

For those uninterested in grape-made plonk, **dog-friendly beer tastings** can be done at Art Is An Ale (artisanale-brewing.fr) in Amboise. The town also has a brilliant Friday and Sunday market, and there's a small tourist train that accepts dogs.

Families will want to head for **La Vallèe Trogloditique Goupillières** (troglodytedesgoupillieres.fr) – a complex of caves 30 minutes from Tours where after the stone was quarried for the region's churches and castles, the workers moved in to create homes and farmsteads. Styled as they might have looked in the Middle Ages, you can now explore the former cave houses and meet the farm animals the residents would have kept.

For great dog walking beyond beautiful châteaux gardens, there's a lovely 5km loop starting in Amboise town centre and heading across the bridge and around the Île d'Or (directions on mypacer.com). Near Tours, take the nearly 5km stroll around **Île de la Métairie** (directions on alltrails.com).

WHAT'S FOR DINNER?

It's not hard to pick your tipple here thanks to the local Vouvray and myriad other local wines available in the Touraine Loire, but choosing what to eat can be tricky – this region is packed with exceptional produce and some truly creative chefs. Regional specialities include *rillettes* (cooked pork preserved in fat), which is best served with a fluffy white baguette, and moreish *rillons* – confit pork belly served as a main course. Excellent button mushrooms come from the neighbouring Saumur region, while there are plenty of Loire cheeses to sample at almost every delicatessen (look out for the ultra-local Sainte-Maure de Touraine goat's cheese).

LIVE LIKE FRENCH KINGS AND QUEENS IN THE LOIRE VALLEY

WHERE TO SLEEP

Domaine de la Tortinière

From £125 per night
sawdays.co.uk

There are few better places to lay your head at night in the Touraine Loire than this fabulous château. A 25-minute drive south of Tours and only 35 minutes from Amboise and Chenonceau, it's the perfect location for day-tripping around the region. There are vast gardens for the dog to enjoy, a swimming pool for those sunny summer days, a beautiful restaurant terrace and a spa. Chef Damien Piochon changes his menu seasonally, using the best local and international ingredients from creamy burrata and zingy yuzu to fish from the region's waterways and succulent French duck, and the sommelier will pair wines to whatever you choose.

Le Relais Chenonceaux

From £75 per night
chenonceaux.com

In the heart of Chenonceau village, this hotel is a handy budget base. Expect simple rooms with original wooden beams and pine-clad ceilings, and a cosy fireplace in the restaurant for those chillier nights. There's an outdoor terrace for al fresco breakfasting and you're just a 10-minute walk from the Château Chenonceau.

Le Parc du Val de Loire

From £18 per night
caravanclub.co.uk

If you're bringing canvas or a camper, this campsite is a brilliant option for families on the road. There are fully serviced grass pitches with hedgerows all round for privacy, brick-built barbecues and picnic benches. There are also self-catering lodges should you prefer something a little more solid for you stay. On-site entertainment for the kids includes bouncy castles and dance performances on the stage, there's a shop selling groceries and rotisserie chickens, and the restaurant does a decent pizza. There's a good dog walk through woodland just next door to the campsite, and the Domaine Cocteaux winery is just around the corner should you need a decent bottle for the evening.

↓ A view of Amboise from across the Loire river

The Kingfisher

From £375 per week
gites-TOURAINE.com

Make like the peasants of the Middle Ages and book into this cave dwelling on the northern banks of the Loire just 10 minutes' drive from Tours city centre. Dug into the rocks on the banks of the river, it's an excellent example of a typical cave home, but with a few mod cons to ensure your comfort. There's a beautiful private terrace with patio furniture, a well-stocked kitchen, and the bedroom has a double and single bed ideal for a small family.

ESSENTIALS

Getting there: Caen is the nearest ferry port for those travelling from the UK (2.5 hrs by car). It's also possible to get to Tours by train with direct trains from Paris Gare d'Austerlitz (2 hrs 20 mins).

What to pack: There's little need for any special equipment here, but you'll want to leave plenty of space in the car to bring home some lovely Loire Valley wines.

> **MAKE IT A ROAD TRIP**
> If coming from the UK, take the ferry to Roscoff and you can stop off on the Breton coast (see page 36) before heading inland to the Loire Valley.

The dog rules: Dogs must be on leads in almost all châteaux gardens unless otherwise specified. It's always best to keep them on leads in nature reserves, too, as there are lots of wading birds around the rivers.

Getting around: Driving is a simple and efficient way to get around Touraine, but cycling is an even more pleasing way to explore. There are several véloroutes in the region – many of which have off-road sections – including from Tours to Amboise (2 hrs). Hire bikes and dog carriages from Rouelib in Tours or Amboise (rouelib.com) and get route information at francevelotourisme.com. It's also possible to explore the region by train: there are stations at Tours, Chenonceau, Amboise, Chinon and Loches.

More information: There's plenty of information and news at touraineloirevalley.co.uk.

6
TAKE IN CITY AND SCENERY IN WALLONIA

When you think of Belgium, you probably imagine medieval city centres like Antwerp and Bruges, or the regal home of the European Union, Brussels. While these cities do indeed have their own appeal, none are quite so charming for dog owners as Dinant – a tiny riverside sprawl with city status but the vibe of a provincial town. Dinant sits almost in the centre of Wallonia, the lesser-known half of Belgium that is all too often overlooked in favour of its high-profile neighbour, Flanders.

But while Flanders is all urban metropolises surrounded by largely flat – and some might say rather boring – landscapes, Wallonia is all drama: undulating hillsides, deep valleys, and precipitous rocky cliffs jutting into the sky. Few places in Wallonia have it all, but Dinant does a cracking job of packing a huge variety of terrain into its metropolitan area and the outskirts. Sitting along the banks of the River Meuse, the city is lorded over by 100-metre-high limestone cliffs, on top of which lies a vast citadel. On the city fringes, brick and concrete houses become less frequent as thick forest takes over on the sides of its sloping valleys.

Dinant

In the centre, you won't find a trace of its medieval past – Dinant has been razed to the ground and fought over more than once. First, it fell in 1466 when Charles the Bold ransacked the once prosperous city whose brass forges and bustling markets were an enviable asset. Then, in the throes of WWI, it was a place of battle between the French and the Germans. Residents were massacred and much of the town was destroyed, including the church and the town hall,

→ Dinant's pretty riverside

↑ One of many saxophone sculptures that line the bridge in Dinant

but eventually, once the war was over, the reconstruction process began and several of its buildings were rebuilt as identical replicas. Today, undoubtedly the most striking of these is the **Collegiate Church** with its Gothic towers and elegant onion dome – dogs can't go inside, but you can take it in turns if you're travelling with others, or just admire it from the outside.

The story of Dinant's rises and falls is well documented in the clifftop **Citadel** (citadellededinant.be), which looms over the city. Park on the site of Citadel on top of the hill and head inside to find immersive exhibits within its walls – most of which are indoors, ideal for a rainy day or a hot summer's afternoon. A viewing platform offers expansive views over the Meuse and the city below – those with a fear of heights might want to refrain – and the replica trench complete with sound effects is quite an affecting

↑ The town of La Roche-en-Ardenne

experience. Don't miss the utterly bamboozling final exhibit: a room that was damaged so severely during shelling that it now tilts at a deeply alarming 30 degrees. If you've never had vertigo, attempting to walk through this part of the fortress gives you a pretty good simulation (if you have suffered from vertigo, give this one a miss).

From the Citadel, you can then head down into the city centre via 400 or so steps, or a short but somewhat rickety cable car. At the bottom, head north along Rue Adolphe Sax, where you should nip into the **Maison Adolphe Sax**, a small but engaging tribute to the inventor of the saxophone whose home once stood on these grounds.

Continuing north, you'll eventually reach Leffe, the village where that now-ubiquitous beer was first made in the 13th century. The abbey where it was originally brewed no longer stands after several fires and various wars, but a new Abbaye Notre-Dame de Leffe has been constructed on the same site and offers tours each Sunday in July and August (dogs welcome, too).

For a proper introduction to the famous Leffe beer, head back to Dinant walking along the River Meuse and cross the Pont Charles de Gaulle – note the flamboyantly decorated giant saxophones along its sides, another tribute to Adolphe Sax – and up the hill to Maison Leffe (leffe.com/en/maison-leffe). Set within a former abbey that has no connection whatsoever to the original Leffe Abbey, this small museum charts the history of this world-famous brewery, from small-scale monastic operation to its place on the global market with world's largest brewer, AB InBev. The detailed exhibit with its touch screens, audio descriptions and even a handful of intriguing olfactory experiences is well worth an hour's diversion before heading out to the garden or into the bar for a taster of one of its modern brews.

At more than 6% ABV, even just one Leffe sample is enough to make you feel a little sleepy, and so a sedate cruise on the

TAKE IN CITY AND SCENERY IN WALLONIA

Meuse is just what you'll need. Book on to a **sightseeing boat** with Dinant Evasion (dinant-evasion.be) to sail south of the city to picturesque Anseremme (where the same company also offers dog-friendly kayaking), or past the majestic **Freÿr Castle** (freyr.be), which is well worth returning to by car to stroll in its beautiful 18th-century gardens.

OTHER ADVENTURES NEARBY

Beyond the compact city of Dinant lies a bucolic region of rolling hills and a patchwork of farmland pockmarked by small, quaint villages and attractive towns. Head north of Dinant and in 15 minutes you can be at the gorgeous **Annevoie Gardens** (annevoie.be), a vast landscaped water garden with French, English and Italian influences, where you'll find artworks by the likes of David Nash and can see myriad water features powered entirely by gravity. The on-site cafe is dog-friendly, and it's the place to try wine made with its own home-grown grapes – a glass of the red goes perfectly with the traditional Liège-style meatballs.

If viticulture is where your interests lie, a few minutes' drive from Annevoie is the **Château de Bioul** (www.chateaudebioul.be). This place has a whole afternoon's entertainment: walk the dog among the gardens and vines, let the kids loose on the hunt for the estate's mascot, collect a picnic from the bar to enjoy on the lawns at your leisure, and indulge in a tasting on the terrace with its small selection of organic red, rosé, white and sparkling wines. There's also a fun museum inside the château, which charts the winemaking process and explores the other endeavours on the estate, including truffle cultivation and beekeeping, and the entire place is dog-friendly (for those on leads).

In the opposite direction, south of Dinant, the pretty little village of Pont-á-Lesse has some of the best walks in the immediate area. You can wander over the hills to the impressive **Château de Walzin**, which perches somewhat precariously on top of rocky outcrops overlooking the River Lesse, or you can roam in the forests that surround the Hôtel Castel de Pont-à-Lesse and gaze up at the brave souls taking on the via ferrata (dogs can be off-lead on both hikes; alltrails.com has several options for walking here).

Even further south, keen beer drinkers will want to visit the only brewery still making its drinks using traditional methods. **Brasserie Caracole** (brasseriecaracole.be) has been a working brewery for well over two centuries, with a short hiatus in the 1930s when it was abandoned after a storm took down its main chimney. Today, its beers are bold, boozy (all around 8% ABV) and brewed on site in huge copper tanks heated by firewood. You can even taste the distinctive, smoky flavours imparted to the liquid during the process. Dogs are welcome on the tours and in the bar for tastings, though beware there are metal steps with gaps for access, so some dogs might want to be carried inside.

A little further afield, a beautiful 15km or so loop around **Nisramont Lake** is well worth the hour's drive from Dinant – expect to see kingfishers and cormorants, and perhaps even beavers at the right time of day (follow the red diamond waymarkers). Refuelling can be done in the nearby town of **La Roche-en-Ardenne** – head down to the riverside for the best pubs and restaurants – where you can also visit a **medieval castle** (chateaudelaroche.be) with the dog for spectacular views over the River Ourthe and a lesson in archery. Also don't miss the fascinating **Musée de la Bataille des Ardennes** (batarden.

TAKE IN CITY AND SCENERY IN WALLONIA

be), where Gilles Bouillon has continued his father's legacy of collecting and displaying memorabilia from WWII and the brutal Battle of the Bulge. His three floors of exhibits are an astonishing array of uniforms, vehicles, photographs and letters, and dogs are welcome to join you to explore (beware, metal stairs abound inside).

Finally, around 30 minutes southeast of Dinant along the River Lesse, you can delve into the unique geology of this region at the **Grottes de Han** (grotte-de-han.be). Guided tours in English, French, Dutch and German head into the caves every 30 minutes and will introduce you to an otherworldly landscape deep in the belly of the hills of Wallonia. Expect stalactites and stalagmites aplenty, and an impressive light projection show cast above an underground river. Above ground, there's an animal park for younger travellers, though dogs aren't allowed into this section of the site. A 10-minute drive from here is a handsome little castle, **Château de Lavaux-Sainte-Anne** (chateau-lavaux.com), which is dog-friendly throughout and has some taxidermy exhibitions the dog will love to sniff around. There's a 30-minute wetlands walk on site, too, which shouldn't be missed.

↓ The unique geology inside Grottes de Han

↑ The unique geology inside Grottes de Han

WHAT'S FOR DINNER?

While Belgium isn't exactly known for haute cuisine, there are lots of excellent independently owned and run restaurants in and around Dinant cooking hearty local produce. A typical Walloon dish is Liège-style meatballs made with pork and beef mince, which come in a warming onion stew best mopped up with chunky bread slathered in salty butter.

There's plenty of good cheese to be had here – Herve is the strongest, made with unpasteurised cow's milk, and has been made in Wallonia since the 12th century. It pairs well with strong Belgian beers, which can be drunk in every bar, restaurant and some cafes throughout Dinant – look out for the Trappist beers, of which there are only seven in the world and three of those are produced here in Wallonia (Orval, Chimay and Rochefort).

But if you don't fancy beer, you can even find a decent glass of Belgian wine. The viticulture here is still in relative infancy compared with its southern neighbour, France, but fresh, zingy white wines and good sparkling wines can be found in the cellars across Wallonia.

WHERE TO SLEEP

Hôtel Castel de Pont-à-Less

From £90 per night
casteldepontalesse.be

Sandwiched between precipitous rock formations where climbers dangle in their harnesses by day and the River Lesse where kayakers can be spotted pootling in the flowing waters, this simple hotel is well placed for adventurous dog owners. It's a 10-minute drive into Dinant from here, or an hour's walk through woodland and then along the main road, and is supremely well priced considering its location. There's little to write home about in terms of decor, but what's outside is fantastic: a huge garden with lawns for games of fetch, and a forest on your doorstep through which you can walk to the likes of Walzin Castle or up to Anseremme village. There's a pool and hot tub for post-walk soaks and the restaurant does a decent meal if you aren't inclined to head into town.

Anhée holiday home (property ref 107152-01)

From £550 per week
en.ardennes-etape.be

Around 6km north of Dinant, this small but quaint stone cottage is a cosy place to retreat after a day out along the Meuse. It's set beside a beautiful woodland and has a log burner for cabin-in-the-woods vibes, plus a sheltered patio sunk into the hillside (and a small non-enclosed lawn above).

↑ Arty relaxing by the moat at Château de Lavaux-Sainte-Anne

Dinant holiday home (property ref 107524-01)

From £1,200 per week
en.ardennes-etape.be

This spacious, contemporary home is a stylish base for adventures in and around Dinant. It's got a metre-high fenced-in garden with a vast lawn, an open-plan kitchen-dining-living area with a sociable breakfast bar, and a substantial gas fire for warmer evenings in winter. There's plenty of provision for kids (including a small dining table with chairs) and it's flooded with natural light, which makes it beautiful on a summer's morning.

TAKE IN CITY AND SCENERY IN WALLONIA

Le Quai Son

From £100 per night
lequaison.be

Right in the centre of the delightful town of La Roche-en-Ardenne, Le Quai Son has a handful of well-kept, dog-friendly apartments. Sleeping between two and four people, each has a comfortable living and dining area and a small kitchenette for simple meals (heartier meals can be enjoyed at the company's own pub by the river, which has great views of the castle from the terrace). There are no gardens here, but parks and riverside walks await downstairs.

ESSENTIALS

Getting there: Public transport connections aren't great in Wallonia, so it's always best to come by car. A roughly three-hour drive from Calais, Dinant is an easy hop if you're travelling over the Channel by ferry or via the tunnel. It's also only 3.5 hours from the Hook of Holland if taking the overnight crossings, or four hours from Amsterdam for those coming on the Newcastle–Amsterdam ferry.

What to pack: You're unlikely to need any special gear or equipment here, unless you're an avid climber and fancy tackling some of the cliff faces.

↓ A view over Dinant from the citadel

The dog rules: There are no specific laws or fines related to dogs in Wallonia, but keeping them on a lead in public places and picking up after their mess is always best practice. Some breeds are banned in Belgium, including pit bulls – full information on this can be found at health.belgium.be.

Getting around: Dogs are allowed on buses here, but it's much easier to get around Dinant and the surrounding regions by car.

More information: There's a tourist office in Dinant at Avenue Colonel Cadoux, but you can also get more detail at visitwallonia.com.

MAKE IT A ROAD TRIP
Only a few hours from the Hauts-de-France coast, you could combine your inland Wallonia trip with a beach break in France (see page 24). Or hit the vast sandy beaches of The Hague, where walks through the dunes and an exciting Ferris wheel ride await (see page 46).

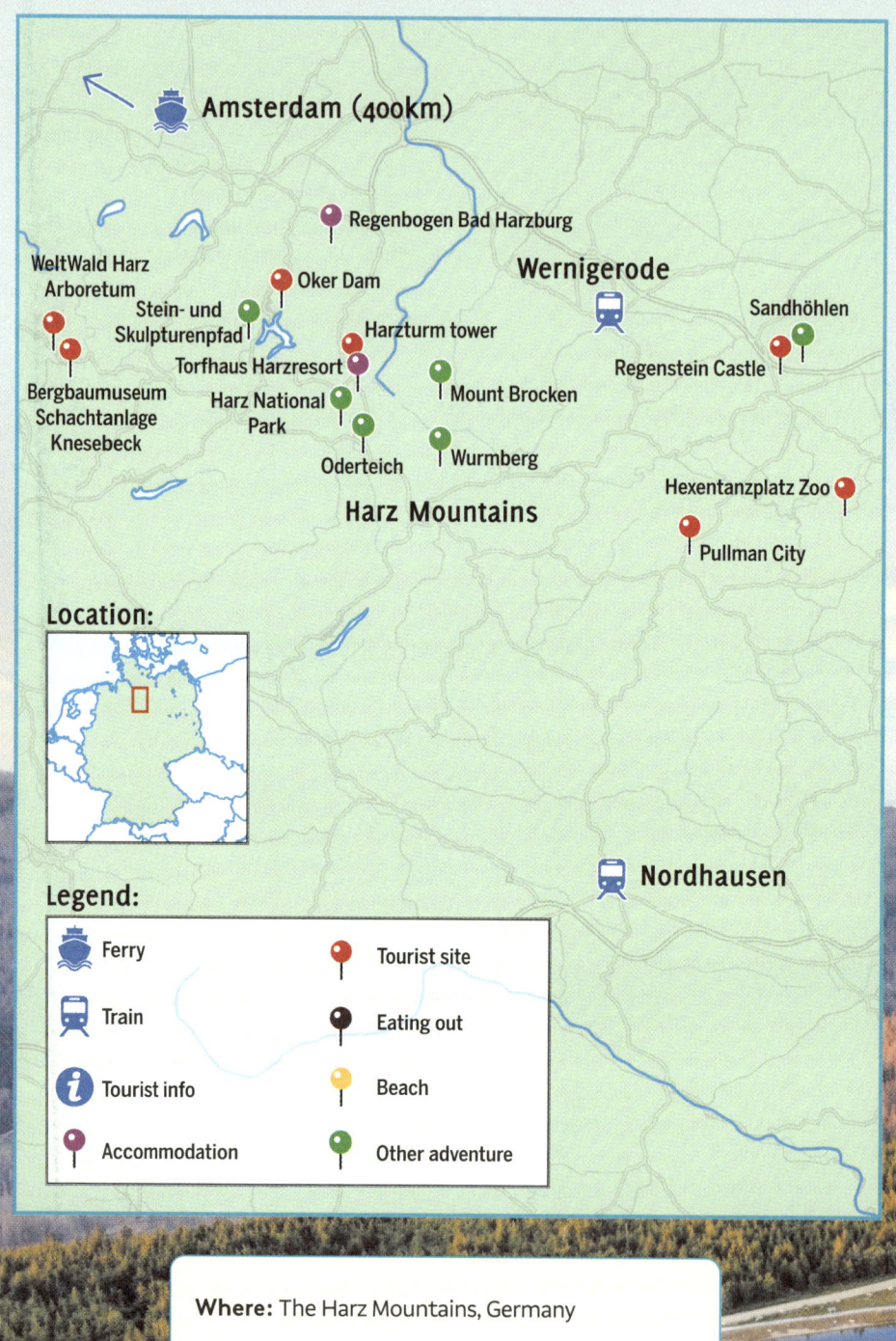

7
RIDE STEAM TRAINS AND HIT THE MOUNTAIN TRAILS IN GERMANY

Harz Mountains

Around three hours southwest of Berlin lies a landscape in recovery: the Harz Mountains, a designated National Park since 1990, has tens of thousands of spruce trees that once flourished on the hillsides. Today, 90 per cent of them are dead, and left behind is an eerie, desolate landscape of lanky silvery trunks and low shrubs.

The spruce was planted in the wake of WWII, when Germany was forced to pay reparations by way of timber and the country's forests depleted. But climate change forests were – largely droughts – and the invasive bark beetle have ravaged this monoculture plantation to create a vast, bare landscape.

It sounds bleak – and in the right weather it certainly can be – but look a little closer and you'll find life is beginning to grow from the dead wood around you as nature is restoring itself. The National Park authority's position is that nature should take its course – the bark beetle has been allowed to spread within reason, and now among the thousands of hollow trunks and towering dead spruces, saplings of other species are starting to take root. Young birch and willow are beginning to thrive, and fungi grows out of crevices and cracks in the dead spruce branches and trunks.

Wildlife is returning, too. You're unlikely to see the stealthy lynx on your travels through this region, but their footprints can occasionally be spotted on the **myriad trails** that track through the forests and up and down the mountains. Come on foot to explore the walking paths of the Harz and you'll want a pair of binoculars, as ring ouzel, spotted nutcrackers, peregrine falcons and black storks can be seen nesting or soaring in the skies. The dog will enjoy tracking the scent of the **wild boar** that snuffle their way through the forest, or the skittish **red and roe deer** (dogs must, of course, be kept on a lead to avoid disturbing any wildlife).

You needn't expend too much energy on your hikes here, either, as a handful of **gondolas** and **cable cars** built for winter skiers offer easy access to the mountain peaks. An excellent 90-minute downhill hike is from the top of 971-metre-high **Wurmberg**, which is served by the Wurmbergseilbahn gondola in nearby Braunlage. From the peak, where a dog-friendly restaurant, kids' playground and small reservoir make for a good pre-walk diversion, follow the mountain road (keeping the reservoir on your left) for almost 3km. Dead trees surround you

↓ The Oderteich reservoir

↑ The woodland trail at the base of Wurmberg

on all sides (don't worry, it gets more attractive as you get lower down the mountain) and, with good visibility, you'll have views out across foothills where the perished forest spreads out.

At a crossroads (///expired.singular.grace), you'll turn right on to a smaller track and head towards the Alfred Rieche Hütte – a leg-resting place for those whose knees are feeling the impact of a downhill trail – and then follow the Große Bode, a small, fast-flowing river with a handful of gentle waterfalls along its way. It's here where things become interesting, as the forest turns from spruce to birch and oak, and the track becomes enclosed by the beautiful woodland before depositing you out in Braunlage once again.

For something a little flatter yet still utterly beguiling, there's a 90-minute trail around the glassy **Oderteich** (parking is at ///jiggle.foxtrot.figures), a reservoir in the western part of the park surrounded

↑ The view from the Wernigerode Castle

Castle sitting atop a rocky outcrop allows dogs in its open-air museum.

Of course, there are longer trails and multi-peak hikes to be done all over this region with the help of the **Harz app** (available on both Google Play and Apple's App Store), which has all the trails listed with detailed information and directions on a helpful map, alongside attractions and more. Plan routes using the desktop version at touren.harzinfo.de, where you can even create your own circular walks using the Rundwegplaner function (translated as 'tourplanner').

For those who don't feel like spending all day, every day stomping on the trails, a far less strenuous day out in the Harz can be found on a different kind of track. At the heart of this National Park by spruce and pine woodland. A combination of root-ridden trails, wider forest tracks and wooden boardwalks that circumnavigate the reservoir, it's surrounded by dead spruce forest before becoming engulfed by lush, green firs. It's here where you'll find intriguing toadstools, artistic carvings made out of the dead spruce trunks, and get to enjoy a little paddle or swim in the water.

Discover a completely different landscape altogether on the edge of the northern Harz, where the Sandhöhlen – a collection of **sandstone caves** in the centre of a pine forest – are a fascinating place to wander. Park at the free car park at **Wanderparkplatz Burg Regenstein** and take the trail through the forest, where you'll walk over sandy tracks that cross ancient fortresses to an area that looks like a giant natural sand pit. There's a dog-friendly cafe and beer garden at Jogys Wald-Kneipe at the eastern end of the forest, and the looming **Regenstein**

↑ Wernigerode Rathaus
→ Riding the rails in Wernigerode

lies the 19th-century **Harz Railway**, an extensive narrow-gauge network that connects the town of Wernigerode on the northern fringes to the southern reaches around Nordhausen. Heritage carriages and locomotives chug their way along hillsides, through the forest and up into the peaks, smoke and steam billowing from their chimneys leaving a white trail behind them.

The most enchanting of the railway's routes is the one that wends its way up to **Mount Brocken**, the park's highest peak at 1,141 metres. Departing Wernigerode – a charming little town on the northern edge of the park – it travels through the low-lying forests of the foothills and gradually climbs before winding around the peak. You'll pass through tunnels and stop at a few smaller stations on the way up, and at the top, on a clear day, you'll get 360-degree views of the surrounding mountains. Dogs are welcome on board for a somewhat princely sum (in the region of around 20 Euros), but the experience is well worthwhile to save your legs – plus there's a great dog-friendly cafe serving lovely German cakes at the top.

Walks abound from Brocken peak, of course, but beware the wicked witch – legend has it that witches once whizzed around this mountaintop on their broomsticks on what is known as Walpurgisnacht. On a foggy day – of which there are many on top of Brocken – this peak becomes an eerie place to roam with the dog, and even riding the railway has a certain spookiness about it as you pass through dead spruce forest shrouded in mist.

OTHER ADVENTURES NEARBY

The Harz isn't just a fantastic hiking area – this region has heritage and intrigue aplenty in the form of mining museums, family-friendly attractions and interesting waterways. Head to Bad Grund for an intimate introduction to the region's mining history at the **Bergbaumuseum Schachtanlage Knesebeck** (knesebeckschacht.de), where the dog can join you on a tour of the museum (available in German and English) and its mine shafts. Nearby, there are stunning walks to be had on the 14km of trails in the **WeltWald Harz arboretum** (landesforsten.de), which has the most spectacular autumn leaves in the region with a strong collection of Japanese acers, as well as gorgeous blossom from cherry trees and magnolias in spring, followed by flowering rhododendrons in summer.

East of Bad Grund in Schulenberg, a **stone and sculpture trail** (Stein- und Skulpturenpfad; oberharz.de) offers a dog walk with a little artistry, and a couple of kilometres from here is the landing for a brilliant **boat tour on the MS *Aquamarin*** with Okersee Schiffahrt (okersee.de). The trip takes in the 75-metre-high Oker Dam and a couple of bridges on the Oker Reservoir, and you'll likely see cormorants and other waterfowl on the shoreline. Dogs are welcome indoors on the boat as well as on the upper deck, and some decent

← The Okersee tourist boat
↓ Inside the engine rooms at the Knesebeck Shaft Mining Museum

RIDE STEAM TRAINS AND HIT THE MOUNTAIN TRAILS IN GERMANY

food is served from the small catering space – don't miss out on the giant choux pastry swan served with cream and jam, named the Okersee Swan (*Okersee Schwan*).

If you've a head for heights, head up the **Harzturm tower** (harzturm.de) that rises 65 metres above the town of Torfhaus, a 30-minute drive east of Okersee. This is Germany's highest observation tower and dogs are welcome to join you should they feel brave enough to step out on to the viewing platforms or the glass walkway. In the eastern half of the Harz, families will discover that **Pullman City** (pullmancityharz.de) – a mock Western cowboy town – is a brilliant dog-friendly day out, as is the **Hexentanzplatz Zoo** (bodetal.de) where you can meet bears and wolves, among other creatures.

WHAT'S FOR DINNER?

This rural region has plenty of local food and drink to try, so come hungry. One of its most famous exports is the tangy Harzer cheese, made with buttermilk or low-fat curd. Of course, with so much wild game in the region, meats like deer and rabbit are popular – often soaked in buttermilk or roasted in the oven – while the region's mountain rivers are brimming with brown trout (*Bachforelle*), usually served up in restaurants with vegetables and potatoes. Mushrooms are big here, too – you'll often see German families take to the forests to forage for porcini mushrooms (*Steinpilz* in German) on autumnal weekends.

There are plenty of breweries and distilleries throughout these mountains. A traditional favourite is Echter Nordhäuser, the country's best-selling grain-based alcohol producer – try the ginger or violet gin, or the sweet green-coloured liqueur, Harzer Grün. Also look out for beers by the Altenauer Brewery, the highest brewery in northern Germany, whose use of the fresh waters from the Oker valley gives its beers an authentically Harz flavour.

↓ The Brocken Railway steaming through an autumnal landscape

WHERE TO SLEEP

Relais & Châteaux Hardenberg BurgHotel

From £164 per night
hardenberg-burghotel.de

Around 25 minutes' drive from the southwestern borders of the Harz National Park, this rural upscale hotel is a delightful hideaway with some intriguing history. Set within a half-timbered 18th-century building at the base of a precipitous rocky hill, it has its very own castle perched right above, which you can walk up to with the dog whenever you wish – ask at reception to borrow the key and you can let yourselves in to explore the thousand-year-old ruins. Dogs are welcomed with open arms here and can dine with you in the exceptional Novalis restaurant and the breakfast room – they also get a welcome pack in the room with a bed and treats. While you're not in the heart of the Harz, the drive to the National Park is through beautiful countryside and mountain roads, so makes being a little out of the way well worthwhile.

Torfhaus Harzresort

From £150 per night
torfhaus-harzresort.de

Right in the heart of the Harz in the ski village of Torfhaus, this resort has a combination of hotel rooms and excellent self-catering lodges. Here, you're in prime position for mountain trail hikes (you can even hike up to Brocken from here), and in a good spot for driving out to many of the region's attractions. Dogs are welcome in both the rooms and the lodges, which sleep up to six people. While there are no gardens as such, you might have a small deck or a patch of grass outside your front door for those late-night loo trips. The lodges have fully equipped kitchens and log burners for extra cosiness, but the highlight is your own private sauna for relaxing those muscles after a long day's walking.

Regenbogen Bad Harzburg

From £30 per night
regenbogen.ag

For campers in the Harz, this site has some of the best facilities – dogs and kids are welcome, there's a swimming pool, and a decent shop and bar. Located on the northern edge of the National Park, it's a 30-minute drive from Wernigerode and just 20 minutes from Torfhaus. There are over 200 pitches here for caravans, campers and motorhomes, so expect it to be bustling in summer.

ESSENTIALS

Getting there: The Harz is located fairly centrally in Germany, a three-hour drive southwest of Berlin. If you plan to come by public transport, the main stations to aim for are Wernigerode and Nordhausen where regional trains connect with the rest of Germany and beyond.

What to pack: You will want a longline for the dog here.

The dog rules: Dogs must remain on a lead at all times throughout the Harz National Park in order to protect wildlife and the fragile, burgeoning ecosystems. They must wear muzzles on all public transport; officially, they must be muzzled on the Harz Railway, too, but this isn't always enforced.

Getting around: The Harz Railway is a scenic service connecting several towns and villages in the centre of the Harz National Park; there is an extensive network of buses in the region, too.

More information: There's ample information about the region, and travelling with pets in the Harz, on the national park's website: harzinfo.de. Also download the Harz app on Google Play or Apple App Store. More information about the two main regions that fall within the boundaries of the park can be found at saxony-anhalt-tourism.com and niedersachsen-tourism.com.

→ Arty posing at the top of the castle at Hardenberg BurgHotel
↓ Lentil and frankfurter soup on the Okersee boat

MAKE IT A ROAD TRIP
Explore both city and mountains by pairing the Harz with a weekend in Berlin (see page 118) or head southeast for a road trip through Saxony (see page 128).

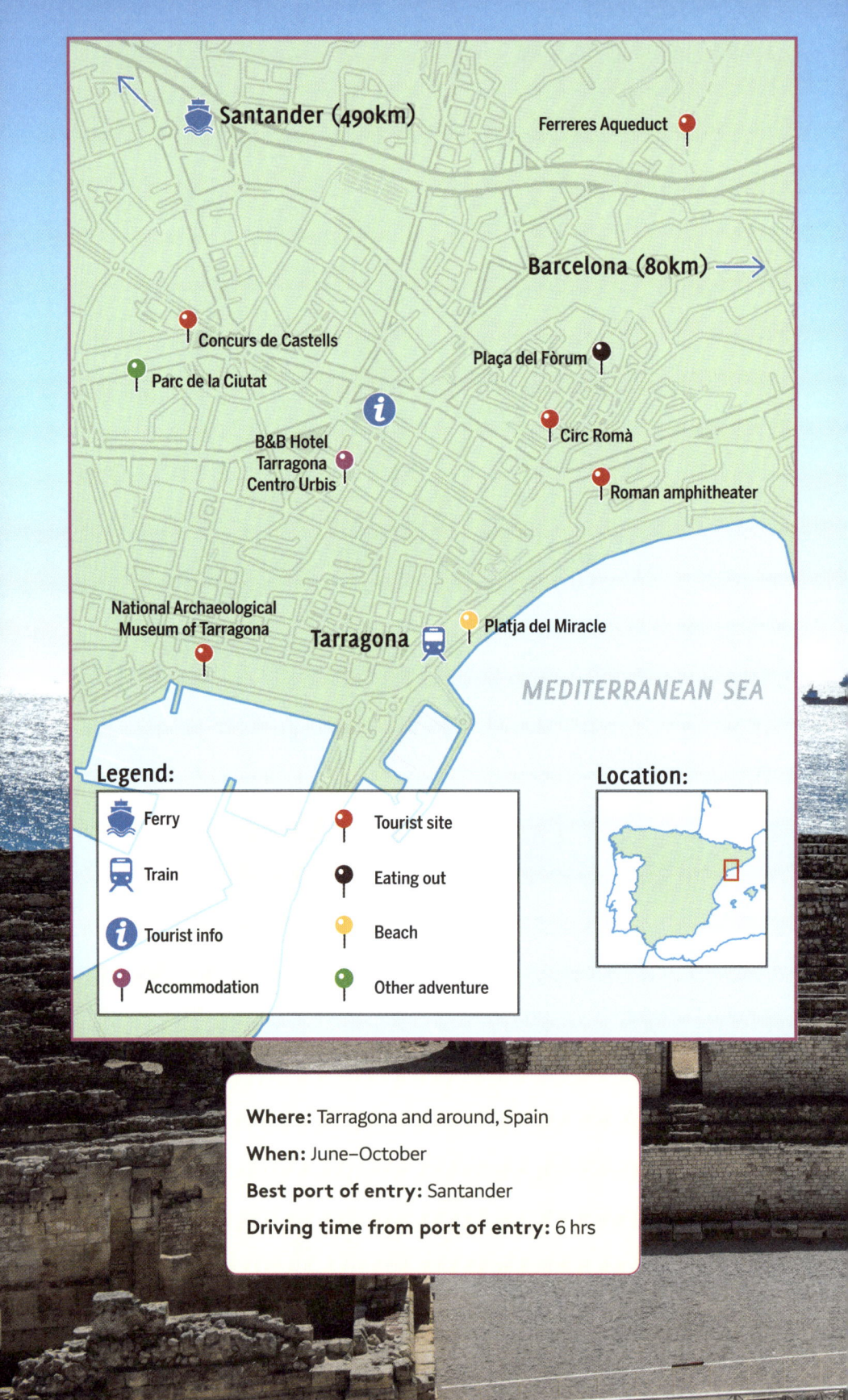

8
WATCH THE HUMAN TOWERS OF CATALUNYA

Tarragona

Spain is known the world over for its somewhat quirky traditions and festivals: the tomato fights in Buñol, the running of the bulls in Pamplona, the satirical papier-mâché sculptures of Las Fallas in Valencia. But few of its traditions are quite as terrifying as the creating of *castells* – vast towers built solely with human bodies, topped with a teetering child in a horse-riding helmet. With somewhat vague origins in the 18th century, what supposedly began as a dancing tradition has transformed into the second-most important sport in Catalunya, after football, of course. There are entire magazines, websites and TV shows dedicated to the *castells*, UNESCO has designated it a spot on the Intangible Cultural Heritage list, and summer performances across Catalunya culminate once every two years in a raucous tournament in the coastal city of Tarragona – the **Concurs de Castells** (concursdecastells.cat).

Castellers – the humans who make up the towers – in modern society are revered as strong athletes, admired for their physical and mental prowess. Great respect is given to those willing to put themselves at the heart of these human Jenga stacks, and even more so for the children who scale its lofty heights in pursuit of the points that will put them at the top of the leader board. Intensive training takes place throughout the winter, and in summer the *colles* (teams) tour the towns and cities of Catalunya taking part in public performances to practise their best towers.

It's at these **summer performances** that you and the dog can take in this utterly ludicrous sport and the thrilling atmosphere it creates. Usually taking place outdoors in plazas large and small throughout the region – check castellscat.cat/en/schedule for the full schedule and locations – there's plenty of opportunity to see a tower or two go up, and sometimes tumble.

You will find it's impossible to draw steady breath as you watch one of these towers gradually rise into the sky. It begins with a *pinya*, a base made up of sometimes hundreds of bodies standing so close to one another they form a sturdy platform on which the next layer can stand. Then there's the tower itself, sometimes made up of a single person on each layer, but more often than not two, three or four people stand together, gripping one another's shirts and shoulders to create a hollow tower. The *colles'* smallest members – usually young teens – create a two-person point at the top, and then the *enxaneta*, the smallest child in the team, must climb all the way up and back down the other side, lifting one hand as they reach the highest point.

→ A group of *Castellers* building a human tower in a public square, Barcelona
↓ The cathedral in Tarragona

All of this is done to traditional tunes played on gralles and timbals (wind and percussion instruments), each part of the song transforming to indicate to those in the tower which stages are in progress. There's a wave of relief among the crowds and *colles* as the *enxaneta* makes their way down once again, but a tower can only be truly celebrated once the entire construction has been dismantled safely, without injury or fall.

And fall they do. Often without disaster, but broken bones, dislocated shoulders and head injuries are not uncommon among the castellers of Catalunya. And yet they continue to create these towers – their practice a symbol of resolve in the face of adversity, of bravery and of the importance of working together as one regardless of their differences. More than just a sporting spectacle, the *castells* are an awe-inspiring reminder of what humans can achieve when trust, strength and teamwork prevail. Of course, much of this will be lost on the dog, but where there's a *castells* performance there's often a barbecue of traditional Catalan cuisine not far beyond, and no doubt the dog will help you seek out some sustenance after all the drama is over.

The practicalities: These free public performances can be enjoyed throughout the year across Catalunya, but the majority – and often the best – take place between 23 June and the third Thursday in November. Locations vary, but the best can be found in the coastal cities of Tarragona and Barcelona, as well as the pretty historic centres of Valls and Vilafranca. The full schedule can be found at castellscat.cat/en/schedule; dogs are generally allowed to attend any outdoor performances. Note that nervous dogs or those of sensitive disposition may find the crowds and loud music distressing.

OTHER ADVENTURES NEARBY

When you're not holding your breath at the human tower performances, this part of Catalunya has lots more to offer. Start in Tarragona, a coastal city famed for its Roman ruins and golden sandy beaches. There's an off-lead dog area in the **Parc de la Ciutat**, but better still, dogs are allowed on specific sections of **Platja del Miracle** all year round. Between this stretch of soft sand and Via Augusta lies a **Roman amphitheatre** – dogs are allowed in as long as they can be carried. Right next door to this is the terminus for the **Yellow Train** – which is actually a blue land train where the dog can join you on a hop-on-hop-off tour of the city's sights. Take the train all the way down to the El Serrallo, the city's fishing quarter, and you can visit the **National Archaeological Museum of Tarragona** (mnat.cat) providing you carry the dog when inside.

Remnants of Roman Tarragona – or Tarraco as the Romans named it when they first landed in 218 BCE – can be seen all over the city. Behind the amphitheatre you'll see the **Circ Romà**, a 1st-century CE circus ground where up to 30,000 spectators would watch chariot races. Wander through the narrow streets of the old city to **Plaça del Fòrum** and you can sip coffee or vermouth at one of its many bar terraces while overlooking the remains of the Roman forum.

Head just 15 minutes out of town and you'll discover one of the most impressive Roman constructions of all: **the Ferreres Aqueduct**. At 26 metres high and over 200 metres long, it's an astonishingly well-preserved piece of architecture, bridging a steep ravine. Surrounded by parkland with trails aplenty, this a cracking place for a

↓ The Ferreres Aqueduct near Tarragona

shaded walk with the dog or a picnic beneath the pines.

If you find yourselves in Valls for a *castellers* performance, be sure to check out the **Museu Casteller de Catalunya** for an immersive history of the practice and an exploration of its modern ways – it's not pet-friendly, but well worth seeking out if you can take turns looking after the dog in a cafe or bar nearby. And don't miss a wander round Valls' old city streets, where 16th- and 17th-century churches tower over terracotta rooftops.

Vilafranca – or Vilafranca del Penedès – is another popular *castellers* town and has little in the way of dog-friendly attractions. But beyond its urban centre lies an undulating landscape of farmland and **vineyards**, and a waymarked 3.5km walking route (the **Camí del vi**; turismevilafranca.com) leads you across the countryside to eight of them, where the dog is generally allowed to join you at each on terraces or occasionally inside tasting rooms. This is cava country, so expect plenty of bubbly as well as red and white wines.

↑ The Mastinell winery
← On top of the Ferreres Aqueduct near Tarragona

Strike out in the car from here and there are more vineyards to visit. **Mastinell** (mastinell.com) is just 1.5km from the town centre and has an excellent upscale restaurant with a dog-friendly terrace overlooking the vines, while **Parés Baltà** (paresbalta.com), another 3km north, offers tours and tastings. Head another 25 minutes into the hills to **Mont Rubí** (montrubi.com) and you'll get a tour of the vineyard and winery (no dogs inside the winery building) where the wines are aged in traditional ceramic pots, and then a pairing experience in the restaurant with up to six wines.

WHAT'S FOR DINNER?

One of the joys of visiting Catalunya in summer is its vast outdoor terraces, where your dog will be welcomed with open arms to join you for a flavour of Catalan cuisine, or perhaps just a *canya* (small glass) of local *cervesa* (beer). Out here on the coast, it pays to take advantage of the seafood and shellfish on offer – prawns, octopus and fresh fish abound. But also look out for some Catalan classics – especially on those **community-run barbecues** that pop up at *castells* performances. Look out for a *calçotada* – large leafy onions blackened on an open fire, served with a romesco sauce – which originate from Valls and are to be eaten with your hands. Or, in Tarragona, order *cassola de romesco* for a warming seafood stew with tomato, garlic, chilli, almonds and hazelnuts.

Spend any time in cities like Tarragona or Barcelona (see page 160) and you'll notice a healthy proportion of vermouth bars (*vermut* in Catalan). The fortified wine made its way to Spain via Italian immigrants in the 1800s and is now a hugely popular aperitif (or *aperitiu*), so make like a local and find yourself a seat in the local square for a strong pre-dinner drink.

WATCH THE HUMAN TOWERS OF CATALUNYA

WHERE TO SLEEP

Mas Passamaner

From £150 per night
maspassamaner.com

Designed to feel like the home of an eccentric friend – all antiques and unusual artworks – Mas Passamaner is a supremely welcoming setting. Sitting amid vineyards just 11km from Tarragona and 12km from Valls, this little countryside escape is a tempting place to languish for several hours in the Spanish sun. Some rooms have their own private patios, while others overlook the pool area and lush gardens. Throw the ball for the dog on the lawned helipad when not in use and enjoy early morning walks around the surrounding vineyards before the heat of the day becomes too much. The nearby town of El Morell has a handful of good restaurants and bars.

B&B Hotel Tarragona Centro Urbis

From £45 per night
hotel-bb.com

Right in the heart of Tarragona, this hotel is a brilliant budget option. Rooms are relatively plain but modern and always clean, and some have small balconies and bathtubs. The light-filled lobby offers free tea and coffee, and while there's no breakfast, the covered market and Tarragona's new town bars and cafes are right on the doorstep.

Casa Rural Camí Romà

From £120 per night
casaruralcamiroma.com

A 35-minute drive from Tarragona city centre lies this country mansion, a five-room hotel with vast gardens where palms sway gently and cypress trees line the driveway. It was out here where the Romans took rest during their expeditions across the Iberian peninsula, and while the buildings in which they might have set down for the night are no longer standing, this house still has some immense history. Parts of it date back 1,000 years and original elements from the 19th century betray its life as a strategic military location during the Carlist Wars. Today, it has been renovated and restored and bedrooms have a pleasing palette of neutral colours and natural woods, some with four-poster beds and vast, inviting bathtubs.

Vilanova Park

From £20 per pitch per night
caravanclub.co.uk

For campers in Catalunya, Vilanova Park is a convenient base open year-round, with a huge array of excellent facilities and pitches for caravans, campervans and motorhomes. A restaurant serving local and international dishes, including a good seafood paella, allows dogs on the terrace (or you can have takeaway), and a large outdoor pool is popular with kids in summer. The site is huge, with lots of seasonal pitches hosting vast, luxury motorhomes and caravans, and it's a short drive to the coast at Cubelles, which has an enclosed dog-friendly beach at Platja de les Salines. There's even a dogwash station behind the beach on Carrer Ramon Llull for excessively sandy paws. From here, it's a 35-minute drive to Tarragona and just 25 minutes to Vilafranca.

ESSENTIALS

Getting there: Tarragona itself is easy to reach by train with direct connections to Barcelona-Sants, where there are direct services that connect to Madrid and Paris. The direct trains from Paris to Barcelona are run by SNCF so dogs are allowed with muzzle and lead, but note that dogs over 10kg are not allowed to travel on all Renfe routes in Spain; check renfe.com for details. Dogs also need their own tickets for travel. The local route run between Tarragona and Barcelona is dog-friendly for 'small pets' (see rodalies.gencat.cat), but no weight restriction is specified. Driving is a much more convenient way to reach the region, though, and Catalunya is just six hours by car from the main ports in Santander and Bilbao; note that there will be tolls for motorways.

What to pack: It's often sweltering in this region throughout the summer months, so bring a portable water bowl or bottle for the dog and consider packing a cooling mat so they don't have to lie down on hot sand or pavements. A parasol could also be a good idea for beach days where there's little shade.

The dog rules: Dogs generally must be on a lead in public places unless you're in a designated dog park or beach. Look out for signs around beaches and parks that say '*No gossos*' (no dogs) to decipher where your dog may or may not be allowed. Muzzles are essential for public transport.

Getting around: There are buses throughout the region linking the towns and cities where *castellers* perform, but dogs may not always be allowed on board; they might be required to wear a muzzle, much like they are on trains. Driving around the region is easy, but be aware that some of the motorways have tolls.

More information: Details on the *castells*' performances and more can be found on castellscat.cat. For more detail on Tarragona and its surrounding regions visit the tourist office in the city on Rambla Nova, or head to tarragonaturisme.cat. Pick up a tourist map of Valls at the tourist information at Carrer de la Cor or download it at valls.cat; Vilafranca's tourist office is on Carrer Hermenegild Clascar and its website has more information at turismevilafranca.com.

↓ Tarragona's Roman ruins

9

CRUISE THE CANALS FOR COASTAL FUN IN THE SOUTH OF FRANCE

If it's a sedate lifestyle you seek, a week or two spent slowly exploring the Camargue by boat is a worthy way to have a holiday with the dog. There's something deeply mesmeric about the slow, monotonous chug of a houseboat on the wide, straight channels of the Canal du Rhône à Sète. Set amid an impressively flat landscape, from the top deck of your vessel you can see for miles into the distance, beyond the marshes, **saltwater lagoons** and tiny waterside towns that punctuate this waterway. Occasionally, a smattering of trees will interrupt the view – bright green, lanky and leafy, they harbour herons and the striking European bee-eater. In the sky, flocks of **pink flamingo** glide, their long, outstretched necks almost as lengthy as their shocking fuchsia legs that dangle behind as they pass overhead.

This is the Petite Camargue. A marshy coastal region of southern France where wild horses roam and black, horned bulls stare menacingly from their waterside ranches, offering plenty of intriguing smells for the dog to enjoy as you cruise. Starting from the marina in Saint-Gilles, you can cruise south towards the Mediterranean Sea, where the canal connects with the Étang de l'Or – the first of a series of coastal lagoons separated from the ocean

↓ An aerial view over the Canal du Rhône à Sète

by a thin strip of land that's punctuated by lively seaside resorts. From here, if you have plenty of time, you can continue though the **Étang de Thau** and on to France's most iconic waterway, the Canal du Midi, which winds through the countryside beyond the Camargue to handsome cities like Béziers or walled Carcassonne.

A better endeavour, though, is to take it slowly – you can't really help it in a houseboat that can only travel a few miles per hour at best – and discover the charms of the Petite Camargue with its pretty little villages and walled towns. Days can be spent cruising, those not behind the wheel languishing on deck in the sun or down below preparing lunch for your chosen captain, or you can take to the towpath on foot to explore the local highlights. By night you can moor up in the heart of the action in towns like Aigues-Mortes, or find somewhere serene to stick your pins along the canal towpath and spend an evening under the stars, listening to the resident frogs and crickets who use the marshes as their amphitheatre.

On the nearly 70km stretch of canal between Saint-Gilles and the Étang de Thau lies a host of intriguing communities and beautiful waterside towns; here are seven of the most enchanting to explore with the dog.

Gallician

Just 12km west of the base at Saint-Gilles, Gallician is a truly tiny little village, consisting of just a few main streets with a handful of restaurants, a boulangerie and a small, attractive chapel. You might be tempted to skip straight past this little community that sits directly on the canal, but you'd miss out on a visit to the Gallician Signature (gallician.com) **wine cooperative** – a warehouse where several of the 95 local producers offer their wines for tastings and takeout. This is your place to stock the boat with exceptional local drinks: bottles, bags and boxes of wine abound here, all from the Costières wine-growing region, which has produced wine since the Middle Ages. The reds, which encompass merlot, syrah and grenache grapes, have notes of balsamic, while the whites and pale rosés (largely chardonnay, viognier, sauvignon) are floral and fresh. The dog may be allowed inside if you can carry them.

Aigues-Mortes

While the Canal du Midi has Carcassonne, the Canal du Rhône à Sète has Aigues-Mortes, a 13th-century **fortified town** with magnificent towering military walls just a 90-minute cruise from Gallician. It's not staid history here, though, as the town has a distinctly festive atmosphere in summertime when flamenco musicians play music throughout the streets and the tiny lanes throng with visitors. Enter via the Porte de la Gardette – a gate flanked by two rounded towers – and you'll be thrown into a warren of streets lined with boutiques, colourful vintage sweet shops and irresistible *boulangeries*. Head to the main square, Place Saint Louis, to sip something cool in the sun on a restaurant terrace and soak up the merriment of the day.

If you've a head for heights, climb up on

↑ Arty walks the towpath at Le Boat base, St Gilles
← Arty on board the Le Boat cruiser on the Canal du Rhône à Sète

to the ramparts for brilliant views across the town and out over the pink-hued **Salins du Midi**, a vast saltworks with its own flock of pink flamingos. Dogs aren't allowed to walk the ramparts with their humans unfortunately, so you'll need to leave your pet with one of your group before you take to the towers, nor are they allowed on the small train that tours the saltworks. They can, however, ride the **Petit Train** d'Aigues-Mortes (petittrain-aiguesmortes.fr) with you, which tours the fortress and has historical commentary in French alongside an English translation on paper. If you're not sick of messing about on the water, the dog can also join you on a **canal tour** with Péniches Isles de Stel (croisiere-de-camargue.com), which has commentary in English and French and offers lunchtime cruises with meals on board.

La Grande-Motte

Not directly on the canal but just a little south of the towpath, La Grande-Motte is the first in a string of seaside resorts, which have the Mediterranean on one side and the Étang de l'Or on the other.

This is a modern seaside town with bulky 1960s apartment blocks overlooking its harbour and a huge **soft-sand beach** spread out along the seafront. This beach is its greatest asset, and you can find the dog-friendly section at entrance 60 (in Le Grand Travers), around a 45-minute walk west of the port. In the town centre you'll find plenty of restaurants and cafes with terraces, and on its fringes lies the pleasant Pinède de La Grande-Motte, a large parkland with pine trees providing essential dappled shade, ideal for walking the dog on a hot day.

Come summer, La Grande-Motte has some exciting **markets**. In July and August you can peruse the crafts by local artisans at the Couchant night market (Esplanade du Couchant) on Mondays, Thursdays and Saturdays, while in Place du Cosmos Mondays are for the wine growers to show off their latest vintages.

Carnon

Sitting 2.5 hours west along the canal from Aigues-Mortes and at the far western end of the Étang de l'Or, Carnon is another busy seaside resort with a 6km-long protected dune system and magnificent beach. Neither of these things, unfortunately, are open for dogs, but they can join you on the **free guided walks** run by the tourist office on the shores of the lagoon, and on the many restaurant terraces for a fine seafood supper.

Palavas-les-Flots

A once modest fishing village that's now morphed into a popular seaside town with high-rise apartments and a vast port, Palavas-les-Flots is a **watersports** hub. The dog won't be allowed on the

beach in peak season, but you can walk along the promenade and enjoy the greenery of Parc Saint-Pierre before settling down for dinner in one of its many fish restaurants. Alternatively, pop into town in the morning to watch the fishermen return from their endeavours at sea and bargain a fair price for a fish supper you can cook on board your boat.

Maguelone

Don't miss a pleasant dog walk on Maguelone, a tiny 430-metre-wide island that connects the canal to a naturist beach on the Med via narrow spits of land. It's home to little more than a vineyard, woodland picnic area, a restaurant (dog-friendly inside and out) and, rather surprisingly, a cathedral. The church is a former **Romanesque bishop's palace**, built in the Midde Ages and still standing in part ruin today. Note that dogs must be on a lead here to protect wildlife, which can sometimes include a small flock of peacocks. Dogs are allowed on the beach here, too, but must be on a lead.

Frontignan

Set between the Étang de Thau and the Étang d'Ingril is Frontignan, home of France's most famous sweet wine, Muscat. The town itself is set back from the ocean on the northern banks of the canal. Sample the local tipple at the **Cooperative Muscat de Frontignan** and enjoy a leafy stroll around **Parc Victor Hugo**, and if you come before the end of April, you can let the dog run free on the beach 2km to the south.

Practicalities: Saint-Gilles is home to a Le Boat base (leboat.com), a reliable company for hiring high-quality, easy-to-manoeuvre fibreglass houseboats for up to nine people and two dogs. Each boat has a fully equipped kitchen, television, heating, and a bathroom with a hot water shower. Many also have upper decks where you can barbecue, lounge on sunbeds and dine al fresco with great views of the canals around you.

Bedrooms are small but comfortable and there's plenty of room in the fridge for all that wine you'll acquire on your

↓ The author's father, Andy, skippering their vessel on the Canal du Rhône à Sète

↑ A cruiser boat moored next to the Château de Ventenac en Minervois near Narbonne
→ A night-time view of Aigues-Mortes

travels. It serves to hire bikes alongside your boat (providing the dog is confident and trustworthy trotting alongside you), as sometimes the walk into towns from the towpath can be substantial, which is less than ideal when you're packing baguettes and cheeses and wines for your on-board catering. Bikes come free with some boats on the Le Boat roster, or you can add them to your booking in advance for a fee.

You'll want to allow at least a week for this sort of trip, but book in for two or three if you want to make it all the way to the Canal du Midi (you may be able to leave your boat at one of the Le Boat Canal du Midi bases and arrange transport back to your car at Saint-Gilles).

Before you set off, you can stock up on supplies in Saint-Gilles, which has a small supermarket in town and an Intermarché on the outskirts, as well as a lovely dog-friendly *boulangerie*.

WHAT'S FOR DINNER?

Aside from the excellent wine, Muscat and fine locally produced salt, there are a handful of intriguing specialties from these parts. The sweet-toothed will want to try an Aigues-Mortes *fougasse*, an orange blossom-scented brioche topped with sugar. Carnivores should look out for *gardiane de taureau*, a stew made with bull's meat that's popular throughout the Camargue region, and seafood lovers will want to try *tellines* (clams) cooked in olive oil, parsley and garlic.

Perhaps unexpectedly to those unfamiliar with this part of France, the Camargue is known locally for its excellent rice – it's grown in paddies across the region and is an industry that contributes a substantial amount to the economy here. Look out for *paella camarguaise* on menus – a dish spiced with saffron, often containing shrimp, chicken and mussels.

ESSENTIALS

Getting there: There is no train station in Saint-Gilles so the only way to reach the Le Boat base is by car. It's a long drive from the nearest French port with UK ferry connections (Roscoff), but just a seven-hour drive from Santander and Bilbao.

What to pack: Aside from your usual dog kit, you might want to invest in a dog life jacket. While it's not recommended to let your dog swim in the canal, sometimes you can't help a pooch going overboard and so a life jacket will keep them safe if they happen to misstep getting on or off the boat.

The dog rules: Dogs should be on a lead around wildlife and livestock, including the wild horses should you come across any.

MAKE IT A ROAD TRIP

If you're reaching the Camargue via Santander or Bilbao, a stop in foodie San Sebastián (see page 54) is a brilliant way to break up the journey. Extend your trip by driving just 90 minutes east of the Camargue to the Luberon Regional Park (see page 220), where the town of Apt is a brilliant base for dog-friendly adventuring in vineyards, Martian landscapes and cedar forests.

More information: For more information and pricing details for a canal boat holiday in the Camargue, head to leboat.com.

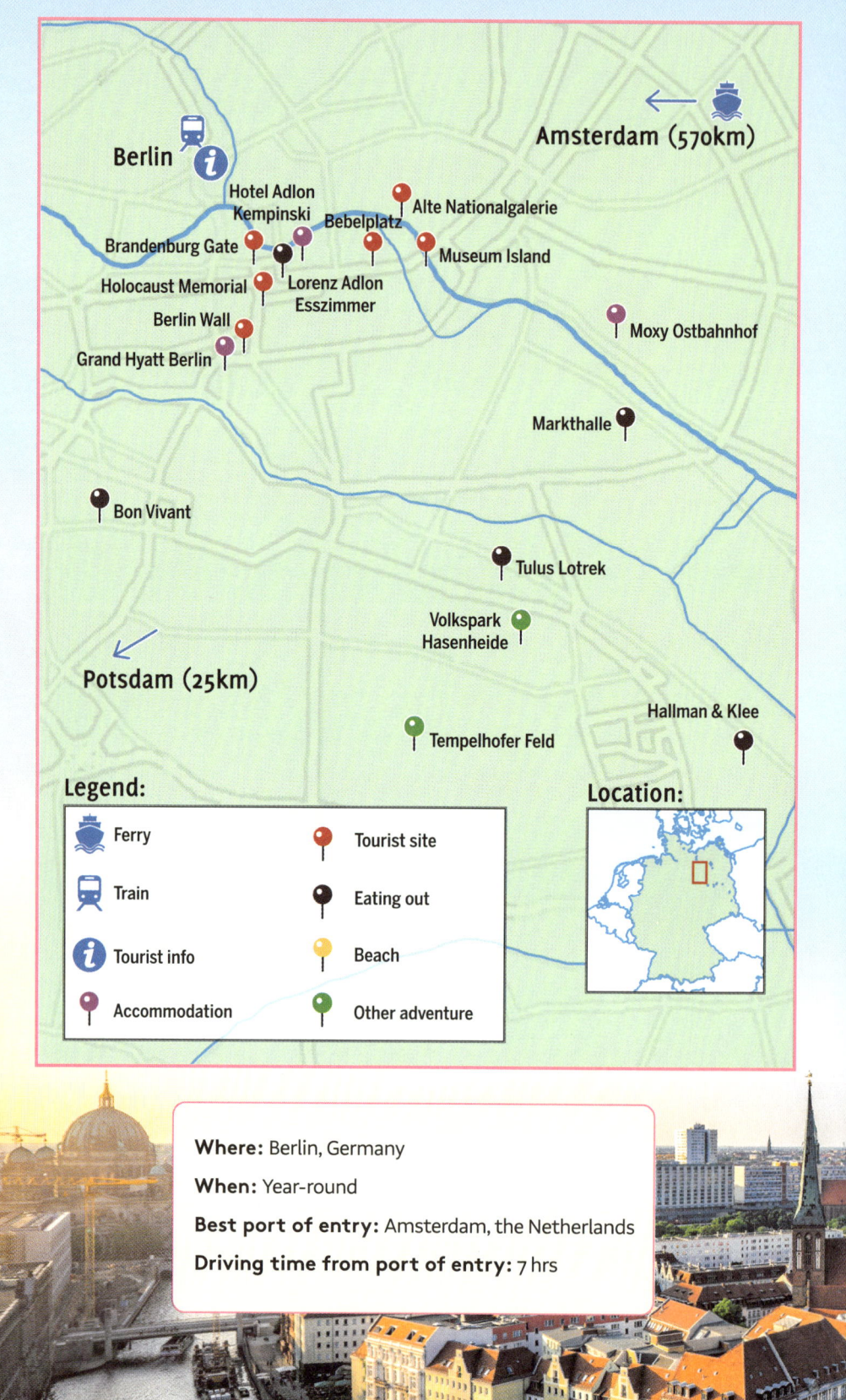

10

GO URBAN HIKING IN THE GERMAN CAPITAL

Berlin

Berlin is both awe-inspiring and intimidating all at once. It's intimidating not because it's difficult to travel around or because it feels like a hostile place, but simply because of its sheer size. This city is inhabited by over 3.5 million people and spreads itself out so widely – it has a span of 45km from east to west – it has myriad exciting and diverse neighbourhoods that could fill entire weekends on their own. Fortunately, having a dog by your side in Berlin does narrow your options somewhat – the city's museums don't allow pets inside, for example – making it easier to decide where to begin, and that's no bad thing. Seeing this city through your dog's eyes will still make for a thrilling urban adventure.

The awe here comes in various guises: it's impossible not to be astounded by the city's relatively recent history of destruction, conflict, segregation and reunification, but it's also a visually arresting place. The architecture is vast, varied and at times utterly spellbinding, from the intricate Baroque buildings of its central Mitte neighbourhood to the post-war tower blocks and blunt, Brutalist constructions elsewhere. And then, of course, you have the **Berlin Wall**, remnants of which are visible at places like Checkpoint Charlie and the colourful East Side Gallery, where artists have painted the wall with bold political murals. It may be innocuous in its height and design, akin to any boarding you might see on an urban construction site, but the wall's remains are a powerful symbol of a country and its population devastatingly split by opposing political ideologies.

And so, with the dog on a lead, walking around Berlin is a visual feast. The best way to see its architectural highlights is on a **tour with a local guide** – and no other local guide offers a better dog-friendly insight into the city than Martin Sauter (toursbylocals.com), doting guardian of a small white terrier called Whiley. Born in the former West Germany and raised in what was then West Berlin, he describes his younger self as 'restless and curious' – perhaps a little like his dog – and today he rarely leaves the house without Whiley when he's not guiding.

You'll most likely meet Martin around Pariser Platz – where one of Berlin's fanciest dog-friendly hotels, the Adlon Kempinski, is located – and start your tour by wandering through the impressive and iconic **Brandenburg Gate**. His tours are always bespoke, so tell him what you're interested in and he'll find a way to work it into your visit – offering titbits of intriguing stories and details about the city's present and past along the way. He will guide you to the **Holocaust Memorial**, an artwork designed by architect Peter Eisenman made up of concrete blocks that create a different atmosphere as the sun moves their shadows throughout the day. Dogs can't join you on the memorial, but it's still impactful from the edge – and you could always take it in turns to stand among the cement structures to feel the weight of their moving symbolism, which is often best done alone.

You'll wander past the magnificent pastel pink opera house on **Bebelplatz**, where you can stop to look down through a glass window in the ground that shows a room of empty bookshelves – a memorial to the 1933 book burning at the Institute for Sexual Research – and on to **Museum Island**, which sits in the middle of the River Spree and has myriad architectural styles, from the ancient temple-style of the Alte Nationalgalerie

→ Suburban Berlin in the autumn

to the classical Colonnade Courtyard. The dog can't join you inside any of these lauded art institutions unfortunately, but their facades alone are worth travelling to see – and the dog will enjoy a sniff around the landscaped gardens, too.

When your feet are tired and you can't walk any more, take to the waters of the River Spree for a **sedate cruise** through the city. Reederei Bruno Winkler (reedereiwinkler.de) allows dogs on board for a small fee and its one- to four-hour cruises meander from Schloßbrücke in Charlottenburg in the west of the city to the waterways around Museum Island, with some longer trips venturing south on to the Landwehrkanal. There are German and English language guides, and if you opt for an evening cruise you'll get an even more magical view on this regal city.

OTHER ADVENTURES NEARBY

Once you've pounded the streets of Berlin's downtown, treat the dog to a run around in the city's lungs: the **Tiergarten**. This enormous park – all 210 hectares of it – is a dog's dream: there are vast lawns, enclosed off-leash areas and towering woodlands that turn all shades of orange and yellow in autumn. Within its twisting trails you'll find a rose garden, an English garden, the impressive Memorial to the Victims of the Berlin Wall and the perfectly mown lawns of the Schloss Bellevue – home of the German president, dating back to the 18th century. An excellent dog-friendly restaurant – Cafe am Neuen See (cafeamneuensee.de) – can be found on the southern edge of the park for those who need to refuel with warming hot chocolates or cheese and charcuterie boards in an upscale setting.

Beyond the centre of the city, aimless wandering around Berlin's diverse neighbourhoods is an equally enchanting

↑ Plush beds and treats for sale in bougie petshop Sonnenberg Berlin
← Arty exploring the Tiergarten

experience. **Charlottenburg**, southwest of the Tiergarten, is where you'll find its shopping high street and fancy boutiques – many of which allow dogs inside. If you find yourselves down here, it would be remiss to not visit **Sonnenberg Berlin** (sonnenberg.berlin), the poshest pet shop you may have ever entered where tweed dog coats and handmade rope leads hang on displays behind eco-friendly toys and an astonishing buffet of natural dog treats and chews. You won't be able to leave without spending a small fortune.

In the southeast of the city is the **Friedrichshain-Kreuzberg district**, where

Bergmannstraße becomes a lively spot at weekends for drinking and dining on the terraces outside the **Markthalle** (not dog-friendly inside) and a flea market offers intriguing finds, from handmade children's clothing to jewellery and vintage photography and artworks. Nearby is the wonderful **Volkspark Hasenheide**, which has an enclosed off-lead area for dogs and beautiful woodlands to explore, as well as the **Tempelhofer Feld** – a former airfield that's become a favourite for locals to exercise their pets in its enclosed dog park.

There are couple of **day trips** worth making time for, too. Head west to **Grunewald**, a vast forest with endless trails and a lake (Grunewaldsee) that has its own dog beach for refreshing summer swims (///green.gosh.packets). Take the train even further west and you'll reach **Potsdam**, where more regal architecture in the form of ostentatious royal palaces abounds. Stroll around the beautiful Park Sanssouci, where Orangerieschloss, Schloss Babelsberg and Neues Palais are among the highlights. There are dog-friendly boat trips on an historic steam ship, too, and dogs ride free (schifffahrt-in-potsdam.de).

WHAT'S FOR DINNER?

While Berlin is a good place to embrace traditional German food, what's really exciting in this city is the fine dining and diverse international cuisines on offer. Google 'most dog-friendly city Europe' and you'll find Berlin is listed at or near the top of many rankings, and that's largely thanks to the dog-friendliness of cafes, restaurant and bars. While it's rare for a dog to be declined from a restaurant here, it's always worth calling ahead to check if there's somewhere specific you want to dine at.

If you want to push the boat out, try Berlin stalwart Lorenz Adlon Esszimmer in the Hotel Adlon Kempinski (kempinski.com/hotel-adlon), which has two Michelin stars, or Tulus Lotrek (tuluslotrek.de), Bon Vivant (bonvivant.berlin) or Hallman & Klee (hallmann-klee.de), all of which have or have had Michelin accolades in recent years.

Of course, you can't visit the German capital without trying a Berliner kebab – a German take on the traditional Turkish doner kebab, which involves succulent grilled meat from a spit stuffed into a soft pitta with salad and tangy sauces. This isn't just an end-of-the-night drinker's snack – Berlin is serious about its kebabs. So much so, there have been festivals dedicated to the dish and it's said there are over 1,000 outlets making them in the city. Another popular street food, which was invented in Berlin, is *currywurst*: smoky sausage chopped up and slathered in a tomato and curry sauce, served with moreish chips.

WHERE TO SLEEP

Grand Hyatt Berlin

From £120 per night
hyatt.com

For the luxury of space and a little five-star treatment, plus an unrivalled location just five minutes' walk from the Tiergarten, the Grand Hyatt is worth splashing out on. Dogs get special hospitality here, too, with beds, bowls and treats left in your bedroom, while you'll enjoy use of divinely soft robes and enormous super-king beds. Dogs are allowed in the restaurant for breakfast, and for humans only there's a fabulous high-rise spa with a pool. On your doorstep is Potsdamer Platz and the Brandenburg Gate and you're just 30 minutes by S-Bahn to Grunewald.

Moxy Ostbahnhof

From £70 per night
marriott.com

Located in edgy east Berlin, the Moxy is a reliable, affordable spot to base yourself. While the area around it isn't so enchanting – though it is minutes from the East Side Gallery – you are handily right next to the Ostbahnhof station, offering easy access into the city centre and elsewhere. Dogs get a bowl with treats in the room and are allowed into the breakfast area, and there's a small grassy square opposite for morning and evening toilet breaks. Note that there's a night light sensor beneath the bed, so you may want to

← Steps lead down to the Spree river near the East Side Gallery

GO URBAN HIKING IN THE GERMAN CAPITAL

stick a plaster over it if the dog is liable to roam in the night and illuminate the room while you're asleep. For excellent food and drink nearby, head to the hip Holzmarkt development on the banks of the Spree just over the road where street food, events and artisan markets pop up regularly.

ESSENTIALS

Getting there: Berlin is easily reached by train (dogs must have their own tickets on German trains and wear a muzzle) or by car, and there are plenty of underground and multi-storey car parks for leaving your vehicle safely (both the Moxy and Grand Hyatt have their own parking).

What to pack: Always bring a muzzle for the dog if you're using public transport – you may not be asked to use it, but if you don't carry one you may be thrown off the train or fined. You might want to bring a longline for the parks where dogs aren't allowed off lead.

The dog rules: Dogs are only allowed on the beaches in town from October to May. They need to be kept under control when in public off lead, and mess must be cleaned up.

Getting around: Berlin's buses, trains (S-Bahn) and subway (U-Bahn) are extensive, connecting all corners of the city with dog-friendly transport. Dogs not placed inside carriers must have their own tickets for travel.

More information: The Berlin tourism board has extensive information on dog rules in the city, and plenty more information on the capital's attractions – visit berlin.de.

↑ The colourful entrance to the Holzmarkt
→ Dog-friendly terraces along Bergmannstraße

MAKE IT A ROAD TRIP
Berlin is just a few hours' drive from the Baltic Coast (see page 180) to the north, where the dog will enjoy beach time and coastal forest walks. Alternatively, head south to Saxony for a road trip (see page 128) via Leipzig and regal Dresden, or to the Harz Mountains for a lofty escape (see page 86).

Where: Saxony, Germany
When: April–October
Best port of entry: Amsterdam, the Netherlands
Driving time from port of entry: 7 hrs

11
CITIES, SWIMMING AND SPECTACULAR SCENERY IN EASTERN GERMANY

Saxony may be small, but its variety of landscapes and rich culture make it quite a dazzling destination. Sitting on the border with Poland and the Czech Republic, it's home to the mighty Elbe River, a handful of cities brimming with art and inspiring architecture – including its elegant capital, Dresden – and has one of the northernmost wine regions in Europe.

For dog owners, there's so much to enjoy in its urban and scenic spaces that the best way to see Saxony is on a multi-stop trip that takes in a variety of its highlights. There's musical history, excellent coffee, swimming, boating and vineyard-touring to be done, plus a whole host of exciting hikes out in the countryside. Whether travelling by car or rail, these are the best stops for a dog-friendly Saxony itinerary.

Leipzig

Start your tour of Saxony in the west, where the region's most populous city, Leipzig, has intrigue of the aural kind. Most famous for its connection to Bach, who did some of his most important work right here, it has myriad musical connections. It was the birthplace of Wagner, Mahler wrote his first symphony here and Felix Mendelssohn founded the Conservatorium of Music in Leipzig in the 1840s. While the city's museums and galleries won't let the dog in, you can still explore its musical history on the **Music Trail** (known in German as the Leipziger Notenspur; directions at notenspur-leipzig.de), where you'll find plenty of information as you go and at some stops you'll be able to press a button to hear samples of the music made within these very streets.

Exploring Leipzig on foot is easy, as the centre is confined to a pleasing 1 sq

km space and informative tour guides can be hired from the tourism office on Katharinenstraße. But those wishing to save their legs can enjoy an entertaining hour's excursion with the **dog-friendly boat trips** by Stadthafen Leipzig (stadthafen-leipzig.com). Departing from the harbour on the Elstermühlgraben and cruising all the way to the Karl Heine canal and back, it's a beautiful way to see the city from the water – and you might spot a kingfisher or heron on your travels, too. Bring your headphones and a smartphone and you can listen along to an audio tour via an app while the live German commentary is given, and prepare to duck as you go under one of the disconcertingly low bridges – health and safety need not apply.

The centre of Leipzig is beautiful, with its mismatched architectural styles from classical to baroque, but it's decidedly concrete – not so exciting for the dog. Fortunately, the west of the city has ample parkland for some lovely walks with the dog, including in **Clara-Zetkin-Park** where they can run free in the open grassy fields. The **Rosental** park also has a dog off-lead area. To the south, pleasant walks can be had around the **Leipziger Auwald**, a riverside forest home to the dog-friendly **Wildpark** (they must be kept on a lead), while if the weather's not playing ball you can nip into the **Deutsches Fotomuseum** (fotomuseum.eu) for exhibitions on photography.

In the city's southeast, don't miss a visit to the somewhat dystopian Monument to the Battle of the Nations within the **Wilhelm-Külz-Park**. The monument itself might look like something out of Margaret Atwood's *Handmaid's Tale*, but there's no denying the views from its staircase are exceptional, especially at sunset. Climb its steps to look out over Leipzig and the surrounding countryside – the perfect precursor to stop two on your trip.

↓ The striking landscape of Saxon-Switzerland National Park

OTHER ADVENTURES NEARBY

Head 20 minutes south of Leipzig by car or 10 minutes on the train and you'll find yourself in mining country – not that you'd know it. The former open mines that once marked this landscape are long gone, and what has replaced them is a series of more than 20 lakes, many of which are connected via canals. This is where the city's residents spill out to on sunny days, as a smattering of beaches offers a chance for **swimming** in fresh open water, or a taster of some high-adrenaline **watersports** – even including diving.

For dogs, there's plenty of walking to be done around the lakeshores and a few dog beaches offering bathing opportunities for you all. Cospudener See has a cracking **10km trail** around its fringes – don't miss climbing the Bistumshöhe viewing tower on your walk – and a **dog beach** on its northwest corner, while at Markkleeberger See there's a dog-friendly stretch of sand at Auenhainer Strand on the eastern edge of the lake. For adventures on the water, **hire a pedalo or kayak** on Markkleeberger See (kanuverleih-leipzig.de), or join the **sedate cruises** (leipzigseen.de) that circumnavigate the lake in a 1950s habour barge built in Hamburg. These two lakes sit either side of Leipzig suburb Markkleeberg, which has a train station for public transport access and plenty of shops and restaurants to keep your energy levels up.

WHAT'S FOR DINNER?

Forget your evening meal – in Leipzig it's all about a mid-afternoon coffee and cake. As a major coffee producer in the 18th century, Leipzig has long had a love affair with the drink. Coffee houses sprung up in the 1700s and 1800s, and the second-oldest in Europe, Zum Arabischen Coffe Baum (coffebaum.de), still stands in the city today. Kaffeehaus Riquet (riquethaus.de) in the city centre is one of the more dog-friendly, allowing pets in its elegant, wood-panelled ground floor cafe. Order your chosen coffee alongside a piece of indulgent gateaux – just don't expect a puppuccino for the dog.

Despite its distance from the sea, one of Leipzig's most well-known traditional dishes is the seafood-based *Leipziger Allerlei*. Crayfish or shrimp are served in a creamy sauce with mixed vegetables and potatoes – a truly comforting dish after a long day on the lakes. To finish, try a *Leipziger Lerche*, a jam and nut pastry, or pick up some *Halloren Kugeln*, a chocolate dome filled with flavoured marzipan made in neighbouring Halle.

More information: Get more detail on travelling in and around Leipzig and the nearby lakes with your dog from the tourism board website, leipzig.travel.

→ Leipzig's towering Monument to the Battle of the Nations
↓ Paddling on the waterways near Leipzig

↑ The Karl-Heine Canal in the west of Leipzig

WHERE TO SLEEP

Townhouse Leipzig

From £90 per night
vagabondclub.com/leipzig

A chic city-centre hotel set inside a timber-framed building, Townhouse has done a great job of incorporating the old with the new. Expect modern bedrooms with nods to the city's history – such as sheet music murals above the beds – and original features, such as exposed brick and chunky wooden beams. Dogs get a bed and bowls in the room, and there's a decent restaurant downstairs serving grilled meat dishes for lunch and dinner and a breakfast buffet in the morning. This place gets bonus points for the sauna and relaxation area (no dogs allowed there). There's a small grassy area for early or late dog toileting opportunities next to the church opposite the hotel.

Seepark Auenhain

From £150 per night
seepark-auenhain.de

Right on the shores of Markkleeburger See and handily located behind the dog-friendly beach, this holiday park is a great place to base yourself for a weekend of fun around the lakes. Dogs are welcome in the holiday homes, each of which has its own equipped kitchen and log burner for those chillier evenings. From here you can easily access the lakeside trail for long walks by the water.

Lagovida

From £65 per night
lagovida.de

Whether you want to be beachside or in a house that appears to hover over the lake's surface, Lagovida has some excellent and unusual accommodation right on the shores of Störmthaler See, a body of water connected to Markkleeberger See by a 1.5km-long canal. Each little home from home is contemporary on the inside, with a fully equipped kitchen and cosy living area. Dogs are welcome in the Dune Houses and the Harbour Houses, and there's also an RV park for motorhomes and campervans (paved, no grass).

CITIES, SWIMMING AND SPECTACULAR SCENERY IN EASTERN GERMANY

Dresden

Set around the curvaceous Elbe, Dresden is Saxony's elegant capital. Visitors flock here for the culture – the world-class performances by the opera or the city's philharmonic orchestra, the art in its state art collections – but for dog owners, the excitement largely revolves around the river. One of the most enjoyable ways to see Dresden and its surrounding countryside is by boat – specifically, on a **paddle steamship** (saechsische-dampfschifffahrt.de). The Saxon Steamship Company, or Sächsische Dampfschifffahrt, has one of the oldest and biggest steamship fleets in the world and their boats cruise up and down the Elbe connecting the urban centre to the rural, as far east as Bad Schandau in Saxon-Switzerland National Park – the final stop on this itinerary.

The **sightseeing cruise** is the shortest option, cruising east to Blasewitz before returning to the city after a couple of hours, and it has a recorded commentary in both English and German. Sip German beers or wines as you pass vineyards, castles and palaces on one side and the Elbe meadows floodplain on the other. To get your steps in, opt to walk back along the southern riverbank for a scenic 6km stroll through the meadows, where the dog can run off the lead.

Back in the city centre it's the **architecture** that will wow you the most: wander with the dog through the old town and gaze upwards at the intricate carvings on the vast cathedral, the Frauenkirche church, or the Baroque Zwinger palace (dogs are allowed in the gardens and courtyard but not indoors). Each has the look of an historic building that's stood the test of time, but instead they are all reconstructions of their former selves, built largely in the 20th century after the devastation caused by bombing in Dresden during WWII. Another excellent and informative way to see the city centre and beyond is on the **hop-on-hop-off bus tour** (stadtrundfahrt.de), which includes English commentary and stops in 22 places around Dresden. Don't miss hopping off near the Großer Garten, a superbly landscaped garden where the dog can enjoy roaming on the lawns (on a lead) and sniffing the floral plantings.

For any dog owner with an interest in wine, Dresden is a dream destination. Not only does the city itself have plenty of excellent wine bars and restaurants (many of which allow dogs), but there's an entire hiking trail stretching for over 90km north and south of Dresden. Grab a map from the tourist office on Neumarkt and plan a walk out to **dog-friendly wineries** like Winzer Lutz Müller (winzer-lutz-mueller.de) or Drei Herren (dreiherren.de), using public transport (buses or boats) to ferry you back to town. This is one of the northernmost wine regions in Europe, so expect to drink plenty of Müller-Thurgau, Riesling and Weißer Burgunder.

WHAT'S FOR DINNER?

Much like Leipzig, Dresden is most famous for its sweets, namely the *Dresdner Eierschecke*. This simple cake has a sponge base, a tangy layer of quark and a creamy vanilla topping. Try it at Sophienkeller in the Taschenbergpalais (a high-end, dog-friendly hotel by Kempinski; sophienkeller-dresden.de), where the dog will be able to choose their own treat from a canine menu. If you visit around Christmastime, don't miss a taste of the city's famous *Dresdner Stollen*.

More information: Get more information on Dresden at visit-dresden-elbland.de, and see the Saxon Wine Hiking Trail at dresden-elbland.de.

WHERE TO SLEEP

Moxy Dresden

From £60 per night
marriott.com

Directly opposite the Dresden-Neustadt train station, the Moxy is a convenient base for getting to and around this city. The hotel – part of the Marriott group – has a decidedly youthful vibe, with dark walls, deep purple accents and graffiti-style artworks throughout. Dogs get treats on arrival, a bowl and more treats in the room, and they're welcome to join you for breakfast in the bar area (which also doubles as the reception). You're just a 10-minute walk from some of the Neustadt neighbourhood's best restaurants – head for the side streets around Königstraße – and it's a 30-minute walk into the city centre (or five minutes by S-Bahn). There's a small grassy area on the corner of Stetzscher Straße for late-night loo trips with the dog; parking is available on site. Use a plaster to cover the night light sensor beneath the bed so the dog doesn't wake you if they fidget while you sleep.

Saxon-Switzerland National Park

The powers that be who are responsible for naming German places seem to have an obsession with Switzerland – anywhere even remotely hilly is often referred to (sometimes officially, sometimes colloquially) as 'Swiss', no doubt because of the German neighbour's lofty mountains. It's often a stretch of the imagination to liken a 60-something-metre hill with a Swiss mountain range, but one place where you might forgive this quirk is in Saxon-Switzerland National Park, which lies nowhere near the border with Switzerland itself but has some of the most spectacular rocky scenery in all of Germany. It might not have the height of the Alps, but it certainly gives the Swiss a run for their money in terms of awe.

Set around the River Elbe, which flows in from the neighbouring Czech Republic, Saxon-Switzerland is a 100-million-year-old Cretaceous sea bed now exposed to the elements, where towering stacks of sandstone have created mesas, cliffs, rock formations, gullies and gorges.

One of the most enchanting places to see this unique geology in action is at

↓ The stunning rock formations of Bastei among an autumnal Saxon-Switzerland National Park

Bastei Bridge, a tourist attraction built in the 1820s for visitors to walk among the tall rock stacks that rise high above the Elbe. Originally, a wooden bridge connected some of the sturdiest stacks, but today a much less alarming sandstone bridge has been constructed to offer access to magnificent views to the Elbe valley below. There are viewing platforms and myriad staircases creating a trail around the rocky landscape, and even a castle dating back to the 1200s. It's an easy 10-minute stroll from the car park to the main attraction, and if you don't mind a breathless return climb, there's an enjoyable descent into the town of Rathen where you can grab some lunch before heading back up.

Further east along the Elbe lies another impressive rock – this time

↑ Visitors admiring the views from Königstein Fortress
← The turrets of the Königstein Fortress

a table-top hill where the mighty **Königstein Fortress** (festung-koenigstein.de) perches in prime defence position. Originally a castle dating back to 1233 when the area was part of the Bohemian Kingdom, Königstein has had various upgrades over the centuries and today it's a collection of fortified walls, guns, drawbridges and around 40 buildings. Dogs aren't allowed inside the buildings, but there's plenty to enjoy outside with 360-degree views over the surrounding landscape where you can gaze down upon an oxbow in the Elbe, lush evergreen forests and grassy plains used for grazing cattle. Get the audio guide available in English to offer some interesting context to what you can see.

Elsewhere there are plenty of excellent hiking areas in Saxon-Switzerland, especially east of **Bad Schandau**, so make use of the local public transport system of riverboats, buses and trams to discover other trails – though note that many may include ladders and steep metal staircases to scale some of the rockiest terrain.

WHAT'S FOR DINNER?

Fuel for hikers abounds in this region, so walkers will never go hungry. Expect to see lots of comfort food on the menus here, from *Schnitzel* to *Spätzle* with venison and cranberry sauce. One regional favourite is *Krautwickel*, which consists of seasoned minced meat rolled in white cabbage leaves. All good hikes should end with a beer, of course, and Saxony has a thousand-year history for brewing. Try unfiltered beers from Pirna's Zum Giesser brewery (the Bastei Pils and Giesser Dunkel are favourites), or for something stronger opt for a glug of Elbsandsteiner, a local liqueur distilled with 45 herbs.

WHERE TO SLEEP

Hotel & Restaurant Forsthaus

From £100 per night
pura-hotels.de

Tucked away in a small valley that follows the Kirnitzsch, a tributary of the Elbe, this rural hotel is a lovely low-key, modest hideaway for a few nights in the National Park. You've got a tram and bus stop right outside the front door for easy access into Bad Schandau, walks from the doorstep into the hills, and a dog-friendly restaurant where you can dine on regional specialties and sip local beers. Dogs get a welcome pack in the room, including a towel, blanket, bowls and treats.

Berghotel Bastei

From £110 per night
berghotel-bastei.de

While staying almost on top of one of the most popular tourist attractions in the National Park might seem less than ideal – thousands of people visit this place each day – there's one good reason to book this hotel at Bastei Bridge: once the day-tripping crowds have gone home, you'll have its staircases, viewing platforms and bridges almost entirely to yourselves. This means stunning sunrise walks or magical stargazing opportunities at night. Note that dogs aren't allowed in the restaurant but can be left in the room while you dine; there are only a couple of dog-friendly bedrooms so you'll need to call in advance to make sure they have availability.

ESSENTIALS

Getting there: Driving to Saxony is easy thanks to the superbly connected *Autobahn*. If travelling by public transport, there are major train stations in Leipzig and Dresden, both served by national rail operator Deutsche Bahn (int.bahn.de) as well as regional networks.

What to pack: If boating or swimming with the dog in the lakes, you might want to consider a buoyancy aid for them. A longline will be handy in places where dogs are not allowed off lead. Muzzles are essential for public transport.

The dog rules: Dogs can only go off lead in certain areas of Leipzig and Dresden, so look out for signage that indicates a '*Hundewiese*' (dog park). Dogs must be muzzled on all public transport.

Getting around: The rail network throughout Saxony is easy to use and regular trains run between Leipzig and Dresden. The best way to get to Saxon-Switzerland National Park is by direct train from Dresden to Bad Schandau; from here, there are bus, tram and ferry services that serve the wider National Park run by Regionalverkehr Sächsische Schweiz Osterzgebirge (rvsoe.de). Dogs almost always need their own ticket, so be sure to check at the station ticket office.

More information: There's a list of dog-friendly hikes on the national park's website, saechsische-schweiz.de.

→ A shopping mall in Leipzig

CITIES, SWIMMING AND SPECTACULAR SCENERY IN EASTERN GERMANY

MAKE IT A ROAD TRIP
You're only a couple of hours from Berlin here so head north to the capital for an urban adventure (see page 118), or beeline for the mountains in Harz National Park (see page 86) where you can go hiking and ride heritage railways less than two hours west of Leipzig.

Where: Parque Natural da Serra de São Mamede, Portugal
When: March–May and September–November
Best port of entry: Bilbao/Santander, Spain
Driving time from port of entry: 7 hrs

12
EXPLORE RAILS AND TRAILS IN THE ALENTEJO

Set north of the Algarve and south of Lisbon is the Portuguese province of Alentejo. This wine-growing, rural region takes up a third of country's mainland, with a dramatic coastline of cliffs and sandy beaches in its west and a mountainous area on the border with Spain to the east. Despite its size, it's the least-populated region in Portugal, and one of the lesser visited, too. While most are beelining for the Algarve or the terraces of the Douro (see page 150), only the truly curious make it to the Alentejo, and the rewards are great.

While the coast might be tempting, its beaches are often largely off-limits to dogs for much of the year. Instead, head inland towards that border with Spain to the Parque Natural da Serra de São Mamede and you'll discover an undulating landscape full of drama, history and hiking trails without any crowds. This part of the Alentejo rises 1,000 metres above sea level and its **microclimate** has created habitats that allow certain species of flora and fauna to thrive here, including rare bats, reptiles and unusual wild flora. Look out for vultures and the Bonelli's eagle in the sky, too.

The park's landscape is characterised by crumbling dry-stone walls, almond and olive groves and **cork oak plantations** whose midriffs are periodically stripped of their bark, leaving behind a striking reddish, bare trunk. Rocky terrain belies ancient history, with menhirs (standing stones) and dolmen dotted around the region – often hidden in plain sight at the side of roads, or within small farmsteads with weather-beaten outbuildings – and steep hills with quartzite ridges are topped with **centuries-old fortresses** that rise above the landscape. These castles with their strategic positions were once used to keep the neighbours out. Today, they instead bring together Spanish tourists and Portuguese locals, as visitors flock across the border to visit the towering keeps and admire the expansive views.

Marvão

Marvão is one of the area's most enticing – and dog-friendly – hilltop castle towns. Just 5km from the Spanish border, it was first established in the 9th century and was expanded and upgraded throughout the following thousand years. It was of great importance during the Reconquista, the Christian campaign against the Muslim kingdoms that had moved into the Iberian Peninsula, and it later protected Portugal from Spanish invasion.

Dogs are welcome to join you on an exploration of its ramparts. See one of the largest cisterns within a Portuguese castle, which contained enough water to supply the village for six months in case of siege, and climb its keep (metal stairs may be off-putting for some dogs) for exceptional views over the **pretty white-washed town** and the surrounding countryside.

Next door to the castle is the small but completely fascinating **Museu Municipal de Marvão** housed inside a 14th-century chapel, where dogs on leads can wander with you around an exhibition that features historical finds from the town and its surrounding areas. See religious figurines from the church's previous iterations and prehistoric stones, carved into icons that are said to depict gods and goddesses of the time.

A couple of the shops in this tiny hilltop town are dog-friendly, as is the O Castelo cafe, and it's generally a beautiful spot to while away an afternoon with a view. Of course, the views *from* Marvão's castle are beautiful, but views *of* the fortress on its dramatic precipitous rock are equally enthralling. You'll get a glimpse of this from the roads as you approach the town, but better still, hop on the **Marvão Rail Bike** and you'll be treated to a truly spectacular sight.

This former railway line that once connected to Spain now operates as **cycle**

↓ The castle of Marvão

experience on four wheels. Your vehicle is a pair of plastic seats bolted on to a metal frame, with four wheels that sit perfectly on the old railway tracks. With pedals at your feet and the dog on your lap (small, calm dogs only for this adventure), you'll power yourselves along the track from the Marvão-Beirã train station to a 1930s bridge, where the turning point allows you to head back to base. It's a scenic 2.5-hour trundle with wonderful views over the region's countryside and towards both Marvão and another hilltop town, Castelo de Vide. Keep your eyes peeled for wildlife both in the scrub and the skies.

For those less inclined to travel on wheels, more thigh-burning fun can be had on the hiking trails around Marvão. Take the fantastic circular **walking trail** that passes through Portagem and back up, via various historic sites, including some anthropomorphic tombs and a medieval bridge. The route, named the PR1 MRV, is well marked with signs (follow yellow and red markers) and is a loop of around 8km (allow four hours). It might be a slower moder of travel, especially on the steep inclines, but there's no better way to get to know this landscape full of intrigue, and the fascinating flora and fauna that thrives here, than on a hike around its hills.

OTHER ADVENTURES NEARBY

For more hilltop beauty, head to **Castelo de Vide**, a 20-minute drive from Marvão. Here you'll find another castle with exceptional views over the town below. Linger here for a few hours to explore its lovely giftshops – Portugal d'Alma, on Rua de Bartolomeu Álvares da Santa, has a vast collection of **handmade cork souvenirs** and owner Manuela is a fount of local knowledge – and try some local beers at the **Barona Craft Beer House** (cervejabarona.pt).

↑ Arty awaits a treat at the dog-friendly bar in Barona Brewing Company

→ The whitewashed homes and cobbled streets of Marvão

This region is a joy for history buffs, as alongside its various **prehistoric sites** – which can be explored using a free guide in Portuguese from the Marvão tourist office (Rua de Baixo) – there's also **Roman remains**. A short drive south of Marvão takes you to the Cidade de Ammaia (ammaia.pt), the ruins of a 1st-century CE city that once had 2,000 inhabitants. Dogs can join you for a wander around the ruins, but they're not allowed inside the museum itself; it's well worth going in to see jewellery and glassware recovered from the digs, though, so take turns with someone in your group to look after the dog outside.

A 10-minute drive from here towards the Spanish border takes you to Lagar-Museu António Picado Nunes, an **olive oil production** factory and shop where you can have tastings with the dog and purchase the rich, tangy oil that's made right here.

Finally, for those with an interest in **hiking**, there are myriad routes throughout this protected Natural Park, including routes between Marvão and Castelo de

EXPLORE RAILS AND TRAILS IN THE ALENTEJO

Vide (9.4km) and an excellent circular half-day hike around nearby Galegos (marked as the PR2 MRV Galegos; 12km). The helpful Natural PT website (natural.pt) has maps and route descriptions.

WHAT'S FOR DINNER?

This rural region is well known as a foodie destination: exceptional olive oil, wine and nuts are produced here, so you've a bounty of exciting local produce to enjoy on your travels. The Alentejo does cakes like nowhere else, too – you must try the *pão de rala*, an almond-based, flourless bread-like cake with an unimaginable number of egg yolk mixed in to give it richness. A very local sweet is the *pastel de castanha de Marvão*, a pastry with ground chestnuts, cinnamon and lemon zest usually made throughout autumn.

Savoury delights abound, too, and *açorda* is a common feature on Alentejo menus – this bread soup with poached eggs and garlic is divine in cooler months. Pair it with an Alentejo white, which is typically acidic with tropical fruits on the nose, and you've got a perfect meal.

WHERE TO SLEEP

Camping Asseiceira

From £20 per night
engcampingasseiceira.weebly.com

This remote, leafy campsite is a gorgeous base for wonderful walking and visits into the nearby hilltop towns. It's a 15-minute drive to Marvão and sits just outside the quiet town of Santo António das Areias. Fig and grapefruit trees surround the grass pitches here and the entire site is enclosed by a traditional dry-stone wall. There are excellent walks on the doorstep (ask at reception for a map) and each morning the bread van comes stocked with cakes, pastries and bread. There's good wi-fi if you pitch up close to the main house where the owners live, and a pool for use in summer.

EXPLORE RAILS AND TRAILS IN THE ALENTEJO

Pousada de Marvão

From £100 per night
pousadamarvao.com

Discover a little slice of historic luxury at this stunning *pousada* – a traditional Portuguese inn. Set within the walls of the town fortress, it's an atmospheric escape. Bedrooms are furnished with antiques and colourful hand-woven rugs, while the restaurant has a spectacular view over the surrounding countryside. Dogs are well loved here, with welcome gifts and plenty of fuss from the staff, though they may not be allowed to dine with you in the restaurant.

Casa da Silveirinha

From £60 per night
casadasilveirinha.pt

This homely guesthouse has just three bedrooms, so make yourself at home here as it's yours to share with just two other parties. There's a shared kitchen and living room, a lovely, leafy garden and it's right in the town of Marvão, offering near-instant access to the castle and museum nearby. Everything about this place is quaint – the cosy armchairs, the trinkets on the shelves – and beyond your windows you'll find spectacular views of the surrounding countryside.

← Arty dodges the puddles left behind after a downpour near Camping Asseiceira
↓ Marvão Municipal Museum

Quinta da Bela Vista

From £90 per night
airbnb.co.uk/rooms/46741509

You may find it difficult to leave this beautiful villa just north of Marvão in the town of Santo António das Areias. Not only does it have an enclosed garden to keep the dog safe, but it's also got a sparkling pool – a very tempting prospect on those sweltering summer days. With two double bedrooms and a sofa bed it's perfect for families, and has play swings in the garden. Here you're surrounded by fruit trees on all sides, and there's on-site parking for extra convenience.

ESSENTIALS

Getting there: Marvão isn't connected to any extensive public transport networks so it's best to bring your own wheels. It's a seven-hour drive from the nearest UK ferry route (Santander or Bilbao), best done over two days.

What to pack: You won't need any specific equipment for this trip, but it's always a good idea to pack plenty of water for the dog on longer hikes.

The dog rules: Dogs can be off lead on some of the trails, but where there's livestock be sure to keep them leashed. Reactive or nervous dogs may enjoy the quieter hikes, but beware that dogs are often still found chained up outside homes in this rural region, so prepare for

↓ The view from Marvão castle

some bark-offs with angry guard dogs if walking through remote villages. You may meet occasional street dogs or free-roaming pets in towns, too.

Helpfully, several of the towns in this region have signage that indicates where dogs are allowed inside restaurants and shops; look out for the blue notices in doors or windows with a section that says '*lotação máxima*'.

Getting around: Driving is the best way to get around this region.

More information: There's a tourist information in both Marvão (Rua de Baixo) and Castelo de Vide (Praça de Dom Pedro); visitalentejo.com and visitportugal.com have further information online.

> **MAKE IT A ROAD TRIP**
> Take your time through Spain and Portugal by stopping off at the dog-friendly highlights en route: San Sebastián (see page 54) is an excellent and delicious diversion in northern Spain, while the Douro (see page 150) offers a chance to get familiar with some of Portugal's best-loved wines.

Where: Porto and the Douro, Portugal
When: March–May and September–November
Best port of entry: Bilbao/Santander, Spain
Driving time from port of entry: 7 hrs

13
TOUR THE TERRACED VINEYARDS OF THE DOURO

The Douro Valley is one of the most enchanting wine regions in the world. With the fast-flowing, broad Douro river running through its heart and an iconic patchwork of terraced vines cloaking the hillsides that surround the waterway, it's a truly mesmerising landscape to travel through. From Porto, where the river empties into the Atlantic after an almost 900km journey across Spain and Portugal, the valley slices its way inland. Its westernmost parts are lush with greenery – towering invasive eucalyptus trees cloak the land and as you drive east from Porto, small farmsteads and vineyards cling to the hills. This is **vinho verde** country, where the white wines have a distinctly crisp character with apple and citrus notes at the forefront and a low alcohol content – an ideal lunchtime indulgence.

In the centre of the valley beyond the Marão tunnel, the landscape and climate seem to shift dramatically. The slopes down to the river become steeper, the valley wider and the vineyards larger, with vines stretching for hundreds of metres interspersed with almond and olive groves and small patches of native woodland. This is the **Cima Corgo** part of the Douro, where the climate feels drier and warmer – perfect conditions for producing the port wine this region is famous for.

Provesende

For a first taste of the region's flavours, the tiny village of Provesende has two tempting diversions: a dog-friendly winery and a traditional wood-fired bakery. If you're brave enough to drive the tiny, twisted streets of Provesende yourself, head to the **Padaria Fátima bakery**, where before 10am you can pick up a loaf of fresh-out-the-oven bread baked in a traditional wood-fired oven. Next, head for the hills above the village where **Quinta do Cume** (quintadocume.pt) enjoys vast views across the valley from its vines. Call in advance to book a wine tasting and you'll be able to bring the dog along to sample their rich reds and lightly oaked whites from a tasting room with panoramic views over the vineyard. It's the sort of place you might want to spend an entire day indulging in cheese platters with wine pairings, but more delicious things are afoot at the **D'Origem's Museu do Azeite** (dorigem.pt) in nearby Casal de Loivos.

Olive oil production has been a key part of life in the Douro for centuries. You'll see the trees planted around the vines, or spot small groves between the vineyards. They not only provide a crop of fruit, but they also increase biodiversity in the region and help maintain the structural integrity of the terraces with their deep roots. At Museu do Azeite you can take the dog on a tour of a former olive oil factory, where centuries-old equipment is on display and a guide will regale you with stories about production and traditions in English and Portuguese. Afterwards, there are olive oil and wine tastings from the D'Origem estate overlooking their sloping vineyard.

↓ The author's father and Arty take a stroll through the vines near Provesende

↑ A train passes through Pinhão

Pinhão

Further down the valley on the riverbank lies the pleasant town of **Pinhão** – home to a beautiful tiled railway station and plenty of restaurants, wine shops and bars where you can find a spot outside with the dog. Right down by the water is **Quinta do Bomfim** (symington.com), another dog-friendly winery for tastings and tours, and adventures on the water can be had with Companhia Turística do Douro (ctdouro.com), whose traditional **rabelo boats** cruise down the river past the Carvalhas, Roêda and Ventozelo wineries.

If it's walking you want to do in the Douro, Pinhão is a brilliant base from which to hit the trails of the PR20 ALJ, an **8km circular route** with red and yellow waymarkers. It wends its way up into the hills to Casal de Loivos (where you can visit the aforementioned olive oil museum), passing almond trees that flower pink and white in February and March, and cork oaks whose soft bark has been harvested for the production of wine corks. The route then gently descends via the Capela do Espírito Santo – a hillside church with beautiful views over the river and a lawn ideal for picnicking. Take a short diversion from here before ending in Pinhão once again and you can nip into Quinta da Roêda, where the world-famous Croft port is made. Tours are dog-friendly, and tastings include three different kinds of port, as well as a can of the quinta's latest invention: white or rose port mixed with tonic.

While many vineyards are dog-friendly in the Douro – plenty have their own dogs on site for security – one of the most welcoming for our pets is **Quinta do Pôpa**. Sitting up a steep hill on the southern banks of the river, just 15 minutes' drive from Pinhão, it's run by brother and sister duo Stéphane and

TOUR THE TERRACED VINEYARDS OF THE DOURO

Vanessa Ferreira. The dog will get fuss and treats on arrival, and a bowl of water on the terrace if you stop for a glass of something. Plus, they can join you for the lengthy but fascinating tour of the winery, where you'll taste up to six different wines, including port, served in different areas of their property from the cellars to among their ageing barrels.

Douro Superior

Further east from Pinhão lies the **Douro Superior** – a wilder region where the climate becomes semi-arid and summers swelter. Fewer tourists make it this far into the Douro – it's several hours from Porto by car and so the day trippers stay away, leaving those travelling a little slower, perhaps on lengthier road trips or on multi-day river cruises, to enjoy the remoteness of this valley. Tiny towns and villages are scattered along the river's twisting waterway, accessed by roads with hairpin bends and steep climbs, but the highlight out here for dog owners is the access to a wilderness that's finding its feet once again.

After centuries of farming that has ravaged the natural ways of the landscape in the Douro Superior, small sections of it are being allowed to rewild, re-establishing nature's status quo with a little help from biologists, botanists and other experts. Take the dog for a stroll through the **Faia Brava nature reserve** (faiabrava.pt), set 18km south of the Douro within the Coa

↓ Vineyards on the banks of the Douro river

Valley – one of the Douro's tributaries – and you might see griffon, Egyptian and Rüppell vultures, meet semi-wild ponies, follow the tracks made by wild boar, or spot a golden eagle soaring in the sky. Park across the road from the entry gate (///vertigo.intentional.consulates) and follow the wide track that bears west to a viewpoint over the river for a light stroll with the dog (plan a route using alltrails. com; dogs must be kept on leads).

The practicalities: For dog owners, there are myriad ways to see the Douro while making the most of its scenery and sampling opportunities. The train line from Porto to Pinhão is a stunning, scenic ride, and self-drive, guided tours and walking holidays are all available options here. Bring your own vehicle and you can wend your way through the valley on its twisting roads and tiny village streets, exploring at your own pace – taking pause at a viewpoint above the river to soak in those vine terraces, or stopping off at whichever wineries take your fancy.

But let someone else do the driving and you'll get to fully sample all the region has to offer, from exceptional red wines to rich, ruby-coloured ports, plus the superb gastronomy that goes along with it all. **Explore Iberia** (exploreiberia. pt) is the favourite: run by two dog-loving Portuguese women, Isabel Sousa and Marina Carvalho, they can craft dog-friendly day tours, multi-day and even guided or self-guided walking tours that encompass pet-friendly hotels along the way.

OTHER ADVENTURES NEARBY

Most visits to the Douro Valley begin from Porto, northern Portugal's biggest city, set between the sea and the wineries further inland. It's here that the port produced in the Douro is aged in vast old warehouses on the southern banks of the river, and the city centre on the north bank has garnered UNESCO World Heritage status for its astonishing presentation of 2,000 years of history.

Get your head around Porto's past – which involves Romans, Visigoths, Normans and Moors – on a **walking tour** of the city centre (dog-friendly options are available to book via getyourguide.co.uk) or take a **boat trip on the river** with Douro Acima (douroacima.pt) to see the city's six bridges.

If it's that sweet **port wine** you're seeking, head to Vila Nova de Gaia across the Douro (the ferry from Cais da Estiva accepts dogs) and take your time touring some of the port houses along the riverfront – most will allow dogs on their terraces where you can enjoy tastings. Further up the hill from here, a vast cultural complex called **World of Wine** (wow.pt) has several excellent restaurants where dogs can join you to dine outside, as well as The Wine School where you can sample yet more Douro wines. There are several museums here worth exploring if you can spend a day without the dog by your side (the Pink Palace Museu do Rosé and Planet Cork Museum are two favourites), and a beautiful shopping arcade with fancy boutiques selling Portuguese crafts and designer items. The complex's very own chocolate factory is not dog-friendly for obvious reasons, but the brand has a cafe in the city centre called Vinte Vinte Cafe on Rua das Flores where you can enjoy **chocolate and port pairings** with the dog by your side.

Further afield from Porto lies a coastline battered by the mighty Atlantic. Head up to surfer-central coast around Angeiras where a vast **sandy beach** is dog-friendly outside of the summer season and you can walk part of the **Camino de Santiago** along the seafront boardwalks. Closer to the city, Praia de Matosinhos is dog-friendly year-round.

WHAT'S FOR DINNER?

It's not only about wine in the Douro – this region has some excellent cuisine worth pairing it all with. With access to the ocean via the port of Porto, the Douro is a great place to try *bacalhau à Brás*, a comforting mix of salted cod, potatoes, eggs and olives. You'll also find what is possibly Europe's most

↑ The picnic prepared by the team at Explore Iberia
← Arty admires Porto's many bridges on a river cruise

outrageous sandwich on menus across the city: the *francesinha* is a doorstep, knife-and-fork affair with pork, sausage, beef and ham inside the bread, topped with melted cheese and a fried egg, often served swimming in a spicy tomato-based gravy.

Also look out for *Alheira de Mirandela*, a chicken sausage that was invented by Jews who settled in Portugal during the 15th century and sought to conceal their religion by hanging what looked like a traditional pork sausage in their homes. Those with a sweet tooth will enjoy indulging on the country's favourite pastry, the *pastel de nata* – a custard tart best eaten warm, fresh from the oven.

Dog-friendly restaurants in Porto and the Douro are a little hit and miss – it's always best to ask before entering – however, most will allow dogs on their terraces for al fresco dining.

WHERE TO SLEEP

The Yeatman

From £280 per night
the-yeatman-hotel.com

Views rarely get better than those from the terraces and balconies at this Porto hotel. Sitting atop the hills of Vila Nova da Gaia overlooking the historic city centre, it has the ultimate vantage point for port cocktails and wine pairings as the sun sets over the Douro. Dogs are welcome in your room here and can wander around the hotel with you, on a lead, but they're generally not allowed in any of the dining venues or at the pool. Breakfast can be ordered to the room, though, and the World of Wine's dining terraces are just a few minutes' walk down the hill.

TOUR THE TERRACED VINEYARDS OF THE DOURO

Octant Hotels Douro

From £160 per night
douro.octanthotels.com

In the western part of the Douro, just a 45-minute drive from Porto, this luxurious hotel sits right on the river's edge with watery views through the floor-to-ceiling windows in many of its suites and rooms. Dogs staying here will love sniffing around the grounds, which are planted with myriad herbs and flowers or playing ball on the lawns by the car park. They must, however, be under 25kg, so note that your average Labrador might not make the cut here. They can dine with you at the À Terra bar and wander throughout the hotel except in the spa, kid's club and by the pool.

Mesão Provesende

From £70 per night
mesaoprovesende.pt

A charming guesthouse right in the heart of the village of Provesende, this homely property is an ideal budget base with a handful of studios with small kitchenettes, some with terraces, and a pleasant pool for summertime dips. Owners Jet Spanjersberg and Ronald Weustink are from Rotterdam but have been living in Portugal since 2001 and can deftly take you on a quaffable tour of the region with their impressive port collection. There's no garden here, but green space isn't far away as the village is surrounded by vines and walking trails.

→ A cork oak that has been stripped of its outer bark for cork production

ESSENTIALS

Getting there: Porto and the Douro are roughly a six-hour drive from Santander, the nearest ferry port with routes to the UK. Porto has direct train connections to the Portuguese capital, Lisbon, as well as Vigo in Spain.

What to pack: The Douro can be extremely hot throughout summer and sometimes into October, so bring plenty of water for yourself and the dog. A parasol for shade or a cooling mat might also go some way to keeping the dog cool when the sun's out. Muzzles for public transport are essential.

The dog rules: Dogs are not required to be on a lead at all times in Portugal, but it's often best to do so – not least because there are a fair few street dogs in Porto and the larger towns. Vineyard guard dogs are common in the Douro and so if your dog is nervous or reactive you might want to call ahead before stopping in for your tasting. You will often see dogs chained in front of houses throughout Portugal or even loose in enclosed gardens, so be aware that your dog may get spooked.

Getting around: The best way to get around the Douro is on a day or multi-day tour with Explore Iberia (exploreiberia.pt), but there are also regular trains serving the region (around five per day) from Porto to Pocinho in the Douro Superior, stopping at Régua and Pinhão en route. Dogs must be muzzled on public transport.

More information: Explore Iberia can advise on dog-friendly trips to the Douro, while visitportugal.com has more information on the region. The local tourist office in Pinhão has walking maps for circular routes around the Douro.

MAKE IT A ROAD TRIP
A few hours south of Porto lies the Alentejo, a region of cork oak plantations, more vineyards and a smattering of hilltop castles and fortifications well worth exploring (see page 140).

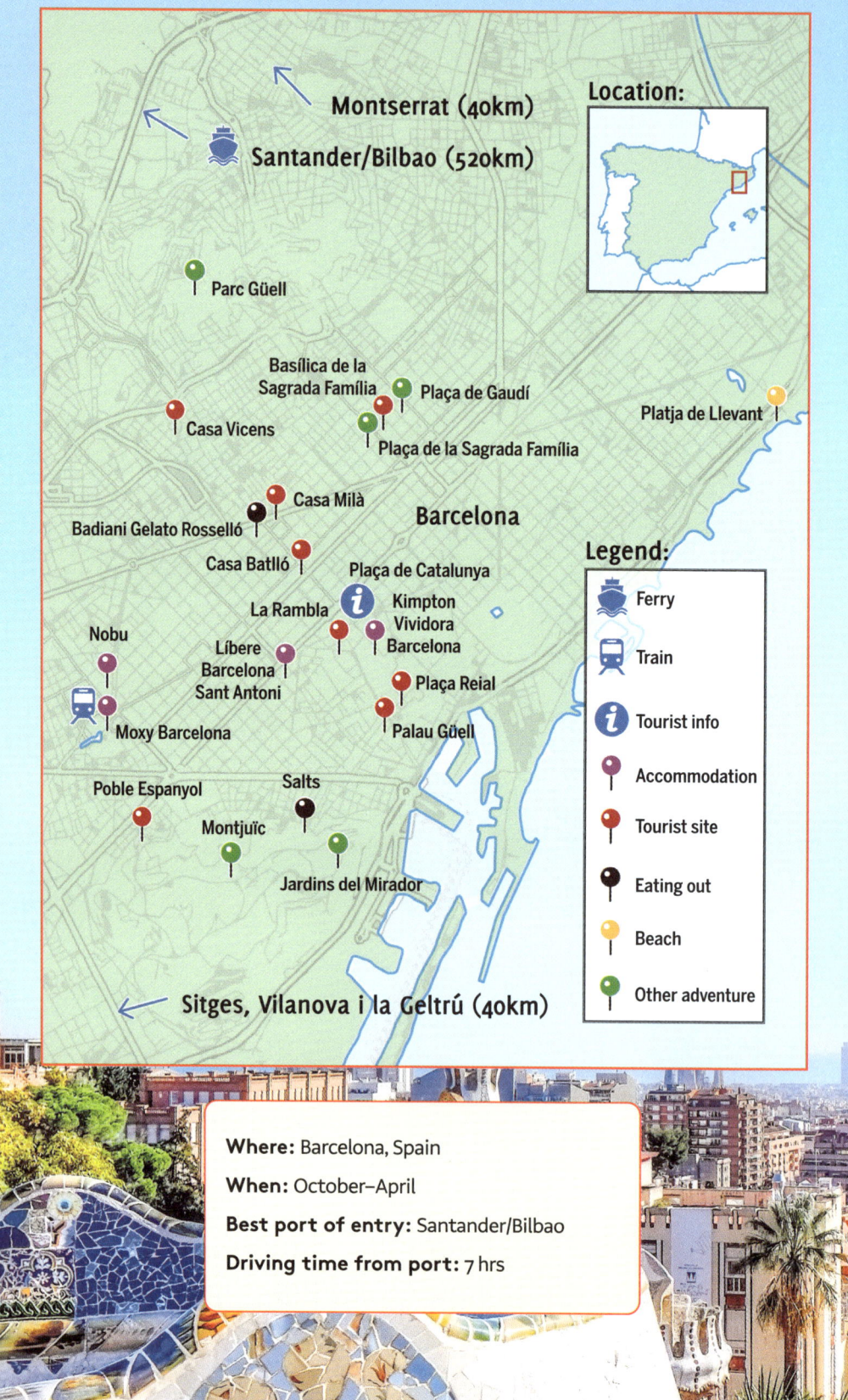

14

SEE SPECTACULAR ARCHITECTURE IN THE CATALAN CAPITAL

There are so many reasons to come to Barcelona. The world-class food and drink, for starters, will tempt anyone with an appetite. The sparkling Mediterranean coastline is a blissful place on a sweltering summer's day. And the culture – the art galleries, the museums, the city's dazzling architecture – draws visitors in their thousands to see works by some of the world's greats. And there is one great who crafted so much of this city's unique fabric that even those visiting with dogs can follow in his footsteps: the inimitable **Antoni Gaudí**.

This city is brimming with Gaudí masterpieces, from his first modest official commission – a series of lamp posts – to the city's central icon, the Sagrada Familia, a behemoth church that is still, at the time of writing, yet to be completed over 140 years after its first stone was laid. The architect, born in 1852 in Reus in southern Catalunya, studied in Barcelona in 1870 and had begun designing for its public and private spaces by 1879. His life's work spanned all manner of constructions, from display cases for Barcelona boutiques to industrial mills and landscaped parkland. And today, much of it can be admired from the outside with the dog by your side – including seven of his buildings given UNESCO World Heritage status.

The best way to take all this in is on a walkabout the city – this suggested stroll could take an entire day or be split across a couple of days should you wish to save your soles. Begin on **Plaça Reial**, where a young, fresh-from-graduation Gaudí designed a series of lampposts as his first ever official commission. This elegant square is surrounded by porticoes with fountains and palms in its centre, and two ornate red and black lamp posts standing out among the rest.

From here, cross over the famous Rambla and on to Carrer Nou de la Rambla where you'll need to crane your neck to see the mosaic spires of **Palau Güell** (palauguell.cat), a mansion of seemingly simple design when compared with Gaudí's more famous works. It's now a museum and while pets aren't allowed inside, you can admire its ornate carvings on the two entry arches from the outside.

Head back across the Rambla and into the tangle of narrow lanes of the Gothic quarter. Linger for a while – perhaps for some tapas or a coffee – and pass the impressive cathedral on Placita de la Seu before heading northwest on Passeig de Gràcia to the next stop: **Illa de la Discòrdia**, also known as the 'Block of Discord'. This block of buildings on the Passeig de Gràcia, set between Carrer d'Aragó and Carrer del Consell de Cent, is one of the most famous collections of **modernist architecture** in Barcelona, home to several constructions showing different designs and tastes from the early 20th century. The most exciting of these is **Casa Batlló** (casabatllo.es) – a rare work by Gaudí that allows dogs inside.

You'll need to book ahead for Casa Batlló – it's one of the most popular attractions in the city and it gets incredibly crowded – but turn up at your allotted time and you'll discover an almost ethereal home that brings together themes of a fantasy underwater world and ingenious functionality. Dogs are well looked after inside by staff who will offer fuss and sometimes treats, and you might find the dog becomes an attraction in itself among the throng of tourists. To keep one hand free for the dog, opt for the audio guide only (the iPad guide is a bit of a faff when holding the lead, too), and don't miss a visit to

→ Arty suns himself at the rooftop bar in Casa Batlló

↑ The cube exhibit at Casa Batlló
→ Inside Casa Batlló

the rooftop – not only will you get to see the home's iconic wonky chimney stacks and enjoy brilliant views across the city, but there's a bar where you can stop for a little refresher – perhaps a local cava or a Spanish lager – and the dog can enjoy a bowl of fresh water. As you leave, you'll have the option to pass through the '**Gaudí cube**', a 360-degree immersive exploration of the artist's mind through light projections; nervous dogs may prefer to wait outside, and staff will happily leave the door open so you can enjoy it from the exterior.

Just four blocks up the road from here is another UNESCO-listed work, the **Casa Milà** – a residential building with a pleasingly curvaceous exterior built from stone, with intricately designed iron balconies. If it's a warm day, cross the street to Carrer del Rosselló and nip into **Badiani Gelato Rosselló** (badiani1932.com) where dogs get their own tubs of the cool stuff. At this point in the day, your legs may be getting weary so to avoid the rather monotonous walk up Passeig de Gràcia, you can hop on the metro (dogs must wear a muzzle) from Diagonal to Fontana to reach **Casa Vicens** (casavicens.org), an altogether very different construction on Carrer de les Carolines.

This was the architect's first house commission after graduation and it shows – the design is a little more geometric and decidedly Moorish, with minaret-like turrets and detailed tile and mosaic motifs, nothing like the later homes he built further south in the city. From here, take a slow, northward amble through the hip Gràcia neighbourhood – perhaps pausing in one of many wine bars for a refresher – to reach a world-famous Gaudí highlight on a hill: **Parc Güell**.

> **TOP TIP**
> Plot all these points of interest on the map on your phone so you can follow it from one to the next.

Designed in the early 20th century, thiTop tipas created at the height of Gaudí's naturalist period, when he was most influenced by the materials and forms of the natural world. This is evident in the cave-like viaduct and porticos built into the landscape among palms and other lush foliage. There are miles of footpaths here for walking the dog, and at the top of the hill you'll find a woodland area where they're allowed to run around off lead.

The park is hugely popular so booking tickets ahead of your visit is essential; this is an excellent place to get some shade during warmer hours of the day, but if you come at dusk you'll get gorgeous sunset views from Nature Square (also known as the Greek Theatre).

Of course, the final stop on this architectural itinerary is the most famous – the **Basílica de la Sagrada Família** (sagradafamilia.org). This gargantuan church sees upwards of 4 million people explore its chapels and towers each year, despite the fact that it remains unfinished according to Gaudí's design. Its first stone was laid in 1882, and it is due to be completed in 2026. Still, it's a truly surreal, almost otherworldly building and a circumnavigation of its exterior is enough to make you appreciate the utterly ambitious vision of its creator.

There are a pair of parks flanking the church, so if you do want to visit inside you can take it in turns to look after the dog in the shade of a tree in either **Plaça de la Sagrada Família** or **Plaça de Gaudí**. Tickets to visit inside must be booked in advance as they are often sold-out weeks ahead.

↑ Arty on the terrace at Salts bar

OTHER ADVENTURES NEARBY

Most of Barcelona's museums don't allow dogs, but one of its more exciting and engaging open-air museums does: **Poble Espanyol** (poble-espanyol.com). Built for the 1929 Barcelona International Expo, this cultural complex has over a hundred different actual-scale architectural replicas, from Romanesque monasteries to Andalusian houses. Within its buildings are a series of workshops where local artisans work on their crafts, making jewellery, textiles, leather goods and more. There are workshops available to take part in, there's often live music in the main square, and you can rest at a handful of restaurants with dog-friendly terraces serving Catalan, Mediterranean and international cuisine.

A visit to Poble Espanyol is well paired with a wander up **Montjuïc**. Head up the hill via popular bar Salts (saltsmontjuic.com) on Avinguda Miramar, where you can stop for a drink overlooking the diving pools built for the 1992 Olympics where there are spectacular views across the city. Then beeline for the Jardins del Mirador, where a terrace offers panoramic sea vistas and top-down views of the busy working port below.

Of course, if you're exhausted by all the walking, you'll find ample opportunity to relax on the coast where **Platja de Llevant** has an area for dog owners to enjoy some time on the soft, golden sand. If visiting in winter, the majority of beaches are open for dog owners to use, so take your pick and let the dog paddle in the gentle surf.

Inland, beyond the urban sprawl of Barcelona itself lies a precipitous mountain range where a network of trains, cable cars and walking trails around **Montserrat** offer an enchanting day trip from the city. Take the R5 line from Plaça Espanya to Aeri de Montserrat, then hop in the cable car to the top, where a vast monastery lies beneath a wall of bulbous, wind-sculpted rocky pillars. There are walking routes aplenty, but one of the best is the 10km Sant Jeroni Summit Loop (allow four hours, alltrails.com), which takes in the fascinating rock formations and views out to the Med on a clear day.

WHAT'S FOR DINNER?

With its mild climate, there's rarely a cold or dull enough day to warrant sitting indoors in Barcelona, but plenty of the more casual restaurants and cafes will allow dogs inside, too – just ask before you enter. This city is packed with tapas bars, so use your time here to sample an array of excellent Catalan and Spanish dishes. Breakfasts should involve a *pa amb tomàquet*, bread (sometimes toasted) with a smooth mixture of olive oil, garlic and tomato on top. A hearty favourite for any time of day is *truita de patata* (or tortilla in Spanish), an egg and potato dish that's reminiscent of a thick omelette. For dessert, *crema Catalana* is a must-try – a custard dessert with a crispy burnt top not dissimilar to a *crème brûlée*.

Drinks-wise, you're in cava country so eschew the Champagne and prosecco for a glass of Spanish bubbles instead, and if the sun's shining, a jug of sangria – a fruity wine punch – won't go amiss.

WHERE TO SLEEP

Nobu

From £210 per night
barcelona.nobuhotels.com

Sitting right next to Barcelona-Sants station, this high-rise hotel has one major asset: a dog-friendly rooftop with views for miles. Dog beds and bowls are provided in the sleek, minimalist Japanese-inspired bedrooms, and dogs can follow you up to the roof in the lift for a menu of small plates and cocktails by the pool. The team here has put together an excellent guide to Barcelona living for dogs, including where your local off-lead areas are and plenty of lovely green spaces for exploring together. Dogs can dine in the ground floor bar area with you, too, but they're not allowed in the main Nobu restaurant so will need to be left in the room. There's a park open 24 hours a day at Parc de l'Espanya Industrial, where dogs are allowed off the lead and will enjoy sniffing in the grass and among the trees.

Kimpton Vividora Barcelona

From £250 per night
ihg.com

In the heart of the Gothic Quarter, this sumptuous hotel has plenty to offer dogs, including a dog-friendly rooftop bar serving Spanish and international plates alongside a cracking cocktail list for the humans, while dogs get their own menu of healthy, home-cooked meals. Bedrooms here are colourful, with bold artworks and accent chairs, and bathrooms with free-standing tubs and marble sinks. Dogs – and cats, in fact – are warmly welcomed here, as Kimpton's only pet-related rule is that they must be able to fit in the lift. All the hotel's restaurants are dog-friendly, and your nearest park is a 15-minute walk away at Parc de la Ciutadella.

Moxy

From £120 per night
marriott.com

This reliable chain has a handily located hotel near Barcelona-Sants station, a short stroll from the Parc de l'Espanya Industrial and just around the corner from the Nobu Hotel where you can take the dog up to the rooftop for a swish meal. Dogs are warmly welcomed and may even get treats on arrival, and they can join you in the bar where the breakfast buffet is served daily. Bedrooms are simple but modern with plenty of helpful hooks for hanging things and cosy cushioned seats next to the beds. Note that the beds have a sensor-activated light beneath, so if your dog fidgets in the night you might want to stick something in front of the sensor to stop it from illuminating the room.

Líbere Barcelona Sant Antoni

From £100 per night
staylibere.com

Get a little hotel luxury with the added convenience of your own kitchen at this serviced apartment block. Studios and flats are contemporary and bright, some with balconies and terraces with privacy screens. There's a living area, equipped kitchen and en-suite in each, and there are two-bedroom apartments for larger groups. Your nearest green space is on Plaça de Catalunya where there's a handful of small grassy areas where the dog can relieve itself if need be; otherwise, the closest parks for a nice walk are Parc de la Ciutadella and Parc del Mirador del Poble-sec, each around 1.5km away.

ESSENTIALS

Getting there: Barcelona is easy to reach by train for humans, but for dogs it's a little complicated. There are direct routes connecting Barcelona to Madrid, Marseille, Lyon and Paris, but only those run by French operator SNCF (which includes TGV high-speed trains) allow all dogs provided they're muzzled and leashed or inside a carrier. Spanish train operator Renfe only allows dogs under 10kg on all of its trains, while those between 10kg and 40kg are only able to travel on some routes within Spain. The best route into Barcelona for most dogs is on the direct Paris–Barcelona line with TGV, which takes around seven hours.

Driving to Barcelona is possible, but the city is a low emission zone, which requires registration before arrival and acceptance can take up to two weeks (see zberegistre.ambmobilitat.cat for more information). If you choose to drive, you might want to consider leaving your car in one of the surrounding towns or cities, such as Sitges or Vilanova i la Geltrú and taking a regional train into the city.

What to pack: Barcelona can still be sizzling even in October and April, with occasional highs of 30°C during heatwaves. Check the weather before you go and bring a cooling mat for the dog if it looks to be hot. A parasol for shade and a portable water bottle are a good idea, too.

The dog rules: Dogs are highly regulated in Barcelona and fines have been handed down to those who don't follow the rules. Generally, dogs need to be kept on a lead at all times unless in a designated off-lead area. There are over 200 off-lead dog areas in the city, a map of which can be found at barcelona.cat; some are referred to as '*pipicans*', which are usually sandy enclosures with some rudimentary agility equipment for dogs to play off lead. Most parks will have signage to indicate the dog rules.

Getting around: Dogs are allowed on the metro and buses with a lead and muzzle, and 'small dogs', weight restriction unspecified, can ride the commuter trains on the Catalan rail system (see rodalies.gencat.cat for information). Dogs must have their own tickets on the commuter trains.

More information: Barcelona's tourism office on Plaça de Catalunya is dog-friendly and can offer information about booking tickets for museums, as well as some dog-friendly activities. Online, look up barcelonaturisme.com.

A note on overtourism: Barcelona has been plagued by overtourism in the last decade and its residents have pushed back through protests, while the government has passed regulations to control the housing issues exacerbated by the holiday let market. The uproar is justified – the crowds in this city make living here stressful, expensive and difficult for residents, and as guests in Barcelona it's our responsibility to be as respectful as possible, while attempting to leave as little negative impact as possible. The best way to do this is to travel out of peak season – ideal for dog owners, as the peak months in Barcelona are often too hot for our pets, anyway, and the crowds are not ideal for exploring with dogs. Consider coming in November after the late-summer crowds have retreated, or in January after the Christmas holiday rush. Spend your money with local independents instead of large brands, to boost the local economy, and avoid booking sites like Airbnb, which contribute to housing problems.

↑ Arty samples some dog-friendly gelato
→ The rooftop of Casa Batlló

MAKE IT A ROAD TRIP
Barcelona is the Catalan capital, and so stick around and you'll find plenty to do in the surrounding areas. Try the beaches of the Costa Brava (see page 170), the human towers events around Tarragona (see page 98), or head northwards to France to explore the Camargue by boat (see page 108).

Where: Catalunya, Spain
When: September–June
Best port of entry: Santander/Bilbao
Driving time from port of entry: 7 hrs

15
SUN YOURSELF ON THE BEACHES OF THE COSTA BRAVA

Whether it's digging holes, sun-worshipping on the sand or simply zoomies on the shoreline and through the waves, the beach is a thrilling playground for most dogs. Europe's coastlines are peppered with pristine sands and pebbly coves, but so many of them are off-limits to our pets, or at least become so in summertime. The Costa Brava, though, is one of the most dog-welcoming coastal regions in the Mediterranean. While many of its beaches do have dog bans, it's often only on certain sections, and a few hundred metres down the boardwalk you'll usually find a '*per gossos*' – 'for dogs' – stretch of fine golden sand waiting to be explored.

This part of northern Spain, which sits on the border with France and faces eastwards on to the pleasantly mild Mediterranean Sea, has over 200km of coast. Its name, Costa Brava, is widely believed to mean 'rugged' or 'rough' coast, and it's certainly no misnomer: it may be a relatively low-lying area, but rocky coves and bluffs decorated with sparse Mediterranean flora make plenty of drama along the shoreline here, and there are ample coastal paths on which to see it.

The beaches range from fine sandy swathes licked by glittering blue sea, or small pebbly coves ensconced by rocks that provide shelter from the breeze, and almost all are on the fringes of charming fishing villages or bustling seaside towns, where shady dog-friendly restaurant terraces serving seafood abound. From south to north, these are the best dog-friendly beaches in the Costa Brava:

↓ Arty exploring the rocky coastline around Palamós

Platja de Sant Antoni, Palamós

Location: ///superego.rebukes.cartoon
Parking: Passeig del Mar

A long stretch of golden sand makes up the beach that fronts the delightful town of Palamós. In winter, dogs are generally accepted all over the beach, but come summertime, you'll need to head westwards beyond the lifeguard hut to find the '*per gossos*' section. Here, dogs can run free all year round (though note there is a road directly behind the sand) and paddle in the clear waters. Beyond the beach, the town itself is a lively place: its modern end has lots of restaurants, bars and shops selling fresh fruit and local wines, and on the seafront you'll find beach bars and kids' rides.

For a pleasant walk, stroll along the seafront promenade towards the harbour. The distinctive seaside smell of salt and fish hits your nostrils as you approach the working docks and the town's **fish market** (open Mon–Fri 4.30pm–7.30pm). Keep following the coast past the marina and you'll discover another **small dog-friendly cove**, where a tiny beach made up of pebbles gives way to yellowish rocks that jut out into the sea – perfect for a spot of rock-pooling and scrambling with the dog.

Keep walking a little further around the headland to find a grassy **dog park** on Passeig Sota Pedró, overlooking a vast marina where boat masts clink as they bob in the sea. From here, it's a short walk back through the old town via the Parc del Convent dels Agustins and Carrer del Pedró, tempting deli shops and boutiques, to arrive at the beach once again.

↑ Arty trots on the sandy beach at Els Griells, L'Estartit

Platja de l'Estartit, L'Estartit
Location: ///baseballs.gymnasium.cranky
Parking: Carrer Tulipa

Around 30km north of Palamós, the sprawling resort town of L'Estartit isn't much to write home about, but the long sweep of fine sand that stretches out towards the south from the main town is a truly stunning swathe of beach. The dog section here is a little more remote, around a kilometre south of the town near a small new-build neighbourhood called Els Griells. You'll know you've found the dog area when you reach a small fenced-in section of beach where dogs are invited to do their business with a sea view. Surrounding this, they can run free on the sand and leap into the water (it gets deep quite quickly so keep an eye on any non-swimmers).

Aside from the vast space you'll have, one of the highlights of this beach is the views of **Illes Medes**, a tiny archipelago of seven small uninhabited islands that jut out of the ocean on the horizon. In summer, a **tapas bar** sets up on the sand here and dogs are welcome to join you on the shaded decking for a bite and a beer.

↓ Calm waters from the beach at Palamós

Platja del Rec, L'Escala
Location: ///photographed.imported.collectives
Parking: Aparcament Rec del Molí

Only 5km as the crow flies from L'Estartit but 18km by car due to some rather rocky hills that rise up in between the two coastal towns, L'Escala is another typical seaside resort on the Costa Brava. Multistorey apartment blocks loom over the town beach, and remnants of the old town exist by way of chunky coastal mooring pillars and a handful of stone buildings. The main beach here isn't dog-friendly and gets wildly busy during the summer months, but just 1.5km north there's a beautiful 350-metre-long stretch of sand at Platja del Rec that's hugely popular with local dog owners.

Access to the beach is via a leafy boardwalk and down some wooden steps on to the sand, and if you fancy a stroll there's a lovely viewpoint via another boardwalk with steps at the northern end of the beach. If you keep walking northwards along the coast path and boardwalks for around a kilometre, you'll eventually reach the area's biggest intrigue: the Museu Arqueològic d'Empúries (macempuries.cat) – an extensive, **open-air ruined Greek and Roman city** with striking mosaics and architectural remains.

Platja de la Rubina, Empuriabrava

Location: ///vivid.bribing.waxing
Parking: Carretera d'en Plus

Set at the northern end of the Gulf of Roses – a nearly 16km-long bay in the northern half of this region – well-heeled Empuriabrava describes itself as the 'world's largest residential marina'. Characterised by a network of canals where leisure boats bob about ready to take to the seas, the town is a pleasingly low-rise oasis with palm-lined streets and whitewashed houses with terracotta roof tiles. Completed in the 1970s, it is very much a purpose-built resort and doesn't try to hide it, but if that's not your scene that's no bother – the dog beach here is at the far northeastern end of the sand away from the man-made hubbub and backed by a network of **dunes and wetlands**.

It's a near 2km walk from the edge of town, or you can drive up to the furthest reaches and leave the car in one of the unmarked laybys. There are no facilities nearby – not even toilets – so bring a picnic, some shade and plenty of water.

Platja de la Ribera & Platja del Port de la Vall, El Port de la Selva

Location: ///avid.snidely.alignment
Parking: Carrer Llançà

The northernmost dog-friendly beaches in the Costa Brava sit around 10km from the French border around the pretty little town of Port de la Selva. Backed by steep hills where holiday homes look out over a glittering Med, this town is a far more sedate escape than the aforementioned sprawling resorts. This comes at a price, though, as its beaches aren't half as impressive either. The north-facing Platja de la Ribera is closest to the town, at the western end of the main stretch called Platja Gran. It's part-shingle, part-sand and is often littered with drying seaweed and broken shells, but offers a lovely space for dogs to roam free right by the car park – ideal for a quick exercise before heading into town for lunch or dinner.

For something a bit more relaxing, though, walk further west along the coast path and after less than 1.5km you'll reach Platja del Port de la Vall, an attractive 200-metre stretch of pebble beach backed by a **low-key, dog-friendly restaurant and campsite** (WhatsApp +34 651 31 62 06 for bookings). Often much quieter than the town beaches, this is a lovely sheltered spot for a swim or picnic on the rocks.

OTHER ADVENTURES NEARBY

Costa Bravan fun isn't confined to the coastline, though it's always a good place to start when you're all beached out. Seafaring adventures on **rental boats** can be had at Cadaqués (cadaquesboats.com), L'Estartit (novaimport.com) and Palamós (rentboatscostabrava.com), all of which have vessels that don't require a licence. **Sightseeing cruises** depart from Lloret de Mar with Dofi Jet Boats (dofijetboats.com), offering an easy way to see the beautiful rugged coastline from the best vantage point.

Inland, though, this region has plenty more to offer, and with a car at your disposal you can enjoy plenty of it in a short space of time. A 45-minute drive from Palamós or L'Estartit, **Girona** is the biggest city in the Costa Brava and is well worth a day trip – especially if you've any interest in medieval history or hit TV series *Game of Thrones*. Its old town is a captivating tangle of alleyways and staircases, and it's all confined by Roman and medieval walls – which today you can walk on with the dog for exceptional

↑ Narrow lanes in Girona

small towns like Pals, Peratallada and Monells, all of which have pretty sepia-stone centres with historic churches. More history can be found at Ullastret (macullastret.cat), an open-air museum set amid the **ruins of an Iberian settlement** that dates back as far as the 6th century BCE.

For an ambitious walk with the dog, head to the trails that lead up a steep 300-metre-high hill to **Castell Montgrí**, from which you'll enjoy panoramic views across the entire region and out to the Mediterranean. Directions can be found on alltrails.com, but read the trail reviews to learn which routes have the least scrambling over steep ledges.

WHAT'S FOR DINNER?

In such proximity to the ocean, it's impossible not to be tempted by the seafood on offer in the Costa Brava. Chunky Mediterranean prawns from Palamós and salty mussels (*musclos al vapor*) steamed and served with myriad sauces abound on menus here, as well as grilled squid (*xipirons a la planxa*) with oil, parsley and lemon. But don't miss out on some other Catalan favourites, too.

Pa amb tomata (bread with crushed tomato and olive oil) is a staple at breakfast and lunch, and is even better when served with piquant anchovies, while *mar i muntanya* (which translates as 'sea and mountain') is a hearty meat and seafood stew perfect for cooler evenings. Desserts are worth saving space for, too, with smooth, moreish *crema Catalana* (similar to a *crème brûlée*) on menus all over the region, and in Girona you must try the locally loved *xuixo* pastries. These sausage-shaped, sugar-dusted treats are stuffed with various fillings, from simple custard or apple to cheesecake, coffee cream or cinnamon and cardamom cream.

views across the city and surrounding countryside. Take a walking tour with a guide from the tourist office (girona.cat) and you'll learn about it all, including the spots where the likes of Kit Harington and Emilia Clarke played out scenes in *Game of Thrones*.

Dining out is a pleasure in Girona – the city has eight Michelin stars – and most restaurant terraces admit dogs, so come hungry. In May, the city comes alive with colour thanks to a **flower festival** that sees its biggest attractions adorned with thousands of floral decorations.

If **medieval history** is where your interest lies, there's plenty more of it in

WHERE TO SLEEP

Hostal Sa Rascassa

From £100 per night
sawdays.co.uk

A homely five-room property, Hostal Sa Rascassa is a pretty place to base yourself on the coast of the Costa Brava. Located in the seaside village of Begur, it has access to exceptional walking trails on the hilly, verdant cliffs above, and a lovely swimming cove below where dogs can join you for a plunge from a concrete dock. Rooms are simple, but the food here is excellent, with meals served in a leafy courtyard outside the main stone building.

Mas Vinyoles

From £900 per week
sawdays.co.uk

Just outside Girona within the Gavarres mountain massif, this cosy whitewashed house has two lovely apartments inside and is surrounded by lush gardens. There's a shared plunge pool outside for those sticky hot summer days, parking on site and you're just a 45-minute drive from Palamós.

Camping Mas Patoxas

From £18 per night
caravanclub.co.uk

Located just outside the town of Pals, a 20-minute drive from Palamós and 90-minutes south of Port de la Selva, this leafy campsite is a brilliant base for adventures throughout the region. Pitches are set on a terraced grassy hill and are hemmed in by low hedges and some stubby little trees. There's a pool on site, a restaurant and takeaway, and a supermarket all open in high season, while in low season the site is a supremely peaceful place to have an extended break in the mild weather. Dogs get a slightly run-down off-lead area for toileting, and it's an easy walk along the main road to historic Pals should you want to go elsewhere for dinner.

Carrer del Mar apartment

From £1,000 per week
booking.com

If sea views and beach proximity are your priority, this apartment in Palamós is a corker. You're right opposite the dog-friendly beach here, with views over the play park and on to the sand from your own balcony. The apartment has the feel of a well-loved home, with paintings hanging on the walls and some vintage furniture and fittings. There are no gardens here, but you hardly need it what with the sand right on your doorstep.

← Arty relaxes on the beach north of El Port de la Selva

MAKE IT A ROAD TRIP
From Palamós, you're only a 90-minute drive to brilliant Barcelona where you can explore Gaudí architecture and indulge the dog in a little luxury (see page 160), or, a little further south, see Roman ruins and human towers in Tarragona (see page 98). In the other direction, boating holidays on the Camargue are a 3.5-hour drive (see page 108). Alternatively, if you're coming into Santander or Bilbao by ferry, stop in San Sebastián for a delicious diversion by the sea (see page 54).

ESSENTIALS

Getting there: There are only a handful of train stations on the Costa Brava, including one in Girona, but none of them reach the dog-friendly coastal areas, so the best way to get here is by car. From the UK, the best port of entry is Santander or Bilbao, which are roughly a seven-hour drive from the Costa Brava.

What to pack: With warm weather throughout summer, a cooling mat or jacket is sensible for the hottest months, and a pup-tent for the beach will offer the dog some shade.

The dog rules: Generally, dogs are allowed on most beaches throughout winter. For summer trips, all of the dog beaches in this chapter are marked by signs indicating whether or not dogs are allowed. Look out for signage with the word '*gossos*', which means 'dog' in Catalan. Summertime on the Costa Brava can be sweltering, so while these beaches are dog-friendly throughout the peak season, they are best avoided during the hottest hours as there's generally no shade. They are most pleasant and reasonably quiet in the shoulder seasons (March to May and late September to October), when temperatures remain in the teens and early twenties. Always bring plenty of water with you for both humans and dogs.

Getting around: A car is essential on the Costa Brava, as dogs are not always permitted on buses and there are no train connections to the dog-friendly beaches.

More information: Get additional inspiration from the Costa Brava's own tourism board website at costabrava.org.

← A boardwalk leads to a dog-friendly beach at L'Escala
↓ Sunset fun on the beach in Palamós

SUN YOURSELF ON THE BEACHES OF THE COSTA BRAVA

16

TAKE A BALTIC BEACH BREAK IN NORTHERN GERMANY

Idyllic island life isn't the first thing that comes to mind when you think of adventuring in Germany, but in the very far north of the country on the edge of the Baltic Sea lies a smattering of isles just off the mainland, accessible by bridges, where beech and pine forests meet soft golden sands and a handful of seaside resorts attract holidaying Berliners from their city pads.

Heringsdorf

It's said that Germany's seaside resort culture was born here on the island of Usedom, when Adelbert and Hugo Delbrück had the bright idea to develop the settlement of Heringsdorf into the **country's first coastal spa town** in the 1870s. What followed was a boom in building as wealthy city folk bought up parcels of land to turn into their own havens by the sea. The result is a dazzling array of ostentatious **seaside villas**, built in the art nouveau, baroque, Palladian and Classical styles, and painted in pastels that make some look like they belong on the shelves of a fine French bakery, dusted in sugar.

All of this can be seen on a self-guided **walking tour** using the Kaiserbäder Erlebnispfad app (**kaiserbaeder-auf-usedom.de/rundgang**), which offers extra insight into the town's most intriguing architectural gems, from the villa owned by Berlin millionaire Benoit Oppenheim to those used by officials in the imperial era to conduct important business. It's clear from the architecture here that Heringsdorf was a destination for the well-heeled. In fact, from the late 1800s up to WWI, this was *the* place for the wealthy to spend their summers, and the town grew into quite the chic destination, with spa hotels popping up to meet the demands of holidaymakers seeking a soothing escape.

Today, while it may not be quite so glitzy as it once was, it still attracts crowds of sea-and-surf seeking Germans to its shores. And why wouldn't it? With a

beach as vast as this – 12km long in fact – it's an oh-so-tempting place to don the swimming costume and feel the healing power of the sea with the dog (they're welcome year-round on the signposted section 2/Y in Heringsdorf, and can enjoy the full length of the beach from October to March).

The island is beautiful in autumn and the beach will certainly be less crowded, but come in summer to escape the sweltering heat of southern Europe – it rarely gets above 23°C on Usedom – and you'll find the sands littered with cheerful chairs known as *Strandkorb*. These sturdy wicker constructions were invented here, supposedly for a woman with rheumatism who was staying at one of the many spa hotels in Heringsdorf and found the classic deck chair too uncomfortable. They're made in Rostock, along the coast on the mainland, and now feature on beaches across Europe. Hire one at the original *Strandkorb* town and bring a mat for the dog to relax on and you'll certainly have a day well spent by the Baltic Sea.

Of course, the dog will need a walk at some point and fortunately, Heringsdorf has that covered, too: this town is one of a handful that sits on the **longest beach promenade in Europe**, and a romp along its pedestrianised pavements is a real pleasure. From Heringsdorf, head eastwards along the prom and you'll pass through pretty Ahlbeck with its much-loved **beachside fish shacks** (ideal for a snack stop) and, if you keep going you'll eventually reach Poland 3km later. In the opposite direction lies Bansin, a beautiful little town whose architecture is dominated by intricate **wooden villas**, largely built in Wolgast on the nearby mainland and assembled here on the coastline like giant pieces of IKEA furniture. Your walking tour app has intel on the most intriguing properties, and the promenade stretches all the way through the town along the seafront until it reaches a beech, pine and oak forest set atop undulating sand dunes.

↓ Sunrise on the beach in Usedom

OTHER ADVENTURES NEARBY

Beyond Heringsdorf and on land, the island of Usedom has a variety of landscapes for interesting dog walks, from forests to small fishing villages. Head to **Wolgastsee** for an easy hour-long wander through beech and pine woodland around a small, calm lake, or drive south to the village of Neppermin where you can walk along the shores of the Achterwasser, a lagoon that separates Usedom from the mainland.

The tiny fishing village of **Kamminke**, on the border with Poland, is a quaint little spot for a stroll and fish sandwich at the lagoon-side *Fischräucherei* (fish smokehouse), while all the way to the northwest edge of the island lies the Peenemünde peninsula. Here, walks amid lush forests abound and a slice of history can be explored at the **Historical Technical Museum** (museum-peenemuende.de), a former power station that built test rockets during WWII, where dogs can join you for all the outdoors exhibits (there's an indoor waiting room where one of your party can wait with the dog so you can take it in turns to explore the main exhibit inside the power station).

Of course, there are adventures to be had at sea, too – there are dog-friendly **boat trips** on the ferries from the various piers in Usedom, including Ahlbeck and Bansin with Adler-Schiffe (adler-schiffe.de; large dogs must wear a muzzle when on board and dog fees apply). Trips track the Usedom coastline and visit various islands of interest, including Greifswalder Oie and Ruden where you might spot grey seals lolling around on the shores or bobbing about in the sea.

↓ Industrial buildings at the Peenemünde Historical Technical Museum

WHAT'S FOR DINNER?

Naturally, there's plenty of excellent seafood to be eaten on Usedom – fishing is a mainstay of the local business here. You'll see everything from herring (often pickled) to fried cod, plaice and flounder on menus in the casual fish shacks by the waterfronts. More interesting, though, is some of the wilder food you can try here. Head to Neu Pudagla and you'll find the Wildbistro (wild-auf-wild.de), a small cafe serving snacks made from locally foraged herbs, vegetables and game meat shot in the nearby forests. Try sausages made with wild boar, venison and reindeer, or traditional German soups. The shop is stocked with locally made produce, too, from *Glühwein* to gin distilled with forest herbs and cured game meats.

→ Game sausage from the Wildbistro in Neu Pudagla

WHERE TO SLEEP

Villa San Remo

From £60 per night
villasanremo.de

Tucked just 50 metres back from the promenade and beach in residential Heringsdorf, this handsome apartment block is a brilliant location for dog-friendly adventuring in Usedom. You're five minutes' walk from the beach, a 20-minute stroll into the town centre, and there's parking on site and a small garden for late-night loo trips. The apartments are mostly modern (some on the upper floors look a little dated), fitted out with kitchens where you can cook on the hob or in the combi microwave oven, and some even have enclosed balconies overlooking the street.

Strandhotel Ostseeblick

From £120 per night
strandhotel-ostseeblick.de

Dogs are well catered for at this beachfront property, where the hotel's own 'Feel Good Manager' Costello (a poodle cross) greets guests when he's hanging about. There are blankets and bowls in the rooms, as well as welcome snacks for the dogs. Humans get to enjoy contemporary bedrooms with walk-in showers and bath robes, and an on-site spa to fully embrace Heringsdorf's spa town history.

← Villa San Remo in Heringsdorf, Usedom
→ The seaside promenade in Heringsdorf

ESSENTIALS

Getting there: The easiest way to get to and around Heringsdorf is by car, but there are train connections, too. It's around three hours and one change away from Berlin Central Station.

What to pack: A longline for the beach is essential, as dogs are required to be leashed at all times. Don't forget a spare towel for any pets liable to take a dip, too, and a muzzle for public transport.

The dog rules: Leads are generally required throughout Usedom, even on the beach, but locals will use longlines or let their dogs off lead in quieter, open spaces (like the forests). You may be asked to muzzle your dog at times (on

boats or public transport) so be sure to carry one just in case. Dog poo bags are freely available at the entrances to the dog-friendly beach sections in each of the main towns (look out for signs at section 1/E in Ahlbeck, 2/Y in Heringsdorf and 3/L in Bansin); it's essential to clean up after your dog.

Getting around: Usedom is easy to explore by car or public transport. There's a great bus service and train connections all the way from the border with Poland (Ahlbeck Grenze) to Peenemünde on the northern edge of the island. To head to the southern reaches of the island and more remote spots like Wolgastsee there are buses, but a car is your best bet. Note that muzzles for dogs are mandatory on all public transport.

Alternatively, make use of the extensive cycle network: e-bikes, normal bikes and dog-friendly trailers are all readily available for hire from the Mietrad Usedom (mietrad-usedom.de) hubs in the seafront towns.

More information: The tourist information hubs in Heringsdorf, Bansin and Ahlbeck are all dog-friendly; more information on the island of Usedom and all it has to offer can be found at kaiserbaeder-auf-usedom.de.

→ Beech woodland on the coast near Bansin
↓ The promenade in Heringsdorf

MAKE IT A ROAD TRIP
The Baltic Sea is a great stop on any trip in Germany – try city breaks in Berlin (see page 118), road tripping in Saxony (see page 128) or hiking in the Harz mountains (see page 86).

17

EXPLORE THE CHRISTMAS MARKETS OF LAKE GENEVA

The origins of the Christmas market might be in Austria and Germany, but Switzerland does this December tradition just as well, and the dog is more than welcome, too. The lakeside cities of Montreux and Lausanne are not only exciting destinations to visit in their own right – there are beautiful parks for walking the dog and cosy restaurants and bars that'll welcome your pets inside for traditional Swiss comfort food – but they also happen to have some of the most spectacular views across Lake Geneva towards the spiky, snow-capped French Alps. This is a truly magical location to do a little Christmas shopping at the myriad wooden stalls set out across each city, selling everything from hand-crafted jewellery and fine knitwear made from yak's wool to kids' clothing and traditional Swiss toys.

Bringing a dog to Switzerland is an easy endeavour – this country loves its pets and both Montreux and Lausanne are well set up for dogs, especially with the prevalence of free dog mess bags attached to most of the bins in parks and green spaces. In December, the twinkle of Christmas lights and warming smell of *vin chaud* carried on the air is enough to make even the Grinch feel festive, and the dog will no doubt have a fabulous time following their nose through the warren of market stalls.

↓ The Christmas market in Montreux

Lausanne

Known as the Olympic capital thanks to the presence of the International Committee's headquarters on the city's riverfront, and the many more international sporting federations that call this their base, Lausanne is a sprawling multicultural city on the shores of Lake Geneva. While it's famous for its sporting connections, come wintertime Lausanne turns its hand to celebration: almost every street is adorned with Christmas lights, and it feels like every square or marketplace hosts some sort of festivity. You can't turn a corner without smelling the sticky-sweetness of a mulled wine or hot chocolate.

Each year here Christmas is slightly different – the organisation responsible for the city's party atmosphere over the festive period, aptly named Bô Noël, is adept at crafting new and unusual experiences with each season. You might find a **city-centre toboggan run** that uses recycled snow with an adjoining bar, or pop-up boutiques for local designers to showcase their wares – perfect for a Christmas gift or two.

Elsewhere there will be fondue and raclette in the **Marché des Papilles** – a food market that thrums with the sound of clanging metal spoons and sizzling crêpes – and anyone travelling with kids will want to seek out the annual **Village des Enfants**, where you might ride a Ferris wheel for city-wide views, get to pet farm animals or meet Santa Claus.

Spread across the city, visiting each Christmas market is a wonderful way to see Lausanne's varying neighbourhoods, from the modern, trendy Flon district to the Rôtillon area, one of the city's oldest. Of course, it could be an exhausting endeavour trying to take it all in in one day, but with the assistance of the dog- and wheelchair-friendly **Petit Train de Noël**, you'll pootle from market to market with ease.

Beyond the festivities, though, this city has other draws for visiting dog owners – most notably its vast array of pet-friendly chocolate shops. Famous for its silky-smooth milk chocolate, Switzerland is one of Europe's top chocolate-producers, and Lausanne really knows how to flaunt its finest with its '**Choco Tour**' (lausanne-tourisme.ch). With a pre-paid voucher of around 30 CHF, you'll get to visit five of its artisanal chocolatiers for a sweet treat and an explanation of their craft, with discounts offered for any purchases. Dogs are welcome in most shops, and some even have cafes attached so you can stop for a coffee or hot chocolate.

Lausanne's centre isn't the greenest of urban spaces (Esplanade de Montbenon is the most central park and it does have a lovely dog-friendly cafe), but down by the waterfront you'll find plenty of spots for walking the dog. The terraced **Parc Olympique** – set in front of the Musée Olympique – is a pleasant amble with steps or a zigzag ramp for wheelchairs, and at the bottom you can join the **Quai d'Ouchy**, a lakeside promenade built in 1901 that connects the former port to the 18th-century Haldimand Tower. In the north of the city, just before the urban sprawl becomes a sprinkle of houses amid green hills, **Sauvabelin Park** is the city's green lung. Climb the 302 steps of the park's tower for panoramic views across Lausanne and the lake.

→ Sledding on fake snow in the centre of Lausanne
↓ Walking along the shore of Lake Geneva, or Lac Léman as it's known in French

↑ Irresistible chocolates on display in Lausanne
→ The Freddie Mercury statue on the waterfront in Montreux

Montreux

While Lausanne might have mountains of chocolate, Montreux has mountain views. This city has an utterly spellbinding location with a waterfront promenade overlooking the snow-clad, spiky peaks of the French Alps across the lake. On a cloudy day, they're often shrouded in a cloak of thick mist, but as the fog clears the mountain ridges become visible and are an ever-present companion on lakeside walks.

Come here anytime from late November to 24 December, though, and those views from the lake's promenade will be partially obscured by rows of wooden huts housing artisans, craft-makers and food producers for the city's famous **Montreux Noël** (montreuxnoel.com). Stretching north along the lakeshore from Place du Marché to the Mona Montreux hotel, the Christmas market here is vast, with activities aplenty for the whole family.

At Place du Marché you'll find a huge **food hall**, where steaming cauldrons of *tartiflette* fill the air with a distinctly cheesy smell and the musty scent of mulled wine drifts by on the breeze. There's *rösti au lard* (potatoes with bacon), *choucroute garnie* (meat and sauerkraut) and roasted ham hock, plus enough dessert options to make your arteries wince. Outside on the marketplace you can't miss the towering **Ferris wheel** (dogs allowed), and down by the lakeside stands the famous **Freddie Mercury statue** (he lived here and recorded several albums with Queen in the city), only slightly overshadowed by a majestic silver and gold deer sculpture on the jetty.

Heading north from here, crowds are

squeezed between an alleyway of stalls on the **promenade** selling myriad crafts, jewellery and local produce. Expect to see wooden sculptures and toys, olive oils imported from the Med, mammoth chunks of nougat and hand-knitted socks and hats made from yak's wool. If you can't fulfil your Christmas presents list here, you've no chance anywhere else.

It's out on the promenade where you'll also get to see the market's main spectacle: the **flying Santa**. Suspended on wires (don't tell the kids), a real-life Santa Claus in an illuminated sleigh with four reindeer guiding his way swoops over the stalls with the lake and mountains in the background. Fortunately for visitors, he makes time to visit Montreux several times a day throughout the festive season, so you can't miss him if you check the schedule online.

With kids' workshops and plenty of events on offer, exploring the market alone could take up several days, but Montreux is a city with appeal beyond its festivities. For a little quiet time, take the train from the main station in the city centre and press the call button to stop at **Haut-de-Caux**. Here, with cinematic views over the city, lake and mountains beyond, you can stop for coffee or hot chocolate with the dog on the terrace at Le CouCou hotel. From here you can join walking paths that head down into the city or connect the hillside villages (alltrails.com for directions), or bring some snowshoes and you can have a go at traipsing along the 2.6km-long Haut-de-Caux snowshoe trail (details at montreuxriviera.com). At the nearby village of Caux, you'll also find a **natural ice rink** where kids can skate as you watch on with the dog.

If your legs don't fancy the workout in the hills, the promenade along Lake Geneva continues south of the Christmas market and offers more enchanting mountain views – you could walk as far as **Château de Chillon** (no dogs inside, but there are kennels on site for those who wish to visit), and then take the ferry back up to the city.

Of course, with the lake on your doorstep here, it's almost impossible to resist a boat trip. Ferry company CGN (cgn.ch) runs **sightseeing cruises** alongside the basic ferry trips, and you can even get a combined ticket to ride the MOB **panoramic trains** (mob.ch) into the mountains above Montreux.

WHAT'S FOR DINNER?

The Christmas markets here have a roster of hardcore comfort food – potatoes, cheese and bacon seem to be the staples. Ultra-cheesy fondue with chunky bread is a must (especially in the fondue tent at Lausanne's food market, where you can even eat while seated inside a giant fondue pot), and it needs to be washed down with a refreshing glass of white wine. The canton of Vaud produces plenty of excellent wine; look out for a Chasselas on the menu.

Raclette is similarly popular (more melted cheese, usually served with meats and potatoes), while *malakoff* – like beignets made with a molten Gruyère middle – are another deeply warming snack. Chocolate is also a Swiss specialty here and it's best had piping hot in a mug at a cafe or on a terrace with a lovely view.

WHERE TO SLEEP

Moxy Lausanne

From £140 per night
marriott.com

A convenient city-centre base with a youthful feel and a free welcome drink at the bar on arrival, Moxy is a reliable choice for your Lausanne break. There are no big views nor especially beautiful bedrooms, but there's clever, contemporary design and a decent breakfast spread should you want something to start your day. It's right next to Esplanade de Montbenon, so is handy for your end-of-day wee walks. There's a movement-activated night light beneath the bed here, so bring something to cover the sensor to avoid being awoken in the night by your roaming dog.

→ A Christmas tree-shaped sculpture made with giant baubles in Lausanne
↓ Arty on the banks of Lake Geneva (Lac Léman) in Montreux

Hotel 46A

From £100 per night
46a.ch

If you'd rather self-cater for your stay, this is a reliable aparthotel where rooms come with small kitchens and living areas, and a pet kit with bowls is provided on request. Dogs are allowed in the on-site restaurant, and there's a gym and wellness area, too. Located in the Vidy neighbourhood, west of the city centre, it has Parc Emile-Henri-Jaques Dalcroze on the doorstep and isn't far from the lakeside beaches.

Grand Hotel Suisse Majestic

From £200 per night
marriott.com

A belle époque masterpiece overlooking the lake and located directly opposite the main train station, this luxurious Marriott-owned hotel is an excellent base for the night. Posh dogs will enjoy prancing down its long carpeted corridors to bedrooms that look out over the lake and mountains – some with balconies for al fresco morning coffee. Dogs aren't allowed in the restaurant, but you can have breakfast sent to the bedroom for a tray charge, or leave them there while you dine downstairs. Directly beneath the hotel on the lakeside is Parc Suisse, where the dog can go for their morning or evening wee walk.

Hotel Bon-Port

From £120 per night
hotelbonport.ch

Located south of Place du Marché and just one block away from the lakeside promenade, this simple, affordable hotel is great if you're on a tighter budget. Bedrooms are basic but always clean and comfortable, and some have kitchenettes with a small hob and microwave. There's a small breakfast buffet, and bedrooms can sleep up to four if you book one with bunk beds.

ESSENTIALS

Getting there: The easiest way to get to Montreux or Lausanne is by car and it's just a 7.5-hour journey from Calais if you're coming from the UK – break up the drive in somewhere like Dijon and use the budget chain Première Classe (premiereclasse.com) for a no-frills stopover. It's possible to get to Lausanne and Montreux by train, too – the best route is via Paris – and the journey can be quite spectacular, especially the final leg that trundles the shores of Lake Geneva from Geneva.

What to pack: You can expect sub-zero temperatures and possible snow at this time of year, so pack thermal clothing for you and something warm for the dog if you've got a pet with a thin coat of fur. Don't forget to bring an empty bag for all that Christmas shopping, too.

The dog rules: Swiss law says that dogs must be kept on a lead in public places, and there's a 150 CHF (£140) fine for failing to clear up your dog's poo. There are other oddly specific fines, too, such as allowing dogs into cemeteries or on to boat jetties (both 70 CHF, which is around £65).

↓ Mesmerising views of the Alps from Montreux

Getting around: If you're driving, it's a short hop between Lausanne and Montreux and there's central parking in both cities. Public transport in and between both cities is excellent, though, with trams, buses and trains all allowing dogs – if you stay overnight in hotels that pay the tourist tax, you'll also get a free transport card in both cities. Dogs must be leashed on transport and in rare cases you might be asked to muzzle them, so it's always best to carry one just in case.

More information: Learn more at montreuxriviera.com and lausanne-tourisme.ch.

MAKE IT A ROAD TRIP
If there's good snow up in the mountains, nip over the French border for a snowshoeing adventure in Morzine (see page 202) or drive further into Switzerland and explore the Jungfrau region's plunging snowy valleys and take the train to the highest station in Europe (see page 210).

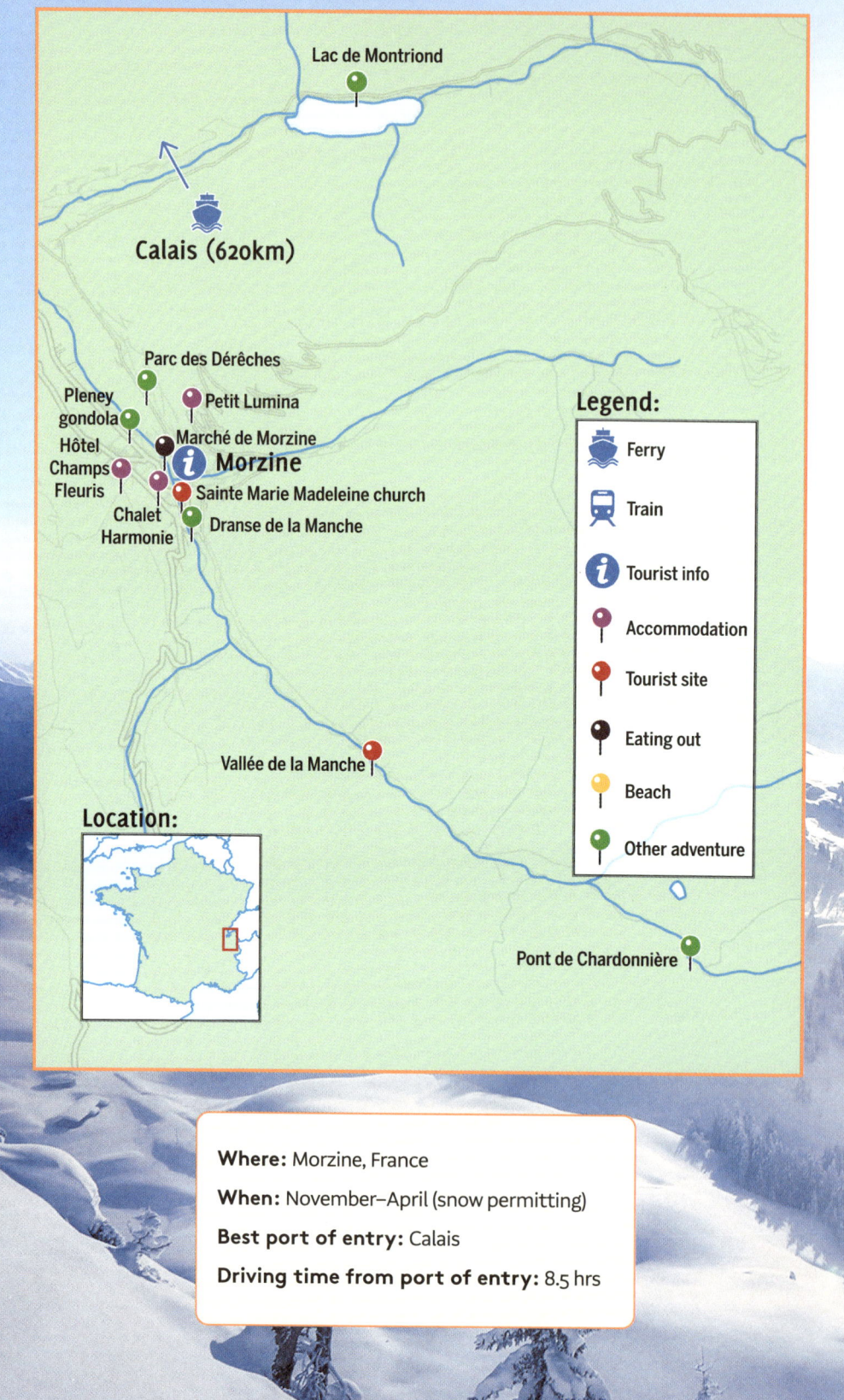

18
GO SNOWSHOEING IN THE FRENCH ALPS

Morzine

No doubt we all expect a certain amount of jeopardy on our daily dog walks when there's ice or snow under foot. On days like this, we are probably more inclined to shuffle instead of stride, and eager dogs on the ends of leads can easily turn a walk into an accidental mushing experience – and that rarely ends well. But, amid the spruce, birch and pine winter wonderland that is the **Vallée de la Manche**, with a pair of snowshoes on your feet you'll find your footing greatly improved – and the dog will love the freedom of the snow-draped forest that surrounds the trails here.

Sitting a few kilometres south of the ski village of Morzine at around 1,100 metres above sea level, the valley here feels gloriously remote but is still easily accessed by road. Park up and you can ramble across what are usually grazing meadows in summer, which become caked in snow come winter, and then into thick woodland where the tree branches droop under the weight of the of the white stuff. The trail then joins the mountain road – closed in winter for cross-country skiers and snow-shoers – which gently twists upwards following the Dranse de la Manche to the Pont de Chardonnière at 1,309 metres above sea level. Here you'll find a small hut – a welcome resting spot after a breathless 2km walk from your starting point and a good point at which to turn back if you're feeling the thigh-burning effects of hiking in deep snow (there's an alternative return trail from here that wends its way through the forest to meet the road again if you don't want to completely retrace your steps). But if you continue, you can add on another few kilometres to Refuge de Chardonnière before you turn back.

As long as they remain under control, dogs can roam off lead as you make tracks on that powder-soft snow, which is extra satisfying when you're the first to step in it, but note that there are some steep cliffsides above the river and some wildlife roaming in the woods. If you're lucky, you might come across **deer** or even a chamois, a **goat-like mammal** with a black-and-white striped face that's part of the bovid family, and while you won't see them, the dog will most likely catch the scent of the magnificently horned ibex that live in the high mountains that surround you on this walk.

Practicalities: Snowshoes can be hired from Morzine's myriad ski hire shops, and maps for local snowshoeing routes are available from the tourist office (morzine-avoriaz.com), all of which are accessible with the winter shuttle buses and various lifts. Beyond Vallée de la Manche, another must-try is the excellent route that travels alongside the glassy Lac de Montriond and takes around three and a half hours – you'd be forgiven for thinking you're in Canada as you gaze across the water to the distant peaks.

If you're a first-time snowshoer, book a guided tour for your first session with DaysAway Adventures (daysawayadventures.com) – Viv and her trusty border collie Gaia will guide you all the way, and provide coffee and cake at the mountain hut stop. Alternatively, she can also guide you on a dog-friendly cross-country ski trip.

→ Arty prepares to go snowshoeing in Vallée de la Manche

↑ Arty on the trails in Vallée de la Manche

OTHER ADVENTURES NEARBY

Tucked away in a steep valley in the Portes du Soleil ski area of the French Alps, Morzine is a pretty little market town and makes a fantastic base for any snowshoeing or skiing adventure here. Running through its centre is the River Dranse, which thunders with whitewater after heavy rains or snow melt, and throughout the village you'll find a smattering of handsome historic buildings – unlike many of the purpose-built resorts in the region – including the charming Sainte Marie Madeleine church, which was constructed in the early 1800s. There's a **market** in the centre on Wednesdays, where you can stock up on local produce – think cured meats, fresh bread, French cheeses – and on the square outside the tourist office you'll find an **ice-skating rink** and carousel for kids.

For a little local history, try out the tourist board's own Géodyssée app (geodyssee.fr), which has a geo-location-specific **treasure hunt** that'll encourage exploration of the village while offering up intriguing little nuggets of history.

During the peak winter season, the village buzzes with skiers and snowboarders – there's excellent access to the slopes with several lifts, cable cars and tramways for any adrenaline junkies in your midst – but for dogs and their owners, it's the **Parc des Dérêches** where the more exciting action is. Down by the rushing River Dranse, this is where the locals walk their own dogs before a day

GO SNOWSHOEING IN THE FRENCH ALPS

hikes relatively level, though, it's worth going up to the top of the runs just to enjoy a little mountain hospitality – there's nothing quite like a **hot chocolate** topped with cream or a steamy *vin chaud* in the middle of a sunny winter's afternoon. Especially as the views are rarely short of spectacular on a clear day.

WHAT'S FOR DINNER?

Morzine has plenty of bars and restaurants in its village and very few of them would decline a dog-towing patron, so you've plenty of choice when it comes to dinner. But knowing what to order here is the key: in this mountainous region, there are three traditional dishes that are a must try, but be warned, they're heavy on the cheese.

The first is perhaps the most famous: the *fondue Savoyarde*. This utterly indulgent and incredibly rich cheesy dish is everywhere in the Haute-Savoie region, so you'll see it on menus throughout Morzine. Generally, the fondues here are a mix of three cheeses – Beaufort, Comté and Tomme de Savoie – with a splash of white wine and garlic, and are served with moreish bread for dipping. There's little etiquette when it comes to eating fondue – it can be a messy business – but know that there are forfeits for those who lose their carbs in the cheese!

With such proximity to Switzerland, it's hardly surprising that raclette is a common feature on menus throughout this French region, too. Another cheese-based dish, there's a ceremonial style to this one, as hefty blocks of semi-hard cheese are melted from above by a piping hot grill and slowly swiped off on to your plate using a metal paddle. The best restaurants let you do the swiping yourself, and dipping morsels are usually served in the form of bread, cornichons, cured meats, boiled or roasted potatoes and vegetables.

at work, and Sunday mornings often see a small gathering of resident Morzine hounds meeting for a mooch around the fields on the eastern side of the riverbank. There's an excellent 4.5km walk through the Dérêches from the François Baud footbridge, which crosses over the river at the sports club and returns through the forest – ideal for a slightly more leisurely morning stroll through the snow (snowshoes optional).

Of course, dogs are welcome up on the mountains, too, thanks to many of the **lifts and gondolas** welcoming pets on board – you just need to buy a pedestrian pass, which is generally far cheaper than the ski pass. While the dog can't join you on the slopes during operational hours, you can walk them on the pistes before the skiers start. If you'd rather keep your

GO SNOWSHOEING IN THE FRENCH ALPS

↑ The author and her dog, Arty, hiding out at a small hut on the trails in Vallée de la Manche

Finally, the ultimate après-ski mountain comfort food: *tartiflette*. A baked combination of sliced potatoes, smoked bacon, onion, cream and – yes – more cheese, it's a favourite among skiers and snowboarders who've spent an exhausting day on the slopes. And there's no reason a day's snowshoeing shouldn't qualify you for this food coma-inducing dinner, either. Whether you choose to share it with the dog is another matter, of course.

WHERE TO SLEEP

Chalet Harmonie

From £5,200 per week
alikats.eu

Right in the heart of Morzine village and conveniently next door to Carrefour, this vast chalet is a chic family base – especially if you plan on skiing or snowboarding during your stay. In true Alpine fashion, the interiors make the most of natural woods, while a splash of colour in the soft furnishings adds a little hotel style to the living room. A large, well-equipped kitchen offers the means to cook for a full crowd, with dining space for 12 at the huge wooden table, and there's chef-prepared meals on delivery if you pay a little extra. There are five en-suite bedrooms here, either with balcony views over the village centre or on the ground floor next to a small patio garden, plus a boot room for drying your sodden snow gear. Outside on the middle floor is a large balcony with a barbecue, dining area and hot tub – blissful after a day's snowshoeing. Operating company Alikats offers a doting concierge service via WhatsApp, too.

> **MAKE IT A ROAD TRIP**
> This trip is easily paired with a foray to some of Switzerland's most magical Christmas markets on Lac Léman (Lake Geneva), which are just a 90-minute drive from Morzine village (see page 190).

Petit Lumina

From £700 per week
alikats.eu

With views across to Pleney and down into the Morzine valley, this mini chalet is a wonderful little hideaway in the mountains. It has a rustic feel about it with a timber-framed vaulted ceiling and mezzanine bedroom, and cosy open-plan kitchen-living room. It's a self-catered chalet, but as part of the Alikats collection you'll get access to chef-prepared meals delivered to your door for you to cook come evening (extra charge). You'll also have access to their concierge, who can answer all and any questions via WhatsApp or over the phone.

Hôtel Champs Fleuris

From £1210 per week half-board
hotel-champs-fleuris.com

Set right next door to the dog-friendly Pleney gondola, you're in prime position here for long days on the slopes or afternoons spent sipping *chocolat chaud* at the top. This handsome hotel operates on a half-board basis (or full-board for an extra 20 Euros per person per day), and you'll be glad of it: the food is excellent, with fondues and hearty stews to warm you up. There's a pool, spa and fitness centre here to keep non-skiers occupied, and the decor is peak mountain chic: expect wood cladding on the walls and soft furs on the beds. The hotel arranges gourmet outings to traditional mountain chalets where a warm raclette dinner awaits at the end, but there's a restaurant on site, too.

ESSENTIALS

Getting there: The best way to reach Morzine with your dog is by car. For those coming from the UK, it's an 8.5-hour drive from Calais, so it might be best to split the journey in half with a stop in cities like Metz or Dijon. Première Classe hotels (premiereclasse.com) are a no-frills, dog-friendly chain offering reasonable accommodation from £30 per night (£5 for the dog).

What to pack: Plenty of cold weather, waterproof gear for the humans, and a thermal coat for dogs with very little fur (such as whippets and greyhounds). Also consider a lightweight waterproof coat for dogs with long fur that might get matted in the snow.

The dog rules: Dogs must be on a lead at the town end of the Dérêches and should always be kept under control in other areas. If you're up on the pistes, always keep the dog on a lead so they don't stray on to the slopes and cause an accident.

Getting around: Morzine is a small village so it's very walkable if you're heading out for lunch or dinner. There are free shuttle buses between Morzine and many of the main ski resorts and snowshoeing locations, as well as gondolas and lifts that welcome dogs on board, too.

More information: Further detail, snow updates and lift or gondola news are available at morzine-avoriaz.com.

Where: Grindelwald, Switzerland
When: December–April
Best port of entry: Calais, France
Driving time from port of entry: 9 hrs

19
TAKE THE TRAIN TO THE TOP OF EUROPE

Grindelwald

If you've not got a head for heights, you may want to turn to the next chapter, for dangling high above pine and fir forests in a glass box with holes in the floor, held up by a just few cables, isn't for everyone. For those who don't mind a little frisson, though, the journey to Jungfraujoch is quite the ride. Of course, there's no real peril involved: the **Eiger Express tri-cable gondola** is a feat of Swiss engineering, whisking visitors from the charming Grindelwald village terminal up to Eiger Glacier in just 15 minutes. It travels at 8 metres per second, hovering above the steep slopes of the Bernese Alps, starting from an altitude of nearly 950 metres and depositing you at just above 2,300 metres. As for the holes in the floor? They're for the skis.

Leave your skis for this day trip, though; today is all about the rails. It's just a minute's walk from the Eiger Express terminal to the Eigergletscher train station, where you can board the **Jungfrau Railway** to the highest rail station in Europe, sitting proudly at a dizzying 3,454 metres. And dizzying it is – not just because of the altitude, either. When you realise these tracks were laid within their tunnels over a century ago, without any of the heavy machinery and automation we have today, you will feel a sense of awe for the people responsible for its construction.

Almost the entire journey on this railway is spent inside one long tunnel that was bored through the Eiger and Mönch peaks at the turn of the 20th century. It took 16 years and a team of hundreds of labourers, engineers and support workers to construct the 9km route to Jungfraujoch. This ride has a similar effect to the Eiger Express, but for very different reasons: whereas in the gondola your heart rate is likely to be raised by the vastness of the space around you and the abyss that looms below, on the railway you might find your anxieties shift to the tightly enclosed space the carriages trundle through with very few stops and seemingly no escape routes.

There is one stop before the top on this railway, though: at Eismeer station. Here you'll disembark for a few minutes to peer out from the side of the tunnel to the **Ischmeer glacier**. In winter, it's usually protected by a healthy layer of powdery white snow, while in summer once much of the snowfall has melted away, it takes on the look of a rushing river frozen in time. There's just enough time to snap a photo before you board the train once again to reach the top.

Whether or not you love the adrenaline rush of being ferried through middle of the mountains on a railway with gradients as steep as 25%, the rewards at Jungfraujoch can be great if you get there on a clear-sky day. While fog and clouds regularly obscure the surrounding scenery, once it clears, you're treated to frankly outrageous views. With the 23km-long **Aletsch glacier** on one side and views out over the Swiss Plateau towards France on the other, there are jagged mountain peaks all around, seemingly at eye height when viewed from the **Sphinx Observatory** deck. If your breath isn't taken away by the panorama before you, you will no doubt be left gasping after a short walk up the stairs thanks to the thin air at over 3,570 metres.

→ Riding the rails from from Jungfraujoch to Kleine Scheidegg

TAKE THE TRAIN TO THE TOP OF EUROPE

OTHER ADVENTURES NEARBY

At the top of Jungfraujoch you'll find a few interesting diversions if you can tear yourself away from the views. It's home to the highest Lindt chocolate shop in the world, an ice palace peppered with sculptures, a Swiss watch store and a souvenir shop, as well as an exhibition detailing the making of the railway and its own power station. There's also an excellent dog-friendly à la carte restaurant at the top serving traditional Swiss mountain cuisine – just beware the booze: the wine might well go straight to your head at such altitude.

While you can't hike from Jungfraujoch in winter, once you've explored all there is to see at the top you can head back down to Eigergletscher and then hop on a train to Kleine Scheidegg, where you'll get staggering views of the Eiger North Face. From here, purple trail markers take you on a **90-minute descent** to Alpiglen, which overlooks the handsome Grindelwald valley. Refuel at the inn here before taking the train down to Grindelwald village, or continue your descent on foot.

Down in Grindelwald itself, there are plenty more walking opportunities. For an easy stroll with the whole family, head down to the **riverside trails** that peel off from Wärgistalstrasse, where a veritable winter wonderland of fir trees cloaked in snow is the ideal place to let the dog run off the lead. Grindelwald's various gondolas offer access to more trails: Head to Waldspitz for a **three-hour hike** ending in Bort, or hop off the gondola in Bort and enjoy a **90-minute walk** down to Grindelwald village.

A 25-minute gondola ride north of Grindelwald lies the 2,168-metre-high First peak. Head up here for more dramatic mountain views, and a chance to take the dog on the **First Cliff Walk** – a purpose-built walkway that hugs the precipitous mountain sides, with a breathtaking and perhaps somewhat terrifying suspended viewpoint at its end overlooking the Grindelwald Valley. Note that some dogs may not cope well with the metal floor, which has small holes in it – often uncomfortable for paws.

Alongside the cliff walk, other adrenaline-fuelled fun can be had, including a **zipline** and a 'glider' – a zipline-style ride where you soar headfirst through the valley like an eagle (jungfrau.ch). The dog can't join you on these, of course, so they'll need to be looked after by someone in your group.

A short train ride from Grindelwald is the small village of Wengen, which has an **ice rink** for kids in winter (no dogs on the ice) and a lovely viewpoint next door to a charming little church where you can look right down through the Lauterbrunnen Valley. For some lower-level activities, head down to the pretty town of Interlaken where you can enjoy **winter cruises** on Lake Thun with BLS (bls-schiff.ch; dogs that measure less than 30cm at the shoulder ride free).

For skiers, snowboarders or those who'd like to take advantage of the region's lovely spas, local **Grindewald dog walker** Andrea will look after your hounds for a fee (dogness.ch).

↓ Arty posing in the centre of Grindelwald

TAKE THE TRAIN TO THE TOP OF EUROPE

↑ Comfort food in the restaurant at the top of Jungfraujoch

WHAT'S FOR DINNER?

Switzerland is famous for its cheese, much of which is made on the alpine slopes in and around Grindelwald, and so it's unsurprising that it features throughout the traditional cuisine here. You almost can't escape it, whether you try a traditional fondue with bread, or raclette with potatoes, vegetables and chunks of meat. *Rösti* – a grated potato dish – is commonplace on menus, often served with bacon and cheese or alongside veal in a rich mushroom sauce, and the Swiss take on mac and cheese is called *Älplermagronen* and is a serious winter warmer with onions, potatoes and crispy bacon on top.

Swiss chocolate is another world-famous export here and you'll find it in various guises, but don't miss sampling the smooth, rich and moreish *Eigerspitzli* – an Eiger-shaped praline chocolate that's made only in this region. You can get them at the top of Jungfraujoch, and in many of the souvenir shops in Grindelwald, too.

WHERE TO SLEEP

Hotel Bernerhof & Residence

From £300 per night
hotelbernerhof.com

Located in Wengen just a short train ride from Grindelwald, this might just be Switzerland's most dog-friendly hotel – not only does it have several of its own dogs on site, but it offers welcome packs for every dog with homemade treats, a toy, poo bags, a bowl and a door hanger to put on your room for when the dog's alone. They even have a little dog boutique in the lobby with handmade collars and more treats.

The property is built in the traditional Swiss chalet style, all wood cladding and cheerful red shutters on the outside and cosy pine panelling in the restaurant and bar. There are two styles of accommodation: typical hotel bedrooms or self-catering apartments. All are simple, no-frills rooms but they have a

homely feel, and the apartments are ideal for longer stays when you might prefer to make your own meals. Bedrooms at the front of the property have balconies with wonderful views over the village and mountains beyond.

Bergwelt Grindelwald Alpine Resort

From £255 per night
bergwelt-grindelwald.com

Posh dogs will love residing at this chic design hotel in Grindelwald village. A 10-minute walk from the train station and a short bus ride to the Eiger Express terminal, it's an excellent base. Bedrooms are supremely cosy with dark wooden flooring and grey walls offset by pops of colour in velvet sofas and purple faux animal skin rugs. With dark, sultry interiors, the views beyond your floor-to-ceiling windows stand out – rooms at the front of the hotel overlook the mountains on the south side of the valley. There's an excellent dog-friendly restaurant in the ground floor, a basement spa and pool and underground parking. Dogs get a welcome pack of treats, too.

Boutique Hotel Glacier

From £200 per night
theglacier.ch

A handsome chalet-style hotel just a 500-metre walk from Grindelwald Grund station, this gorgeous design-centric hotel is a wonderful retreat. Bedrooms are modern and swish, with headboards painted with mountainscapes inspired by the region, and gold touches to add a hint of glamour. Almost all the rooms have brilliant views across the valley, and some have balconies with their own hot tubs on outdoor decks. Dogs are allowed in the lounge where there's all-day dining, but don't miss out on the fine-dining experience: the food is exceptional, with tasting menus on offer and an extensive wine cellar to boot.

↑ The ice caves in Jungfraujoch Ice Palace
← The village of Grindelwald in the snow

TAKE THE TRAIN TO THE TOP OF EUROPE

ESSENTIALS

Getting there: Swiss trains are famously reliable and incredibly comfortable, so taking public transport here is easy and enjoyable. Driving is also possible providing you have winter tyres or are carrying snow chains, but you may not want to tackle the roads above Interlaken. Leaving your car in town and taking the train up to Grindelwald is a much better option.

What to pack: In the dead of winter, it can get extremely cold in the Jungfrau region, and the higher you go, the colder it'll be. Many dogs will benefit from wearing boots in this weather to keep their paw pads protected and their body heat contained. While your huskies and Great Pyrenees dogs will relish this cool climate, most will not and so a thermal coat for your dog is also an essential – especially any terrier, whippet and greyhound types.

The dog rules: Dogs must be kept off the ski slopes in winter, but they can enjoy free running on the hiking and sledging trails, providing they're kept under control. Dogs are allowed to join you for free skiing (off-piste), but this is only for experienced, knowledgeable skiers with a reasonable understanding of these mountains.

Getting around: Dogs ride free on all the public transport in Switzerland, except on the Jungfrau Railway, where they'll need their own ticket.

More information: Your hotel will have maps of all the pistes, sledding and hiking routes and the tourism office at Grindelwald is an excellent source of further information. Online, head to jungfrauregion.swiss or myswitzerland.com for further travel inspiration, and details of the Jungfrau Railway and gondolas can be found at jungfrau.ch.

MAKE IT A ROAD TRIP
More winter wonderlands can be found in Switzerland and Lausanne and Montreux, where Christmas markets make for a suitably festive break (see page 190), and over the French border in Morzine you can try snowshoeing with the dog (see page 202).

↓ The Sphinx Observatory on Jungfraujoch, the highest observatory in Europe

Where: Luberon Regional Park, Provence
When: March–June and September–October
Best port of entry: Caen, France
Driving time from port of entry: 9.5 hrs

20

HIKE OTHERWORLDLY LANDSCAPES IN THE SOUTH OF FRANCE

Purples and lilacs, rust-reds and sunny yellows, and greens of all shades are the colours of the unique and varied landscapes of the Luberon Regional Park. This 1,850 sq km area of protected land around an eponymous mountain range has some of the most bewitching scenery in the south of France. Sitting in the western half of Provence, it is a microcosm of the Med's best offerings: charming market towns like its capital, Apt; vineyards dripping with plump grapes; lavender fields that turn the landscape purple from May to early August; dappled olive groves and verdant forests – all of which sit around the towering 1,125-metre-high Luberon mountains at the centre.

Despite its vastness, thanks to the main D900 highway coursing through its middle from east to west, it's possible to experience much of what the Luberon has to entertain visitors in just a few days if you don't mind whizzing between towns and sights by car. But a much slower pace is recommended – not least because the highlight here is to be found on foot. Walking with the dog in the Luberon allows time to soak up the lustrous sunshine amid landscapes that often feel out of this world. You'll find yourself reaching for your camera more than once on the footpaths that criss-cross this regional park, but you'll probably never quite capture the astonishing scale of its astounding topography.

↓ The unearthly landscapes of the Colorado Provençal

THE TERRACOTTA TRAILS

Colorado Provençal

Perhaps the most striking of all the landscapes in the Luberon is its **ochre quarries**. Between Goult and Viens, a 25km-long band of ochre stretches across the protected park and beyond, formed millions of years ago after an ocean that once covered the region retreated and left its minerals behind to turn all manner of rusty-reds and dirty oranges as they were exposed to the atmosphere's life-giving oxygen. Between the 1800s and 1930s, mining of the ochre – which is used as a pigment to create paint or dye clothing – tore into the landscape and has today left behind gaping red, orange and yellow cavities amid the rocky terrain.

The flushed slopes of the **Colorado Provençal** (coloradoprovencal.fr; dogs must be on leads) in Rustrel (10km from Apt) are one of the most impressive places to walk with the dog: here, the quarries closed in 1991 and you can now wander along a choice of two trails (2km and 4km). It's sandy under foot, which gets a silken texture after rain when the water runs along the footpaths. You'll begin in pine woodland and almost out of nowhere huge cliffs and mounds of red, orange, yellow and pink rise from the Mediterranean scrubland. On a blue-

sky day, you'll delight in the shocking contrast between the terracotta land and cerulean sky.

Further west lies the red-tinged village of Roussillon, which sits atop one of the most significant ochre deposits in the world. **Les Sentier des Ocres** (roussillon-en-provence.fr; dogs must be on leads) has two easy-to-follow trails: one takes around 35 minutes to complete and the other is just short of an hour's amble. Here, blazing red and orange cliffs are topped with lush greenery, and pillars of ochre jut upwards from the land, like reddish stalagmites reaching for the skies.

Need to know: All the routes are well marked and easy to follow at the ochre quarries. Dogs must remain on leads at all times and you must only walk on the specified paths due to the fragile nature of the landscape. Poisonous pine processionary caterpillars can sometimes be found at these sites in spring; keep a close eye on your dog and seek veterinarian help if they come into contact with one.

THE LILAC WAYS

Claparèdes plateau

The region of Provence, for most people, conjures into the mind two things: that pale, pastel-pink rosé wine that the area's winemakers are famous for, and those violet-striped lavender fields that yawn out into the horizon. The former is always best enjoyed in a tasting room or on a vineyard terrace (see page 226), while the latter make for superb dog walking ground when the plants bloom into colour between May and August.

Lavender has been a commercial crop in France since the 19th century, when the burgeoning perfume industry led to farmers switching out traditional crops for the so-called 'blue gold'. Today, around 62,000 acres of Provence's land is used for the cultivation of this sweet-scented plant, and there are over 1,500 producers turning it into myriad products, from soaps to perfumes to herbal teas that are said to have calming properties.

And calming it can be – walking along the boundaries of these fields, or through the foot-wide alleyways created by the precise planting of each lavender plant is indeed a soothing experience. There are entire farms you can visit for tours of the plantations, but even more enjoyable is an amble across the purple-hued landscape with the dog by your side.

One of the best lavender routes is on the Claparèdes plateau, just 6.5km from the centre of Apt, where a 9km trail passes through oak woodland, juniper forests and along the edges of fragrant lavender and lavandin (a highly productive hybrid type) fields that sing with their fresh floral scent. Allow 2.5 hours and you'll have ample time for stopping at viewpoints where you can snap pictures of the majestic Mont Ventoux in the distance, and explore the dry-stone *bories* (cabins) built as shelter by shepherds in centuries gone by.

Need to know: Directions at cheminsdesparcs.fr or ask in a local tourist information centre; the car park and start point can be found at /// envision.cooked.ecologic. You may pass livestock on this route, which may be protected by guard dogs – they are largely harmless but it's best to avoid bringing nervous or reactive dogs on this hike in case of interactions with unattended guard dogs. Do not pick the lavender – if you'd like to take some home, there are plenty of shops at the distilleries throughout the Luberon.

HIKE OTHERWORLDLY LANDSCAPES IN THE SOUTH OF FRANCE

CEDAR-SCENTED TRAILS

Forêt des Cèdres

Provençal summers can get torrid at times – the dryness in the ground and the air can make the heat of the day feel oppressive. But up in the hills of the Petit Luberon massif on the southern fringes of the regional park, beneath a canopy of **aromatic cedars**, you'll find a delightfully cool spot for walking the dog – and up here you've got prime position for views out across the Luberon's undulating landscapes.

The Forêt des Cèdres sits south of villages Lacoste and Bonnieux, rising up above the valleys at 727 metres high. First planted in the 1860s, the cooling, slightly musky scented cedar trees now cover an area of 250 hectares, and within this are myriad marked trails for exploring. A highlight is the Portalas Trail, which begins from the main car park (/// unacceptable.rams.rifling) and tracks south towards a ridge and viewpoint overlooking the lower hills.

Along the 3km route you'll walk through masses of boxwood and burning bush (*Fraxinella*) that has scented flowers in May, and from the Portalas viewpoint you might spot the rare and protected Egyptian vulture soaring in the sky. The walk ends on a straight, wide track through the middle of the cedar forest, where the centuries-old trees tower high above and daylight dances, dappled, on the dusty forest floor – a perfect place to linger with a picnic.

Need to know: Directions at cheminsdesparcs.fr or follow yellow waymarkers. There may be livestock grazing within the forest so dogs must be under close control.

→ Arty hikes through the cedar forests of Luberon Regional Nature Park

OTHER ADVENTURES NEARBY

Beyond hiking, the Luberon has myriad experiences for exploring dog owners. At the heart of the regional park is its 'capital', the little town of Apt. Here you'll find an ample number of cafes and restaurants for whiling away mealtimes or long Sunday morning coffees, but the town's highlight really is its **Tuesday and Saturday market**. Up to 300 stalls set up throughout the town's cosy pedestrianised streets, touting wares from ceramics and candles and clothing to rotisserie chickens, cheese, olives and olive oil, and soap made from the region's lavender.

Lavender isn't the only crop you'll see sprouting from the ground throughout summer, though – Provence is a major wine-growing region in France and the Luberon has a **host of vineyards worth visiting**. Head to Aureto (vignobles-coquillade.com) for dog-friendly tastings, cheese and charcuterie boards on the terrace and guided and self-guided walks around the vines between April and September, or stop in at a tasting rooms like Cave de Lumières (for organics and local distilleries; instagram.com/cavedelumieres) and Sylla (try the surprisingly tasty 0% sparkling rosé wine; sylla.fr) – all along the D900 west of Apt.

Alongside wine, **olives and olive oil production** is common throughout the region, and you'll get a clear understanding of how it all works at La Royère Huile & Vin (royere.com), where you can do tastings of three types of oil and gain entry to a small exhibition on the making of the stuff for around €5. There are also wines to taste from their vineyards. Beware, though – the farm cat can often be spotted guarding reception and so any dogs with a feline rivalry might be sent in a spin.

↑ The tiny streets of Lacoste
→ Inside the Écomusée De L'ocre Roussillon

If just walking among the rust-red quarries isn't enough for you, a visit to the **ochre museum** near Roussillon (okhra.com) is a worthy afternoon activity, where you can see the manufacturing process in an old 20th-century plant and meet modern-day creatives making use of its striking pigments in a handful of workshops. A mooch around the pretty streets of nearby **Roussillon** is a must, too. Pick up handmade ceramics and ochre paints and climb to the top of the hill to Bals'Art (balsart.com) for tastings of locally distilled balsamic vinegar – there are around 30 varieties to try, including white balsamic and flavoured versions recommended for pouring over ice cream.

Historians will enjoy a stroll down by the 1st-century **Pont Julien**, built by Domitius Ahenobarbus, where the dog can roam freely and **swim in the river** (swimming and picnicking opportunities

are also available at Étang de la Bonde, 40 minutes' drive southwest of Apt). Then climb the steep streets of charming, cobbled Lacoste to see an 11th-century castle. Finally, escape modernity entirely with a stroll around the intriguing **Village de Bories**. Rescued from ruin over the last 300 years, the dry-stone houses set across this small site are a fascinating insight into the lives of rural Provençal communities. From here, there's an excellent 6km walk along trails flanked by dry-stone walls and Mediterranean plants (search for Village des Bories - Croix des Baux on alltrails.com).

For more serious walking, those with strong thighs won't want to miss a **hike up Mount Ventoux** – the local tourist office in Apt (luberon-apt.fr) will be able to assist with directions. There are also myriad cycle routes throughout the region taking in those vineyards and lavender plantations, and dog-friendly bike hire with trailers is available from RentBike Luberon in Bonnieux, 11km southwest of Apt.

WHAT'S FOR DINNER?

A productive region, Provence is a place to eat and drink well. Don't miss trying the local wines –the region is famous the world over for its pastel-pink rosé, light in body and perfect as a refresher on a sunny afternoon. There are also some excellent full-bodied reds and elegant whites, using grapes such as Syrah, Grenache Noir, Mourvèdre, Carignan and Cinsault. Also look out for the locally distilled olive oil gin by Manguin (think dirty martini with tonic), and local beers by Les Ouailles du Luberon.

Candied fruit is big business here, too, and Apt is famous for its natural sweets – you'll find plenty in the town's Tuesday and Saturday markets, but you should seek out a slice of *galapian*, an almond tart stuffed with chewy candied fruit. If you've a serious sweet tooth, pick up a jar of *berlingots* (a hard-boiled sweet that's been made in the Vaucluse department for over 150 years), and look out for *Papalines d'Avignon*, a chocolate-coated sweet with an Origan du Comtat liqueur centre.

↓ Arty atop the hills near Village de Bories

↑ Dry stone walls in Village de Bories

WHERE TO SLEEP

Camping des Cedres

Motorhomes, campervans, caravans and tents welcome
From £15 per night
escapade-vacances.com

In a region so well suited to outdoors pursuits, camping is a great way to experience the Luberon. This small but more than sufficient campsite on the outskirts of Apt is a brilliant base for seeing it all. Fresh bread and pastries are delivered daily, and there is a small shop, an occasional pizza van and the pleasing sound of a rushing river going right past the site. Pitches are either on grass (for tents) or sandy, dusty hard ground beneath towering cedar trees, and the town centre is a five-minute walk away.

Bastide du Mourre

From £225 per night
lesdomainesdefontenille.com

A 30-minute drive west of Apt set beneath the foothills of the Petit Luberon, this is a serene rural boutique hotel with earthen decor and a small but refreshing outdoor pool. There are gardens for wandering with the dog and terraces for al fresco *petit déjeuner* in the sun. Dogs go free here and can dine with you in the restaurant, too.

La Bergerie

From £425 per week
clevacances.com

A 10-minute drive north of Apt town, this villa is a wonderful base for any Luberon holiday with the dog. There's an enclosed patio directly outside the back doors, and a pool just beyond it with lawns and terraced gardens for games of fetch (this area isn't enclosed, so no escape artists off lead in this section). The views are magnificent, with a small terrace overlooking the verdant hills, and inside you'll find natural stone walls, plenty of places to relax, a dining area and two double bedrooms.

ESSENTIALS

Getting there: The Luberon is in the far south of France, so it's a long drive from ports like Caen and even further from Calais (just over 10 hours). Break up your journey with a couple of stops, though, and it's well worth the effort to get here. Avignon is the closest train station should you prefer to go by rail; car hire is available here, too.

What to pack: A longline for the dog so they have more freedom in areas where they're required to be leashed.

The dog rules: Dogs must be on a lead throughout most of the regional park due to its fragile ecosystems, but you can let them off for a run around Pont Julien.

Getting around: The Luberon is best explored by car, though if you have or rent a bike and have a suitable means to transport your dog on it, there's a vast network of cycle routes (francevelotourisme.com) throughout the region and cycling here is a real joy.

More information: Head to destinationluberon.com for further details and news.

→ Part of the old ochre quarries at the Colorado Provençal
↓ The unusual landscapes around the Colorado Provençal

MAKE IT A ROAD TRIP
From here, you're only a few hours' drive from the Costa Brava (see page 170) for a beach break, or you could swap the car for a boat and hit the canals around the Camargue or Carcassonne (see page 108).

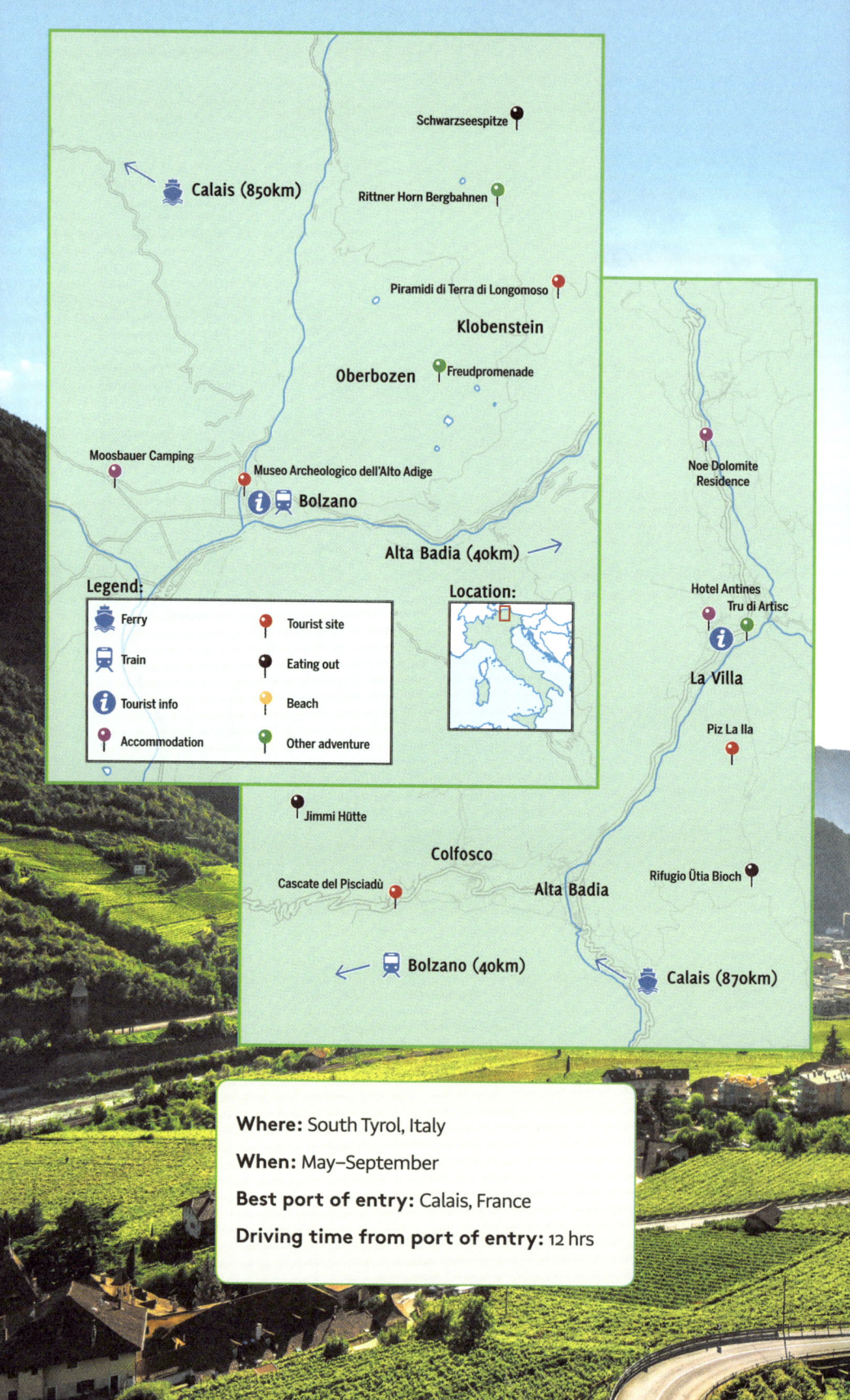

21
SEE CITY AND SUMMITS IN THE STRIKING DOLOMITES

There is nothing quite like waking first thing, opening the curtains of your hotel room and being faced with the jagged, toothy peaks of the Dolomites lighting up in pewter as the sun rises. The view is so shockingly beautiful, so deeply invigorating, that it's almost enough to replace your morning coffee – almost; this is Italy after all, so coffee is always a good idea.

Dog walks at home will never be the same after you've trekked the trails of this German-speaking region of northern Italy, where wildflower meadows swish in the breeze and there's almost always a staggering view ahead of you. What's joyous about South Tyrol, too, is the ease of travelling and walking here – the trails can be tough in terms of elevation, but with a well-organised network of waymarked paths, there's little chance of getting lost. You needn't be an expert mountaineer to explore these idyllic alpine slopes, and you don't even have to be ultra-fit to tackle some of its trails, as a public transport system comprising trains and gondolas will whisk you up to some of the highest plateaus for gentle strolls among the meadows.

High above Bolzano

The capital of this autonomous region is Bolzano, a city at around 230 metres above sea level at its lowest point where you can get high – to around 1,100 metres in just 12 minutes, in fact – via its hefty gondola. The journey up into the mountains is enchanting: you'll glide over apple orchards and vineyards on the slopes of the foothills. You can see hikers and mountain bikers making their way down the mountainsides as you get higher, and you'll hear the quaint tinkle of cowbells from the

↓ Wildflower meadows with views of the mountains around Alta Badia

grazing cattle that keep the slopes' lawns in check.

Once at the top, there are myriad options for exploring, made even more accessible by an electric light railway that connects Oberbozen (or Soprabolzano, to give it its Italian name), where the cable car stops, to the village of Klobenstein (Collalbo). For a gentle wander with plenty of shade, the **Freudpromenade (Passegiata Freud)** is a charming trail. Named after famed neurologist Sigmund Freud, who spent significant time here with his family in Hotel Bemelmans-Post in 1911, it's a pleasant 7km, two-hour walk starting from Oberbozen and ending in Klobenstein. You'll pass meadows, farmsteads and small churches, while views of the Rosengarten massif and Schlern peak will draw your attention beyond. In the woodland and along the footpath, elderberries and apricots grow wild, and a series of benches offer insights about Freud and his work. Finish with a refreshing drink at Hotel Bemelmans.

Up here, a network of buses connect you to other towns and villages in the area, including to the **Rittner Horn Bergbahnen**, a gondola that travels up to Schwarzseespitze (Cima Lago Nero) at 2,070 metres above sea level. There's a restaurant and a kids' play area at the top, and yet more brilliant walks abound here, with a 6km trail signposted as the Panoramaweg. Allow two hours and bring a picnic to enjoy at the panoramic table towards the end of the walk – from here, you can snack with several peaks in sight, including many over 3,000 metres.

Back in Klobenstein, geology enthusiasts will want to beeline for the **Piramidi di Terra di Longomoso** (accessible by bus), a landscape of sedimentary rocks weathered into thin, spiky pyramids over millennia.

↑ The quaint town of Klobenstein on the Ritten Plateau
→ Striking Dolomites views near Corvara, Alta Badia

Alta Badia

Heading deeper into the Dolomites you'll find yet more precipitous peaks and beguiling views. A 90-minute drive from Bolzano city, the ski resort of **Alta Badia** is a popular high-octane sports hub in winter, but in summer it takes on an entirely different personality. Once the snow has melted away, carpets of lush green grass and wildflowers cloak the plateaus here, and a series of trails criss-cross its valleys and slopes. It's most famous for its Maratona villages – the locations that see thousands of cyclists pass through during the one-day race in early July each year – such as Corvara, Badia and La Villa, which sit within a valley at around 1,400 metres, while gondolas ferry you up to altitudes well over 2,000 metres for walks with immense views.

It's not just the walking here that's a highlight, though. Up in the high mountains lie a series of 'huts' or '*rifugio*'. Their modest name belies the **fine cuisine** that's produced inside them, as each is home to an innovative chef, with guest chefs from elsewhere who have lofty accolades – think Michelin stars – regularly taking stints in the kitchen. Up at Piz La Ila, a ski and hiking area reached by gondola from La Villa, stop to let the dog cool off in its 'bau bau' pool (a dog-friendly paddling pool) before you walk over the grazing pasture and wildflower meadows to Rifugio Ütia Bioch (allow an hour for the walk; bioch.it).

Here, Markus Valentini and his team of talented chefs have crafted a menu that celebrates the ingredients that can be foraged from these very mountains – think fruity spritzes with mountain herbs and flowers, or traditional crispy pancakes filled with ricotta and spinach. The views across the plains to the silvery Dolomite peaks are spectacular, and on a summer's day you'll be reluctant to move on – especially as the wine cellar is home to 500 bottles.

Back down in La Villa, a gentler walk is on the Tru di Artisc, or 'path of the artists'. Following the Rio Gadera, this footpath is an easy 6km stroll amid fir trees. It's a popular dog-walking trail, evidenced by the presence of dog mess bins at certain points, with free bags provided.

For another delicious excursion in Alta Badia – this time from the village of Colfosco, a 10-minute drive from La Villa – take the Frara gondola to the foot of Mount Cir, where Jimmi Hütte (jimmihuette.it) is surrounded by the Sella massif and has sofas, loungers and dining tables on a vast deck, making the most of those sensational views. The restaurant serves **exceptional lunches** of traditional local cuisine – the red wine risotto is divine – and has a wine list that champions local vintners. Dogs are allowed inside and out, and from here, you can walk it all off on a trail that leads back to Colfosco. Alternatively, take the gondola back down the mountain and hop off at Plans to see the Cascate del Pisciadù, an **80-metre waterfall**, before walking back into the village.

OTHER ADVENTURES NEARBY

It's never a bad idea to spend some time in Bolzano when you're up in this region, as this city has plenty to keep dogs and humans entertained. Explore its history and culture on a **walking tour** with Airbnb guide Gianluca (airbnb.co.uk/experiences/1180236), or delve into its unique fusion of German and Italian food on a **gastronomic tour** with Daniele (airbnb.co.uk/experiences/3312058).

Don't miss the main event in Bolzano, either: Ötzi the Iceman, a more than **5,000-year-old mummy** who was discovered by hikers in 1991 in the nearby mountains. His body was preserved in the ice and snow for millennia and is now on display in the city's Museo Archeologico dell'Alto Adige (iceman.it), along with myriad artefacts and clothing discovered alongside him.

Within the city there are gorgeous riverside walks that track alongside the Torrente Talvera, but just beyond its limits is a **wine trail** in the hills beneath the Ritten Plateau. It takes an hour, beginning among the vineyards of tiny Signato (accessible via the 163 bus from the gondola station) and wends its way down the hill to the city limits, past wineries where you can stop in for tastings with the dog.

WHAT'S FOR DINNER?

The Alta Badia region is part of an area called Ladinia, a series of valleys within the Dolomites where people have spoken the unique Ladin language for over 2,000 years. The traditional Ladin way of life leaks into the modern day, through both architecture and food. The cuisine is wholesome and warming, with barley soups made with smoked speck, and dumplings served alongside game, such as venison.

→ The terrace at Jimmi Hütte
↓ A red wine risotto with wild mushrooms at Jimmi Hütte

It has some similarities with both German and Italian cuisine, with apple strudels featuring on dessert menus and fried pastries filled with cabbage and herbs (*tutres*) a favoured snack. Try *cajincí arestis* – a potato donut – and don't miss the handmade spinach ravioli (*cajincí te ega*). You'll eat well here, and drink well, too – crisp chardonnays and gewürztraminer are medicinal on a summer's day, while a *radler* (similar to a shandy) is an essential mid-hike refresher when you're up on the trails.

When you're not sampling the Ladin cuisine, look out for fresh trout from the local rivers, apple juice made from the orchards around Bolzano, and for dessert, don't miss the *Apfelkiachl* (apple fritters).

WHERE TO SLEEP

Hotel Hanswirt

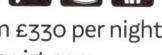

From £330 per night
hanswirt.com

Sitting on the edge of the small village of Rabland, Hotel Hanswirt is a veritable haven in the mountains. Views from its bedrooms look over an apple orchard with mountain peaks in the distance, and warm days spent by the pool – where the dog can laze around next to your lounger – are the perfect respite for a weary hiker's soles. The hotel has real character, with parts of it dating back to the 14th century, and it has been owned by the same family for the past 400 years. The dining here is exceptional, too: book half-board and you'll get a four-course set menu each evening featuring local river fish, excellent stuffed pasta and traditional South Tyrol dumplings, plus an extensive salad bar with several kinds of pickled cabbage.

SEE CITY AND SUMMITS IN THE STRIKING DOLOMITES

Hotel Antines

From £150 per night
hotelantines.it

Located in La Villa, a charming little village in Alta Badia with access to the Piz La Ila cable car, Hotel Antines has mesmerising views of those iconic Dolomite peaks. Bedrooms at the front of the hotel have balconies fringed with colourful flowers, where you can sit to watch the sunset tinge those toothy peaks a pinkish hue. There's a restaurant with excellent dining on offer: beautifully presented dishes from a set menu are served each evening, and the dog might even get a home-cooked meal from the hotel's canine-loving owner. Breakfast is a feast, too – a vast spread of meats, cheeses, fruit and breads complements cooked-to-order eggs from the kitchen. Dogs get a welcome pack of biscuits, bowls and a blanket. The hotel has the feel of an alpine lodge, with amber wooden flooring and pine furniture in the rooms, and there's a wellness centre in the basement with an indoor pool, saunas, a jacuzzi and a steam room.

Moosbauer Camping

From £20 per night
moosbauer.com

If you're bringing your own caravan or motorhome, this campsite on the outskirts of Bolzano is the perfect base. With a pool, shop and playground for kids, it has everything you could want for the days you're not spending on the trails. There are tent pitches here priced per person, and some of the caravan and motorhome pitches have their own en-suite bathrooms. Shared facilities are well-kept and the bathrooms are decorated with interesting stories and facts about the region's landscape, culture and traditions, so you can learn while you shower and shave. The restaurant serves regional cuisine and has plenty of vegetarian options, and there's a vast beer selection, too.

SEE CITY AND SUMMITS IN THE STRIKING DOLOMITES

MAKE IT A ROAD TRIP
With direct trains from Venice to Bolzano, it seems only fair that you pair this adventure with a little escape to the lagoon (see page 242).

Noe Dolomite Residence

From £70 per night
noeresidence.com

A swish apartment block in the village of Badia, Noe Residence is an ideal base if you're staying longer than a few nights. With your own kitchen and a little extra living space in each apartment, you've got the freedom to eat what you want, whenever you want. The property is a few kilometres from La Villa, but also has access to the La Crusc cable lift. There's a supermarket on site, a wellness area with a sauna and relaxation room, a gym and a kids' play area.

↓ Dramatic views of the Dolomites

ESSENTIALS

Getting there: The drive to the Dolomites is long, but the rewards are great once you arrive, though the region is very well connected with public transport, too. Bolzano has a train station with direct services connecting to Verona and Venice to the south and Innsbruck in Austria.

What to pack: The dog will need a muzzle for many of the gondolas, trains and buses. If you're going to be doing serious hikes, consider packing some boots for the dog as the trails can be stony.

The dog rules: It's mandatory to have your dog on a lead on the trails of South Tyrol unless otherwise stated. This is to protect wildlife, livestock and the ecosystems that exist within the region. The region is also particularly hot on dog mess, even turning to DNA testing to call out local dog owners when they fail to clean up after their animal. Local police will hand out fines if you're caught, so be vigilant and always carry bags. Dogs must wear muzzles on public transport.

Getting around: Even if you drive, it's worth taking advantage of the vast public transport network of gondolas, cable cars, trains and buses, all of which allow dogs to travel with you, though they will need to be muzzled. Many hotels in the region offer a free Südtirol Guest Pass for the duration of your stay, which means you'll travel for free; the dog may need a separate ticket.

More information: There's a tourist information office in Bolzano (Via Alto Adige), as well as an information point for Alta Badia in La Villa (Strada Colz); for planning in advance, use suedtirol.info and altabadia.org.

22

SUN, SAND AND A SIDE OF CULTURE IN ITALY

Venice

Venice is a city that needs little introduction to us humans – its history, its architecture and its art are all well-known and well written about. Venice for dogs, on the other hand, is a whole different ball game.

This city is busy. There's no getting around that. The tourist hubs of San Marco, Rialto and around the Santa Lucia train station are a hive of bumbling tourists that is likely to overwhelm the senses of almost any dog. These are places to be visited early in the morning, before the day trippers whose presence has become so controversial in the city descend on the cobbled streets.

Get away from these busy hubs, though, and you'll find enchantment around many a corner, as visiting Venice with a dog gives you cause to step away from the crowds and explore beyond the big-hitting sights. Stay inside the city itself and you'll garner an appreciation for Venetian life unseen by day trippers who are often gone before dusk falls, and early morning walks with the dog can be magical as the city wakes up around you.

This is a place made for aimless ambling, where narrow alleyways lead to small bridges that cross canals where gondolas gently mosey on by. There are piazzas where terraces beckon for a refreshing *ombra* (a small glass of wine, usually at aperitivo hour), and views across the vast, flat lagoon to neighbouring islands. Green space is at a premium in this rather concrete city on stilts, but a handful of charming gardens offer a pleasant space for the dog to enjoy sniffing about with grass under foot. If arriving by train, the closest park is leafy **Parco Savorgnan**, but better yet is **Giardini Papadopoli** where lawns surround sculpted statues and box hedging ensconces large, centuries-old trees. It has the air of an English garden in places, but with ever-enchanting views of the grand canal through its gates.

If you find yourselves at Piazza San Marco, you will discover a relative haven of peace in the **Giardini Reali**, which has pergolas dripping with foliage for shade, benches for lingering and plenty of planted beds for the dog to take an olfactory tour. Further east lies **Giardini della Biennale**, the focal point of the Venice Biennale cultural festival, where you'll see 30 pavilions owned by different countries scattered among the lawns, each of which becomes its own exhibition space during the Biennale. Just across the Ponte de Giardini lies the **Parco delle Rimembranze**, the jewel in Venice's green crown, a 500-metre-long park large enough to let the dog roam free and run for the ball.

While walking around Venice is indeed a joy once you've escaped the crowds, there are other exciting ways to see this city – the most sedate (and perhaps clichéd) of which is by **gondola**. Cliché (and an eye-watering price tag) aside, these traditional handmade boats have

↑ Arty on the dog beach in Lido, Venice
→ A Venetian canal

their origins in the 11th century and have been used as a means of transport ever since. Today, they are very much a tourist attraction – one that can cost you as much as £80 for a 30-minute ride – rather than a practical means of getting about, but they still offer a completely beguiling way to see this watery city. Plenty of the gondoliers will allow dogs on board; just ask at the gondola stations around Piazza San Marco or the Rialto Bridge or look out for gondoliers touting for business in the many squares throughout the city – you can identify them by their uniform of black trousers, striped T-shirts and a straw hat.

Of course, if it all gets too much for you – or the dog – there are myriad islands you can escape to around the Venetian Lagoon. To really get away from it all, take the vaporetto number six from Giardini Biennale and in a matter of minutes you'll find yourselves on the far quieter isle of Lido. This is **Venice's beach resort** – an 11km-long island with a yellow sandy beach that runs the length of its eastern side.

In summer, most of the beach here is off-limits for dogs, but the northernmost section is home to the dog-loving **Pachuka Beach Club** (pachukabeach.com; a short bus ride from the vaporetto station), where you can sit with your dog in the restaurant for a bite to eat before heading out on to the sand to rent a lounger and parasol. Dogs are welcomed with much fuss and many treats, and will get a bowl of water delivered to the lounger as you settle in. They can join you in the surf to cool off, and there's even a dog shower for washing off all the sand and salt at the end of the day.

OTHER ADVENTURES NEARBY

More intriguing adventures can be had around Venice's lagoon on islands like Murano, where you can watch **artisanal glass-makers** craft chandeliers and decorative pieces in their traditional workshops. Or head to the home of Italian **lace-making** and take the boat to Burano, where its canals are lined with brightly painted houses and women work on fabrics embroidered with their delicate lace. For more green space for the dog to enjoy some freedom, take the vaporetto to Isola della Certosa, where a

2.5km trail circumnavigates this largely green island. It's a somewhat uninspiring place compared with Venice itself, but the openness is a breath of fresh air and there's a small restaurant offering excellent seafood from beyond the lagoon.

SEE INSIDE VENICE'S MUSEUMS WITH BAUADVISOR

Of course, so much of Venice's beauty is to be found inside its buildings – the galleries, historical palaces, the museums where works by great painters and sculptors sit for all on two legs to admire. Four-legged explorers are less welcome inside most of Venice's attractions, but that shouldn't stop you from enjoying them. Thanks to a **pet-sitting service** set up by BauAdvisor (bauadvisor.it) and MUVE (the Foundation of Civic Museums of Venice; visitmuve.it), it's now possible to book a one-off professional dog walker and sitter to take care of your pet for an hour or two while you delve into the storied culture of this city. The following sights carry the service, bookable on the BauAdvisor website:

Palazzo Ducale (The Doge's Palace)

One of the most iconic buildings in Venice, this Gothic masterpiece dates back as far as the 14th century and housed Venetian political leaders throughout its history until the 18th century. It dominates the waterside between Piazza San Marco and the Grand Canal, all impressive archways and geometric patterned bricks, and inside it's home to works by Italian painters such as Paolo Veronese and Domenico Tintoretto. If you visit only one museum in Venice, this is a good bet, though you'll need to book in advance for a timed ticket.

Torre dell'Orologio

A true Venice landmark, the 15th-century clocktower that sits next door to the Basilica di San Marco is as interesting for its architecture as it is for its engineering. Of course, it's free and easy to stand outside and gaze up at its lofty heights with the dog, but if you book the BauAdvisor service you can take a guided tour of its interior to see the inner workings. Narrow spiral staircases may put off those with a fear of heights and small spaces.

Correr Museum

At the opposite end of Piazza San Marco from Doge's Palace and the Basilica lies this regal museum, housed in what was formerly Napoleon's Venetian home in the 19th century. A collection of ancient statues, maps and artworks is displayed throughout its elegant halls, and there are fantastical frescoes in the striking Biblioteca Nazionale Marciana.

Ca' Pesaro

Set right on the Grand Canal, this 17th-century palace is home to two deeply intriguing but very different art museums – a modern art collection and the Museo d'Arte Orientale. The former has 19th- and 20th-century works by the likes of Gustav Klimt, Joan Miró and Matisse, while the latter is a warren of artworks and objects from Asia, from weapons to armour to one of the largest collections of Japanese works from the Edo period.

Natural History Museum of Venice Giancarlo Ligabue

While Venice's art museums are less likely to capture the imagination of younger travellers, this collection housed within the handsome classical Venetian Fontego dei Turchi palace is perhaps a little more engaging thanks to its taxidermy sea creatures, skeletons and fossils.

Mocenigo Palace Museum

If textiles are your thing, you'll find this collection an interesting diversion from the tangled streets of Venice. It features ancient fabrics and clothing, elaborate costume from the 16th to 18th century – including a pair high wedge shoes from the 1500s. There's also an entire exhibition dedicated to perfume, with sensory experiences alongside historical artefacts.

↓ The view from Piazza San Marco

Fortuny Palace Museum

A truly eclectic museum filled with art, design and fashion inspiration, this is the collection of Spanish artist and designer Mariano Fortuny y Madrazo. Housed in his former home, the exhibition spaces can feel more 'eccentric artist's attic' than intentional galleries, but it's all the more charming for it.

Carlo Goldoni's House

Explore the elegant former home of one of Italy's most famous playwrights, Carlo Goldoni. Known for his comedic stage productions in the 18th century, he helped reform the way Italian theatre worked both on and off the stage with his innovations. There's original period furniture as well as sets built to resemble the plays he wrote.

Murano Glass Museum

Delve deeper into the craft and history of glassmaking by exploring this beautiful little museum on the island of Murano. There's an archaeological exhibit on the first floor, with pieces dating as far back as the early Roman period, while the rest is a vast array of glass – both decorative and functional – made in Murano itself. The 20th-century exhibition is particularly pleasing, with innovative, fashionable works by modern artisans.

Burano Lace Museum

Set inside what was once the Burano Lace School, this is the place to explore the origins of Venetian lace and meet modern lace makers in action.

WHAT'S FOR DINNER?

Unsurprisingly, fish and seafood are stars of the menu in many a restaurant in Venice. Expect to taste goby fish or softshell crab, and don't miss the *risotto al nero di seppia* – squid ink risotto. Polenta is more traditional than pasta here, so order it with prawns (*polenta e schie*) as a starter. Before you dive in for any big meals, though, don't miss sampling some *cicchetti* alongside your *ombra* (wine). These are essentially small snacks, often displayed in vast cabinets like a carb-heavy pick-n-mix; try crostini with salted cod paste on top or tapenade, or sardines served with pickled onions. Drinks-wise, if you're not indulging in Italy's wealth of wonderful wines, the local version of an Aperol spritz is a Select spritz – a bright red cocktail made with prosecco.

↓ Arty in the gardens of the JW Marriott, Venice

WHERE TO SLEEP

JW Marriot Venice Resort & Spa

From £450 per night
marriott.com

A wave of relief will wash over you every time you arrive at JW Marriott Venice, whether it's your first time here or you're just coming back after a long day of sightseeing. This hotel, set on its own private island a 15-minute boat trip from San Marco, is a true haven of tranquillity compared with the city. The hotel itself is set inside an old hospital but has been given a much-needed facelift inside, but it's the outside space that will wow here. There's an outdoor pool, ball games courts, an indoor-outdoor spa, a rose garden and a 40-acre garden where the dog can run around between palms, beech and oak trees.

The breakfast restaurant and the rooftop bistro are dog-friendly. The latter has glorious sunset views come evening – small dogs will even be allowed to sit up on the sofa with you if you take a booth. Getting here is simple – the hotel has its own boat service from San Marco that leaves every half an hour during the daytime. This is certainly a blow-the-budget option, but you won't regret it one bit.

Corte del Tintor Apartment

From £220 per night
airbnb.co.uk/rooms/53470620

Airbnb be a real issue in Venice: not only does it create a housing shortage for locals, but the platform is not entirely safe from scammers either – beware hosts who claim you need to cancel your reservation but offer alternative options. Having said that, for pet owners it can be a real asset in places like Venice, where finding truly dog-friendly accommodation can be tricky. This apartment is hosted by a pair of siblings from Venice, Davide and Chiara, who have their own dogs. Alongside their beautiful, modern apartment not far from the Rialto Bridge, they can offer advice on where to go with your dog.

NH Collection Venezia Grand Hotel Palazzo dei Dogi

From £210 per night
nh-hotels.com

On the northern edge of Venice proper lies an opulent palazzo turned hotel, dripping with ornate furnishings and sumptuous textiles. But not only does this hotel have all the old-world glamour you'd hope to find in Venice, it also has its own small garden – which will save dog owners from having to trek across the city to find a patch of grass for any fussy pups to pee on. There's gorgeous lagoon-side dining here, and a private daily shuttle to San Marco when you're ready to explore the sights.

ESSENTIALS

Author's note: This city is sinking – and not just on its stilts. It's sinking beneath a tide of tourists and has had to implement strict measures over the last decade to try and curb the issues. A housing crisis, raised crime rates and overcrowding in the city streets has alienated Venetians and now there's a deeply fraught relationship between visitors and Venice residents. It begs the question for many: 'Should I even visit Venice?' This book can't answer that question for you. But if you do choose this as your next dog-friendly break, there are ways you can be a better tourist.

↑ Arty on Piazza San Marco
→ Arty enjoys freedom in the gardens of the JW Marriott

Come in the lowest of seasons – winter is quieter and calmer. But if you must come in summer, avoid July and August and opt for May, June or September, when temperatures are marginally cooler. Staying inside the city itself and for more than just a couple of nights will also help. It means you won't be part of the hordes of tourists coming for the day (and you won't need to pay the tourist tax), and you'll end up spending your money far wider than the crowds do. Finally, respect the locals: don't barter beyond what's reasonable, don't take photographs of people without asking, and certainly don't point your cameras into the private homes of the people who live here.

Getting there: Driving to Venice is done in a few days' travelling across France and Switzerland (parking is easiest at Mestre train station, which is a nine-minute ride from Venice by rail). However, getting the train here is a much more enjoyable experience, especially if you take the sleeper service from Stuttgart that deposits you right at Santa Lucia station. The Nightjet service (nightjet.com) allows dogs in its private compartments of the sleeping cars only; you'll get earplugs, an eye mask and slippers, plus a bottle of German bubbly, and breakfast is brought to your room the following morning. Some compartments have an en-suite shower and toilet. Most dogs will hold their bladders overnight, but if you're concerned your dog will need to toilet during the journey, you could either bring puppy pads or speak to the train manager on board to find out if there will be any extended stops at stations along the route.

What to pack: You'll need a muzzle for your dog if they don't travel in a carrier on the vaporetto (water buses) or trains. A dog life jacket may be useful for any heavier, less buoyant dogs – they're highly unlikely to fall in when navigating the water buses, but it pays to be cautious. It goes without saying that you should avoid the hottest months, but cooling vests and summer shirts will help dark-coated dogs stay cool in heat waves.

The dog rules: Dogs should be on a lead in Venice in most places unless otherwise specified. Swimming in the canals is banned throughout Venice, and that goes for dogs, too. Muzzles are required for those not in carriers on public transport.

Getting around: Dogs travel free on the vaporetto that serve Venice and its surrounding islands; small dogs can travel in carriers, while larger animals must be leashed and muzzled.

More information: The internet is a rabbit warren of both good and terrible information on Venice, but the official tourist board is a reliable resource for the basics (visitvenezia.eu). The Lonely Planet guidebook to the city is a great companion, and read anything on Venice by local journalist Julia Buckley and you'll come away well informed and inspired.

SUN, SAND AND A SIDE OF CULTURE IN ITALY

MAKE IT A ROAD TRIP
Venice is paired well with a trip into the mountains of northern Italy – head to the Dolomites (see page 232) by train or car from here and the dog will love stretching its legs on the trails.

23
TAKE A TOUR OF QUINTESSENTIAL ENGLISH COUNTRYSIDE

The Cotswolds is a living cliché. Golden-hued stone cottages, topped by heavy thatch are fronted by picket fences and perfectly planted gardens that buzz with bees inspecting lavender and wildflowers in summer. Dry-stone walls criss-cross its undulating rural landscape, creating a patchwork of grazing pasture and farm fields. And in winter, cosy pubs with cavernous fireplaces, where flames flicker on locally felled wood fill the room with that comforting musty scent, are a welcome retreat from the cold. The Cotswolds is a vision of chocolate-box England with postcard-perfect scenery and quaint towns and villages.

But it's also so much more than all this. It's a dynamic region with an ever-evolving personality – and a healthy number of well-known personalities making their homes here, too. The Beckhams, of Spice Girls and football fame, and TV presenter Jeremy Clarkson reside out here. Damien Hirst has his own £3-million manor house in the Gloucestershire Cotswolds, and former prime minister David Cameron has been part of the so-called 'Chipping Norton' set since 2001. Along with all these well-heeled residents comes a new kind of Cotswolds culture – one of bougie cafes, upscale pubs with costly tasting menus and zen yoga workshops.

The traditional Cotswolds ways – wool making, sheep farming, agriculture – are now interwoven with a well-established, countryside-chic drinking and dining scene, making a road trip through this National Landscape a delicious experience. And with so many of the Cotswolds' residents accompanied by their own dogs – Clarkson has two Labradors, the Beckhams have four canine family members – there's a great dog-friendly attitude throughout. Follow this itinerary for a fine week or so in England's largest National Landscape.

Tetbury

Set in the southern Cotswolds, handsome Tetbury is a thriving town with a deep-rooted history that goes as far back as the Iron Age. It's also home to the Cotswolds' most famous resident: **King Charles III** has owned and lived much of his adult life in Highgrove House and Gardens (sometimes open to the public but no dogs allowed). The town centre is packed with antique shops, cute cafes and boutiques – don't miss a visit to the colourful **Tetbury Pet Shop** (thetetburypetshop.co.uk) – and there are plenty of traditional dog-friendly pubs to satisfy any thirsty dogs. Plus, there's the dog-friendly, completely free-to-enter **Tetbury Police Museum** & Courtroom (tetburypolicemuseum.org.uk).

But it's beyond Tetbury town centre where this area's real asset for dog owners lies: the **Westonbirt Arboretum** (forestryengland.uk). This 600-acre forest is home to over 2,500 different species of trees, with British native woodlands and plants from all over the world. See Japanese maples turn iridescent reds and oranges in autumn, stand beneath grand old walnut trees whose voluptuous foliage creates a glorious green canopy in summer, and meet some of the UK's 'champion trees', whose great girth or lofty height is the largest in the country.

For dogs, this forest is an enthralling place to run free. The Old Arboretum is a dog-free area, but head into **Silk Wood**, west of the visitor centre, and they can enjoy off-lead time among the trees. Don't miss a stroll along the treetop walkway, which offers a bird's-eye view on the treetops, and families will want to download the OS Maps app (on Android

→ Arty at Ellenborough Park Hotel, near Cheltenham

TAKE A TOUR OF QUINTESSENTIAL ENGLISH COUNTRYSIDE

or Apple) to tackle the 2.7km **Wallace and Gromit-themed trail**, which has puzzles and challenges to solve as you explore with the dog.

Dogs must remain on leads around the visitor centre, shop and the Downs fields, and when Great Oak Hall is open they can join you on a lead to see the special exhibitions. The restaurant is not dog-friendly, but the outdoor areas are.

Cheltenham

A 45-minute drive north from Tetbury, the Regency town of Cheltenham has been attracting visitors for centuries, not least thanks to King George III who visited in the 1780s, spending five weeks here drinking the waters pumped up from the springs beneath the town in an attempt to cure his mental illness. In the decades that followed, hundreds more flocked to its regal townhouses and inns to indulge in the waters, cementing its position as a spa town in the Cotswolds.

Today, the spas are no longer – most had closed down by the 1830s – and instead its pump rooms lie as relics of Cheltenham's heyday. Take the dog for a stroll in **Pitville Park** and you'll no doubt pass the Pittville **Pump Room**, a sandstone Regency building with a copper dome atop its roof where the mineral waters were once siphoned up through a borehole. Surrounded by ornamental lakes and manicured lawns, it's a charming spot for a wander and picnic with the dog before heading 20-minutes' walk north to another slice of Cheltenham history: the **Gloucestershire Warwickshire Steam Railway** (gwsr.com).

Located at the famous **Cheltenham Racecourse** (which also happens to be good dog-walking ground; thejockeyclub.co.uk), this volunteer-run service will take you and the dog on a scenic 45km, 90-minute journey from the former Cheltenham Spa station to Broadway, a pretty little village at the base of a steep hill. Its locomotives – both diesel and steam – hail from various eras, as far back as 1905, and you'll travel in carriages that are up to 70 years old to experience the golden age of rail travel.

Take the train all the way to Broadway to hike up its hill and see **Broadway Tower**, once the favoured holiday retreat of textile designer and writer William Morris, or hop off in Gotherington and take the **five-mile trail** to Winchcombe (directions at winchcombewelcomeswalkers.com), where you can refuel before hopping back on the train.

Burford

A 45-minute drive east from Cheltenham lies Burford. Of all the cute little Cotswolds towns with their sepia-stone cottages, it is perhaps one of the most striking – especially when viewed from the top of The Hill, where you can gaze down upon its charming high street. It's this high street, which used to be a major thoroughfare and gateway to the Cotswolds before the bypass to the south was built, where you'll find a higher number of **independent shops** than on any other street in the region. Aside from a small supermarket chain and a handful of nationwide clothing brands, the tiny boutiques and gift shops are all locally owned and entirely independent. This makes for a delightful afternoon of retail therapy, and plenty of Burford's shops will welcome your dog to browse by your side.

→ The sloping high street of Burford

TAKE A TOUR OF QUINTESSENTIAL ENGLISH COUNTRYSIDE

Artisans abound here, from **Burford Woodcraft** where you'll find one-off pieces carved from British wood, to the **Cotswold Cheese Company** whose counters are awash with locally made cheeses. Browse books by local and global authors at the **Madhatter Bookshop** and seek out trinkets and treasures at **Antiques at the George**. Even the local charity shops, Sue Ryder and Helen & Douglas House, are a cut above your usual second-hand store, so go bargain hunting and you won't be disappointed.

Of course, not all family members will be so thrilled by an afternoon of shopping, and so for something completely different – and better suited for younger travellers – head 10 minutes south of the town by car to **Cotswold Wildlife Park** (cotswoldwildlifepark.co.uk). It might seem like an unlikely pairing – dogs meeting giraffes, monkeys and meerkats – but four-legged visitors are just as welcome here as the two-legged kind. Keep them on a lead and follow the rules around where dogs can go.

Chipping Norton

The hungry will be well fed throughout the Cotswolds, but it seems that the landscapes that surround well-heeled Chipping Norton proffer some of the finest produce in the region. On the 20-minute drive from Burford, you'll pass a handful of the farms that are growing, rearing and, in many cases, cooking wonderful local treats. The most famous of these is undoubtedly **Diddly Squat Farm Shop** (diddlysquatfarmshop.com), owned by former *Top Gear* TV presenter and motoring journalist Jeremy Clarkson.

Featuring regularly on his hit Amazon TV show, *Clarkson's Farm*, his farming trials and tribulations – and occasional successes – have been widely documented in the media, which has led to something of a cult following for the shop. Queues of cars can often be seen waiting to enter the infamous car park (see season three of the show), and thousands of visitors come from all over the country to buy his produce, from

tonnes of potatoes to 'bee juice' (honey). Come with the dog to browse his latest crop, and sample it all from the **Baste food truck** (Instagram.com/bastefood) that cooks up comfort food from the farm – think hot dogs and bavette steak on toast.

Clarkson wasn't the first farmer here, of course – the Cotswolds has a long history of farming. One long-established estate almost next door to Chipping Norton is **Daylesford** (daylesford.com), whose vast organic (and most importantly, dog-friendly) farm shop is a cornucopia of plump produce grown locally, from leeks to lettuce and carrots and cabbage. Beyond fresh veg, there's organic meat, dairy and eggs, and it even has its own range of dog treats and wet food. Stop in for a bite to eat at The Legbar or The Old Spot before tackling the signposted walking trails that explore the farm and surrounding villages; the Kingham walk is just 40 minutes, while the Lower Oddington and Bledington trails are a good two-hour hike.

For something a little less bougie and more down-to-earth, drive 15 minutes south of Daylesford to **FarmED** (farm-ed.co.uk), a part working farm, part educational centre, part cafe. Here it's all about **regenerative farming**, which focuses on giving back to the soil and natural world as much as you take from it by planting crops and rearing animals. Run by passionate, responsible farmers Ian and Celene Wilkinson, it's open for **guided tours** on Fridays, when dogs on leads are welcome, too, or self-guided tours if you come another day. Their cafe is dog-friendly and open Monday–Friday for sweet treats and vegetarian light lunches made from the farm's produce.

↑ A bookshelf in the chic interior of the Bull Burford hotel

WHAT'S FOR DINNER?

The Cotswolds is a brilliant region in which to try some English classics. With so many excellent cosy pubs, a roast dinner is the perfect way to end a week here – expect Cotswold lamb or locally reared beef and chicken, with crispy roasted potatoes, vegetables and a salty, moreish gravy. Or start your day a very British way with a traditional fry-up – bacon, sausages and eggs cooked your way, often served with mushrooms, grilled tomato and black pudding. If it's something sweet you're craving, a cream tea never goes amiss – look out for Cotswolds chain Huffkins (huffkins.com), whose cafes are usually dog-friendly and offer excellent afternoon teas with scones, clotted cream and jam.

As local produce goes, cheese is perhaps the most exciting thing here, with several types made by small-batch, artisanal producers. Don't miss the Ashcombe, which has a distinctive line of ash through its middle, or the tangy, citrusy Windrush Valley goat's cheese. Pair it with crackers from The Fine Cheese

Co based in Bath and a Pot of What chutney and you've got a brilliant cheesy picnic on your hands.

On a sunny day, a pint of Jeremy Clarkson's famed Hawkstone lager or cider goes down a treat, while Hook Norton and Donnington breweries are purveyors of excellent English ales. Woodchester Valley Vineyard is an award-winning winery based near Stroud – try the sparkling Blanc de Blanc.

WHERE TO SLEEP

The Close Hotel

From £120 per nigh
aylesfo-inns-hotels.co.uk

This is a rather regal hotel right in the centre of Tetbury, with a glorious lawned garden at its rear and plenty of spaces for dogs to relax while you drink and dine. Bedrooms are thoughtfully decorated, each with their own individual design and colour palette, and the restaurant on site has fantastic roast dinners on a Sunday, indulgent afternoon teas and an inventive menu of upscale dishes and favourites with a twist – think homemade tater tots served with truffle and aged Italian cheese.

Ellenborough Park

From £220 per night
ellenboroughpark.com

Located right on the edge of Cheltenham Racecourse and beneath the undulating Cleeve Hill, this 500-year-old manor house is a sublime stopover. Not only does it have a dog-friendly bar, but there are expansive grounds where you can tire them out with off-lead ball games before dinner or breakfast. Dogs get a welcome pack in the bedrooms, which includes a meal made by the ubiquitous Sir Woofchester, a dog treat brand you'll find served in many pubs in this area, and muddy paws can even be washed off at the hotel's own dog spa. Humans get some pampering, too, with a beautiful spa well worth spending some time in and an outdoor pool. Bedrooms are understated but still feel luxurious – especially those with enormous free-standing tubs – and many of the dog-friendly bedrooms have their own entrances so you've immediate access to a lawn outside for late-night loo trips.

Bull Burford

From £200 per night
bullburford.com

If browsing Burford's art galleries doesn't satisfy your culture craving, a night or two at the Bull will no doubt see your inner arts connoisseur content. Dripping with works by major artists – including a Banksy in the front window and a Dalí above the fireplace in the lounge – this former coaching inn is now the side project of PR mogul Matthew Freud, great-grandson of Sigmund Freud. With just 18 rooms and a communal dining table for breakfast, it's an intimate affair where everything is executed with a quiet flair. Expect exceptional cocktails from the marble bar, a theatrical performance from the chefs at its unique eight-cover wood-fired Wild restaurant, and a smattering of Damien Hirsts throughout the hallways. Rooms are soothing spaces with simple, organic decor and a small book collection instead of a TV. Dogs get comfy beds and bowls provided, and can join you for breakfast in the morning.

The Kingham Plough

From £195 per night
thekinghamplough.co.uk

Just a 10-minute drive from Chipping Norton town centre and on the edge of the Daylesford estate, The Kingham Plough is a gorgeous Cotswolds pub with rooms. Bedrooms are small but beautifully finished, with light linens and pretty printed wallpaper – book Room 6 for a luxurious bathtub at the end of your bed. Dogs get bowls and treats in the room, and can dine with you downstairs in the pub where regional and national produce is made into Mediterranean-inspired dishes. There's no garden here, but a large village green directly opposite the pub is the perfect spot for morning toilet trips with the dog.

→ The high street in Burford
↓ A public footpath on farmland in the Cotswolds

ESSENTIALS

Getting there: Just over an hour from London by train, the Cotswolds is a well-connected region – Kingham and Cheltenham have the best-placed train stations for arriving from the capital. There are also trains from Birmingham via Worcester. Driving here is a breeze, with several A-roads connecting to the M4, M5 and M40.

What to pack: Waterproof hiking boots will be essential for a trip to the Cotswolds in any season – the trails can get extremely muddy after just a few days of rain. A bodysuit for long-haired dogs in muddy conditions will ensure your dog remains clean and isn't turned away from any cosy pubs for being too soggy.

The dog rules: Dogs are allowed off lead on the trails of the Cotswolds providing they're kept under strict control – this means perfect recall, even in sight of a pheasant. Livestock are prevalent throughout this region, so if you've an inkling your dog loves the chase, keep them leashed. Farmers have been known to shoot at pets if they chase sheep.

Getting around: All public transport throughout the Cotswolds is dog-friendly, including local buses; there are train stations with direct connections to London in Cheltenham and Kingham, near Chipping Norton. The easiest way to navigate this area is by car, though, due to the rural nature of its various attractions.

More information: Most of the visitor centres in the Cotswolds are now closed unfortunately, but there is a tourist information service at the Municipal Offices in Cheltenham. The Cotswolds Tourism initiative has a reliable website at cotswolds.com.

MAKE IT A ROAD TRIP
The Cotswolds is a handy diversion en route from southern England to Scotland, where you can go island hopping to see ancient sites (see page 272), or Northern Ireland, where a striking coastline awaits (see page 262).

24

WALK IN THE FOOTSTEPS OF GIANTS ON THE NORTHERN IRISH COAST

Giant's Causeway

Do you prefer tales of love and loss, or stories of unending grudges and violence? At the Giant's Causeway, you can **choose your own adventure** on the stones as you step out towards the ocean across its hexagonal basalt columns.

Pick love and you'll find yourself standing on top of the bridge built by **Finn the Irish giant**, whose love for a Scottish maiden had him so sick he couldn't bear to be apart from her. Legend has it he crafted these columns so he could step across the sea to Scotland and be with his true love forever, but his plan was thwarted by his grandmother who feared she'd lose her descendant forever should he cross the sea for his beloved. She summoned storm after storm to destroy his efforts, but her plan ended in tragedy: when Finn finally made it across the Irish Sea to meet his maiden, he died from exhaustion in her arms.

Choose a tale of violence and you'll discover a causeway destroyed by **angry giants**. The story goes, Finn McCool built the structure so he could have it out with his greatest enemy, Benandonner, a giant from Scotland. After their mighty clash in the ocean, the pair went their separate ways with Benandonner demolishing the causeway as he travelled back, leaving behind just the small section we can see today.

Of course, there's a third story behind this striking section of coastline, where lanky towers of basalt rock lurch into the sky with their perfectly defined corners. It's the story of science. Perhaps not as sexy as the legends tour guides revel in telling visitors, the scientific explanation for this seemingly magical phenomenon involves volcanic eruptions, erosion, lava and glaciers, and more than 60 million years of geology.

Regardless of which tale takes your fancy, there's no denying the Giant's Causeway is an extraordinary natural wonder – and how many dog walks finish at such an arresting sight? Take the 3km red **waymarked trail** from the National Trust Visitor Centre (nationaltrust.org.uk) to get there and your journey will begin along the clifftops on the coast path. Yellow coconut-scented gorse lines the trail in spring and summer, and wildflowers in pink and purple jostle in the sea breeze. The views of the bays and rocky outcrops below are truly breathtaking, and several viewpoints are worth stopping off at to admire the coastline that expands before you.

The cliff path ends at the so-called Amphitheatre, a series of tall hexagonal columns that loosely resemble an open-air theatre. From here, you'll turn back and follow the same red markers to the Shepherd's Steps – a 162-step staircase that ends down by the waterfront at Port Noffer. Down here, the sheer height of the basalt columns above you is remarkable and within the bay you'll find more curious geological formations, including a rock said to be Finn McCool's boot. The footpath follows the water's edge until you reach the magnificent causeway itself, where climbing on and around the dark grey hexagonal rocks is a thrill for all ages – and the dog.

From here, it's a short walk along the lower coast path to the **Visitor Centre** (dogs allowed), where exhibitions await to offer insight into the fascinating geology and history of the area, and a dog-friendly cafe supplies warming Irish stews and moreish scones.

→ The hexagonal basalt rock formations at the Giant's Causeway in Northern Ireland

WALK IN THE FOOTSTEPS OF GIANTS ON THE NORTHERN IRISH COAST

OTHER ADVENTURES NEARBY

The County Antrim coast isn't only about drama and legend. Beyond the folklore and basalt columns lie a smattering of **tempting beaches**, many of which are dog-friendly, with a few welcoming pets year-round. A 15-minute drive west of the Causeway is the fun little town of **Portrush**, where traditional seaside resort activities abound, from arcades to kids' rides on the seafront, to good old-fashioned sandcastle building on the beach. There are three beaches here: West Strand, East Strand and the vast Whiterocks, which is backed by white cliffs topped with tufts of rich green grass. Out of peak season, these beaches are some of the finest in County Antrim, with soft yellow sand perfect for picnicking on. But there are dog restrictions in Portrush (from June through to mid-September), so come peak summer you'll want to head east to **Ballycastle** (30 minutes' drive) for a year-round dog-friendly stretch.

The beach here is just over a kilometre of sugary sand where dogs can run free all year and you'll often spot locals fishing from the shoreline. There's a chippy in the marina nearby, making it a popular spot for a fish supper on the sand. The beach is north facing and looks out over the rugged **Rathlin Island** – if you've got a day or two here, it's well worth taking the short ferry journey over with the dog. The 7km-wide isle is a haven for seabirds, most of whom nest in the rocky outcrops at the western end of the island. Dogs aren't allowed in this part of the island as it's a nature reserve for nesting seabirds, but you might still see them elsewhere on its coastline. Head to the southern tip of the island for a gorgeous walk out to the black-and-white Rue Point Lighthouse. Look out for seals on the rocks around here. Dogs should be on leads at all times.

↑ Arty posing at the Giant's Causeway
← The waterfall trail at Glenariff

South of Ballycastle lies the Antrim Coast and Glens Area of Outstanding Natural Beauty, a region designated for protection thanks to its dramatic geology. Come here for the **Glenariff Nature Reserve waterfall walk**, a 3km circular route along boardwalks and footpaths that cross waterfalls, a deep gorge and through woodland with rare ferns and plump green liverwort (directions at walkni.com). Afterwards, take the 30-minute drive south to Glenarm Castle to explore the grounds around an imposing 17th-century castle. Here, you'll find an enclosed field for dogs to run free in, and a dog-friendly cafe where they'll get a well-earned puppuccino to finish.

Inland, *Game of Thrones* fans won't want to miss a wander down the iconic Dark Hedges filming location in Stranocum. Park at the Hedges Hotel and make your way on foot down the avenue of beech trees, whose curvy branches extend in all directions. It's especially atmospheric in summer when the trees are flourishing with greenery, creating a gloomy tunnel-like experience.

WHAT'S FOR DINNER?

Northern Ireland isn't quite like the rest of the UK when it comes to dog-friendly dining – it's just not as common here. However, pubs will often allow dogs in the bar area and they're also usually welcome to sit with you outside in beer gardens and cafes. It's all about comfort food here, and few dishes are as warming as the Ulster Fry – the Northern Irish fried breakfast that kicks off each day with bacon, sausage, egg, mushrooms, grilled tomato, black pudding, soda bread and potato bread. For something marginally lighter, a Belfast bap is an on-the-go alternative with bacon, sausage and egg inside.

Beyond breakfast, the highlight in County Antrim is the seafood. Look out for chowder and classic fish and chips on menus, and don't miss some tangy Irish oysters. All Irish food goes down well with a pint of Guinness, which is brewed just a couple of hours' drive south in Dublin, but for a Northern Irish beer try something by County Antrim's Hilden Brewery. The region is also home to the famous Bushmills Distillery, which has been making Irish whiskey for over 400 years.

WHERE TO SLEEP

Galgorm Resort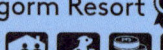

From £180 per night
galgorm.com

Blow your budget on a stay in this vast spa resort and you won't regret it. There are several accommodation options here for dog owners, including shepherd's huts overlooking the river as well as log cabins, forest dens and holiday cottages. Some sleep up to six and have their own kitchen facilities, and many come with their own private hot tubs for long soaks after a day spent walking the coast path. There are a handful of restaurants around the hotel, including The Barn where you can dine with the dog, and the Mulberry Garden; takeaway options are also available for those who prefer a private dining experience.

Forget the dog for a minute, though, as the highlight here is the huge thermal spa. This indoor-outdoor spa is vast, with whirlpools, hot and cold plunge pools, swimming pools and riverside tubs. There are several treatment rooms for massages, facials and scrubs, and a variety of intriguing salt grottos and scented steam rooms. If you can bear to leave the dog in your room for a few hours while you indulge, you'll be ready and raring to hit the coast path together again in no time.

Drum Gatelodge

£175
irishlandmark.com

Sleep inside a little slice of 19th-century history in this former gate lodge. Part of the Ballylough Estate, this small house was home to the workers from the estate, which was and still is owned by the Traill family. Set at the end of an avenue of lanky beech trees, it's in a beautifully remote location amid farm fields. It's a five-minute drive from the village of Bushmills and a 15-minute drive from the Giant's Causeway Visitor Centre. Inside it's decorated with period furniture and antiques, and has a small, well-equipped kitchen.

Marine Hotel Ballycastle

From £110 per night
marinehotelballycastle.com

Set right on the seafront in Ballycastle, this hotel offers probably the warmest welcome to dogs on the County Antrim coast. Not only will your dogs get plenty of fuss on arrival, but they'll also be able to order from their own menu in the restaurant. Humans can enjoy locally sourced seafood on the Marconi's Bistro menu, with crowd-pleasing favourites like steaks, chicken supreme and fish and chips, too. Bedrooms are contemporary, bright and airy, and many have glorious sea views.

↓ Gorse in flower on the coast of Northern Ireland

ESSENTIALS

Getting there: You'll need a car to get to the Giant's Causeway as public transport isn't extensive in this rural region of Northern Ireland. The closest ferry port to the Giant's Causeway is Belfast, which has direct ferries from Liverpool in England and Cairnryan in Scotland.

What to pack: A longline for the beaches might be a good bet to stop your dog from bothering children or picnickers who perhaps don't fancy a dog nose in their sandwiches.

The dog rules: Dogs are welcome to walk the coast path with you on a lead, but they won't be allowed on all the beaches throughout summer, so keep an eye out for signage.

Getting around: Driving is the best way to get around this region of Northern

↓ Arty on the beach in Ballycastle

Ireland, but there are some local bus services serving the coastal towns and dogs are allowed on board.

More information: There's visitor information at the Ballycastle marina and in Portrush Town Hall, but there's lots of detail online at visitcausewaycoastandglens.com.

MAKE IT A ROAD TRIP
If you're heading out to Northern Ireland, you might decide to pass through the Cotswolds (see page 252) on your way for a delectable diversion of home-grown produce and quaint, cosy pubs. Alternatively, take the ferry from Belfast to Cairnryan and explore some Scottish Islands (see page 272).

Where: Shetland and Orkney, Scotland
When: May–October
Best port of entry: Newcastle, England
Driving time from port of entry: 5 hrs (plus 14-hour ferry)

25

GO BEACH HOPPING IN THE SCOTTISH ISLANDS

It is without doubt that the UK has some of the most dog-friendly beaches in Europe. While in France, Spain, Portugal and Italy many beaches ban dogs throughout summer, the UK has a healthy proportion of coves and miles-long sandy stretches where dogs can run, play in the surf and catch some rays no matter the time of year.

While on the country's southern coastlines you'll find crowds of families lapping up the seaside fun throughout the summer season, on Scotland's islands it's all quite different. Here, where remote coves and sandy stretches aren't hard to come by, go to the right places and you will often find yourselves alone on a beach – even in June and July. For reactive dogs, this country is often a blissful escape from the busier regions further south, and heading all the way up to Shetland – the northernmost islands in the UK – owners of anxious dogs will find respite on relatively empty trails.

But there's more than just solitude to be sought out on Scotland's islands – the geology, birdlife, marine life and astonishing historical sites offer more reasons to get out and about with the dog. Great skuas, puffins, gannet colonies, elusive otters and whales may catch your eye, while sea stacks and ruined villages from prehistoric civilisations create a landscape of drama and intrigue. It's all best explored by car, so pack the dog in the back and hit the road using this dog-friendly itinerary.

Shetland

Scottish adventures rarely get more remote than a trip to Shetland – a 12-hour ferry journey and 177km from mainland Scotland, this archipelago of over a hundred islands is the northernmost part of the UK, with Muckle Flugga Lighthouse marking the very tip of the country on its own jagged rock just off the inhabited island of Unst.

The region's 22,000-strong population lives largely on the island of Shetland, the largest in the archipelago and home to the capital, **Lerwick**, where the ferry docks. Start here and you'll discover a small but creative little town, with plenty of dog-friendly pubs and restaurants (The New Harbour Cafe opposite the Albert Dock is a breakfast institution) and the 18th-century **Fort Charlotte** – an excellent place for a wander with the dog after the long ferry journey.

At the southern tip of mainland Shetland, a 35-minute drive from Lerwick, lies the **Sumburgh Head Lighthouse**, where puffins are often seen nesting in spring and summer and occasional orca sightings get visitors excited between April and September. It's here where you'll get your first experience of those white-sand beaches of which this archipelago has so many, plus a little Iron Age history. After visiting the lighthouse, head to **West Voe** just 3km away and let the dog loose on this clamshell-curved swathe as you look out for planes coming in to land at the Sumburgh Airport. Just over 500

↓ A lighthouse sculpture near Hermaness, Unst

↑ Skidbladner, the Viking longship replica on Unst

metres up the road lie the remains of **Old Scatness Broch** and its village, built over 2,200 years ago and now home to a small visitor centre.

Shetland is prime walking country and one of its finest strolls is around **St Ninian's Isle**, connected to the mainland with a sandspit lapped by iridescent turquoise waters that glisten with temptation on a warm day. A trail around 4km circumnavigates the island – there are often sheep roaming so dogs must be on leads – and you'll pass the ruins of 14th-century St Ninian's Chapel. Further north on Shetland's mainland, the **Eshaness circular walk** (start point at ///enforced.tailwind.burst; directions on shetland.org) is a three-hour hike filled with geological drama amid volcanic sea cliffs.

If you want true solitude in the Shetland archipelago, though, make your way up to **Unst** via the island of Yell (the western road on Yell is fastest, but the eastern one via Hamnavoe is more scenic) and base yourselves here for a few days. This is the UK's northernmost inhabited place and offers an opportunity to see the Muckle Flugga Lighthouse from the boardwalks and trails of **Hermaness Nature Reserve** (dogs on leads only), where puffins totter on the cliffs and great skuas (also known as bonxie) breed and nest from March through July – they can dive-bomb people and dogs if feeling threatened, so turn around if you sense their distress.

Unst's beaches are all white-sand and pleasingly few souls. From the Belmont car ferry terminal go west for the sands of **Lund Beach**, which is overlooked by the 12th-century St Olaf's Chapel, or eastwards for **Easting Beach** where you'll find Viking history in the form of a cemetery just north of the sand strip. If it's otter sightings you're after, head for **Westing Beach** – bring binoculars, a picnic and plenty of patience and you might just get lucky.

Further north in the village of Haroldswick, a small curve of sand sits next door to the Viking Unst Project's replica **Skidbladner ship and longhouse** reconstruction, offering insight into how the island transformed after the Vikings first landed here to conquer Britain. On your way up, don't miss a stop at **Bobby's Bus Shelter** on the A968, an unlikely popular attraction after a young boy campaigned for the local authority to build him a shelter from the rain so he could wait for the school bus in the dry. Locals filled it with furniture and two decades later is has curtains, a table, seating and decoration that changes regularly depending on the season. Don whatever is in the fancy dress box and take a picture with the dog in Bobby's honour.

WHAT'S FOR DINNER?

One of the joys of travelling around Shetland is the proliferation of honesty boxes on its islands. Get off the main roads and on to the quieter tracks and you'll no doubt spot ramshackle constructions – sometimes made of old pallets and rusty nails, or occasionally entire fridge-freezers left by the roadside – peddling local produce and wares. Expect to pick up local eggs and home-grown vegetables (and sometimes garden plants), and don't miss a visit to the Cake Fridge on the B9071 near

→ Coming into Lerwick Harbour on the ferry to Shetland

East Burrafirth on Unst for baked goods.

In pubs and restaurants, expect to find plenty of seafood and shellfish on the menu, with the usual suspects such as halibut and haddock and a few more unusual additions, like John Dory and pollack. Look out for Shetland black potatoes, too – they make a cracking roastie to go with Shetland lamb. Distilleries abound here, too – try the Shetland Reel Gin produced in Saxa Vord or the whisky from Lerwick Distillery.

Getting there & around

Overnight ferries for Lerwick, Shetland depart from Aberdeen daily with Northlink (northlinkferries.co.uk); the journey is around 12–13 hours and there are dog-friendly cabins available to book in advance. You'll arrive in Shetland by around 8am; getting around the archipelago is easy by car, with a combination of main and single-track roads and car ferries – booking in advance is possible but not always necessary unless travelling in peak season.

More information: There are several more enchanting islands to explore in Shetland and plenty more walks – get more intel at shetland.org/visit.

WHERE TO SLEEP

Shorehaven

From £120 per night
stay.shetland.org

Set inside the tiny storehouse that once belonged to the lighthouse shore station above it, this little self-catering cottage on Unst sits right on a boat slipway where otters can sometimes be seen rolling around in the surf. A short walk down the road and across some fields is the gorgeous Burrafirth Beach and its sheltered

bay – an idyllic spot for a summertime swim. The house is on a working croft, so the dog must be always kept under control due to nearby livestock. Dog bowls are provided and there will be baked goods for your indulgence on arrival, too.

Viewcliff

From £120 per night
airbnb.co.uk/rooms/51811370

Just a 10-minute drive from Lerwick, this Scalloway cottage is modern on the inside, surrounded by a handsome, mature, enclosed garden that's a suntrap in summer – ideal for dogs who need time off lead without worrying sheep. You'll have views over the harbour, Scalloway Castle and Clift Sound, and can enjoy spectacular walks on the Ness of Westshore to its lighthouse.

↑ An old coastguard hut on a hill in Shetland
← The rocky coastline around St Ninian's Isle in Shetland.

Orkney

The Orkney archipelago is only marginally less remote when compared with Shetland due to its proximity to the Scottish mainland – its southeastern corner sits just 10km across the North Sea from John O'Groats. But much like Shetland, its 70-odd isles feel like a faraway place and its landscapes often betray a mystical quality, bolstered by any sea mist that rolls in on a chillier day and the presence of some truly awe-inspiring Neolithic sites – some of the largest and best-preserved in the entire UK.

Coming from Shetland you'll make land in Kirkwall, the capital of mainland Orkney. There's little of interest here for dogs aside from a smattering of pet-friendly pubs, cafes and restaurants – and the **Orkney Distillery & Visitor Centre** (orkneydistilling.com), which allows dogs if you want to pop in for a wee dram – but it's a good place to stock up on supplies before you strike out for wilder corners of the islands. The closest beach to Kirkwall where dogs can enjoy time off lead is **Scapa**

Beach, a fine stretch of golden sand just a 10-minute drive from town. But head a little further southwest and seek out **Waulkmill Bay** (parking and toilets at ///buzzards.starlight.likes), a huge swathe of yellow sand that stretches 300 metres wide and 500 metre long when the tide is out, ensconced by high cliffs and a stream that flows down from the Loch of Kirbister. The beach is accessible via steps opposite the public toilets, but it disappears entirely when the tide comes in so check timings before you arrive.

For a beach that's easier to access and doesn't disappear under high tide, head all the way out west to **Skaill Beach** to find one of the best stretches of sand on the mainland – all soft white sand, blue surf and a shelf of large, flat pebbles that look made for skimming. This sheltered curve of sand is idyllic on a summer's day, but out of season during the cooler months this bay is often almost entirely empty, which seems criminal but feels magical when you find yourself alone on the sand. Let the dog run free, and when the tide goes out, discover a layered rocky seabed harbouring rock pools and marine life.

It's what's behind Skaill Beach that is most exciting, though: just beyond the sand dunes lies one of the most pristine prehistoric villages in Western Europe. **Skara Brae** (historicenvironment.scot) was first occupied over 5,000 years ago and eight of its houses remain visible today, furniture and all. The dog is welcome in the informative visitor centre and to walk around the site on a lead, where you can stand inside the single-room homes to see where people in 3,000 BCE slept, cooked and prepared their bait for a day's fishing. Pair this with a visit to 17th-century mansion **Skaill House** (skaillhouse.co.uk), which is dog-friendly inside and out.

Skara Brae is just one of several sites that has been awarded Orkney UNESCO World Heritage Status, as these islands are littered with sites from the Neolithic period, both domestic and ritualistic. A 20-minute drive from Skaill Beach and Skara Brae is the mighty **Ring of Brodgar**, a stone circle far larger than Stonehenge, once made up of 60 stones, with over 30 still standing today. There's an easy 3.5km wander to be enjoyed here from the car park (///archives.refutes.committed), around the stones and then along the shoreline of the Loch of Stenness (directions available on alltrails.com). The landscape surrounding Brodgar might look unassuming, perhaps even bleak at times, but beneath the surface lie several ancient cairns, burial chambers and settlements.

It's not just mainland Orkney that's blessed with such fascinating sights and pearly beaches – one of the joys of visiting here is the easy access to the archipelago's other islands. Four ports – Kirkwall, Houton, Stromness and Tingwall – on mainland Orkney offer access to 13 other communities. Beeline for Hoy to visit the region's most dramatic beach, **Rackwick**. A nearly 1km walk from the car park over fields, past an old bothy

↓ The beach near Skara Brae, Orkney

MAKE IT A ROAD TRIP
These islands are some of the most remote in this book, so while there's nowhere nearby to continue your journey in these pages, you can keep the adventure going by exploring part of the North Coast 500 route (take the ferry from Stromness to Scrabster and head east along the A836 for more stunning beaches and dramatic scenery). Dog-friendly tips for the NC500 route can be found in *Dog Days Out*, a guide to the UK by this same author.

and a quick scramble over the Rackwick Burn, this soft, sandy beach has one utterly spectacular feature: an imposing sandstone cliff at one end that lords it over the beach like a giant. Let the dog run free on the beach, then take the path from the car park towards Rora Head to wander over the hills and out to a viewpoint for the **Old Man of Hoy**, a 136-metre-high skinny sandstone sea stack that looks poised to topple at any moment.

Elsewhere, striking white sands can be found on **Westray** (Grobust is the local favourite), **Stronsay** (try Mill Bay), and on the causeway between **Burray and South Ronaldsay**.

WHAT'S FOR DINNER?

Seafood and shellfish are a mainstay on the menus of Orkney's restaurants, pubs and cafes, with salmon, **hand-dived scallops** and locally caught crab firm favourites. But there are a handful of intriguing delicacies from the land here, too, including lamb from the **seaweed-fed sheep** on North Ronaldsay and high-quality beef farmed throughout the archipelago. Whisky has its place here, too, and the distillery in Kirkwall is just the beginning for those arriving on the ferry. Sample Scapa's single malts, the smoky drams from Deerness, or try something completely different and seek out a bottle from the **UK's most northerly winery**, The Orkney Wine Company.

Getting there & around

You can reach Orkney with Northlink Ferries (northlinkferries.co.uk) from Lerwick in Shetland; it's a 5.5-hour journey and there are dog-friendly cabins available. Northlink also runs a service from Stromness, mainland Orkney, to Scrabster on the Scottish mainland, which takes 90 minutes; pre-book a spot in the pet lounge or leave the dog in the car. Getting around Orkney is easy by car, though many roads are single-lane outside of the more popular areas. Orkney Ferries (orkneyferries.co.uk) connects the islands with regular services from four ports on mainland Orkney.

More information: The VisitScotland Kirkwall iCentre (visitscotland.com) has maps and information on travelling in Orkney; online you can also get extensive guides to the islands at orkney.com.

WHERE TO SLEEP

Skaill House Apartments

From £750 per week
skaillhouse.co.uk

With Skaill Beach on your doorstep, Skara Brae next door and the gardens of Skaill House available for the dog to roam, you'd be forgiven for spending your entire Orkney stay right here. There are

just two apartments, so you'll probably get the beach to yourselves once the day trippers have headed off. Inside they're modern with fully kitted kitchens and cosy lounges with log burners or electric fires, plus Fairtrade, organic bed linens for luxurious sleeps.

Kirkwall Hotel

From £100 per night
kirkwallhotel.com

Set right on the harbour in Kirkwall, this hotel is a convenient base for being right in the action of Orkney's capital. Dogs are beloved here, with beds, treats and tennis balls in the rooms, plus a walking map for local trails. Dogs can dine with you in the bar at breakfast, lunch and dinner; note that dog-friendly stays must be booked by phone (+44 1856 872232) and there's no garden for toilet trips. You'll need to wander down to the Model Yacht Lake if your dog needs a patch of grass for its business.

ESSENTIALS

What to pack: Longlines can be helpful for beach days if your dog's recall isn't reliable, but don't use them in the nature reserves or near cliffs. For the cooler months, lean, short-haired dogs will likely need extra insulation.

The dog rules: It's almost impossible to state the importance of having your dog on a lead in most places in Shetland and Orkney. These islands not only have a healthy population of sheep, which can be spooked and harmed by dogs, but they are also havens for some of the UK's rarest plants and wildlife. Keeping your dog on a lead ensures they stick to footpaths with you and cannot harm livestock or wildlife. Bring a longline for beaches where sheep graze nearby, and only let them run free if you're confident they cannot cause harm.

↑ Colourful shells found on an Orkney beach
→ Arty posing at Skara Brae ruins, Orkney

Colorado Provençal – the
    Terracotta Trails 223–4
  dog rules 230
  food and drink 226, 228
  Forêt des Cèdres – Cedar-
    scented Trails 225
  getting there and getting
    around 230
  Pont Julien 226, 228, 230
  Roussillon 224, 226
  Village de Bories 228
  where to sleep 229–30
Northern France
  Baie de Somme 26, 31
  beaches 26, 27, 29–30
  Berck-sur-Mer 29–30
  Boulogne-sur-Mer 27–8, 32
  Calais 26–7, 32, 34
  Côte d'Opale 26, 45
  dog rules 34
  food and drink 31
  getting there and getting
    around 34
  Le Touquet 28–9
  Montreuil 31
  Pas-de-Calais 26, 30, 31
  Saint-Valery 31
  where to sleep 32–3

Germany
  Baltic Coast 127
    dog rules 187
    food and drink 185
    getting there and getting
      around 187–8
    Heringsdorf 182–3
    Kamminke 184
    Usedom 184
    where to sleep 187
    Wolgastsee 184
  beaches and lakes 124, 132,
    182–3, 184
  Berlin
    bespoke dog-friendly walking
      tours 120, 123
    dog-friendly River Spree boat
      trip 123
    dog rules 126
    food and drink 125
    getting there and getting
      around 126
    recommended
      accommodation 125–6
    Grunewald 124
    Harz Mountains 52, 88–97,
      127, 139

  Bad Grund 93
    dog rules 96
    food and drink 94
    getting there and getting
      around 96
    Harz Railway 90, 92
    Schulenberg 93–4
    where to sleep 95–6
  Potsdam 124
  Saxony 127, 130–9
    Dresden 134–5
    food and drink 132, 134, 137
    getting there and getting
      around 138
    lakes and beaches 132
    Leipzig 130–3
    Saxon-Switzerland National
      Park 135–7
    where to sleep 132–3, 135, 138

hiking
  the Dolomites, Italy 234
  Douro Valley, Spain 153
  Dresden, East Germany 134
  the Hague, the Netherlands 49
  Harz Mountains, Germany 88–90
  Luberon Regional Park, France
    223–5, 228
  Montserrat, Spain 166
  Morzine, France 207
  Parque Natural da Serra de São
    Mamede, Portugal 142, 144, 146
  San Sebastián, Spain 60
  Saxon-Switzerland National
    Park 135–7
  Scottish Islands, United
    Kingdom 276
  Waldspitz, Switzerland 214
  Wallonia, Belgium 81
hot weather 20, 22, 168, 179, 250

Italy
  dog culture 15
  the Dolomites 234–41, 251
    Alta Badia 236–7
    Bolzano 234–5, 237
    dog rules 241
    food and drink 236–7, 238
    getting there and getting
      around 241
    where to sleep 238–40
  Venice 240, 244–51
    dog rules 250
    food and drink 248
    getting there and getting
      around 250

  Isola della Certosa 245–6
  Lido beach resort 245
  Murano and Burano 245, 248
  museums and landmarks
    246–8
  overtourism 249–50
  where to stay 249

kayaking and canoeing 81, 132

language barriers 9–10
Le Pet Express 16
leads and harnesses 21, 22
LeShuttle car train 16

museums and tourist attractions,
  dog-friendly
  Casa Batlló, Barcelona 162
  castells, Catalunya, Spain 102
  Charlottenburg shopping, Berlin,
    Germany 123
  Château de Bioul, Belgium 81
  châteaux, France 68–70
  Cotswold Wildlife Park, England
    257
  Ferris wheel, Montreux 196
  Giant's Causeway Visitor Centre,
    Northern Ireland 264
  La Roche-en-Ardenne, Belgium
    81–2
  Orkney Distillery & Visitor
    Centre 279
  Petit Train d'Aigues-Mortes,
    France 113
  Poble Espanyol, Barcelona 165–6
  Prinsestraat shopping, The
    Hague, the Netherlands 50–1
  Regenstein Castle, Germany 90
  Tetbury Police Museum,
    England 254
  Van Kleef Museum, the
    Netherlands 50
  see also beaches; parks, gardens
    and woodlands; walking tours;
    wine tasting and vineyards
muzzles 16, 18

the Netherlands
  beaches 48–9
  dog culture 15
  dog-friendly shopping 50–1
  dog rules 53
  food and drink 51
  getting there and getting
    around 53
  Gouda 51

INDEX

INDEX

accommodation etiquette 19
archaeological sites
  Alentejo, Portugal 142, 144
  Brittany, France 42
  Catalunya, Spain 103–4, 178
  Costa Brava, Spain 174
  Scottish Islands, United Kingdom 274, 276, 280

beaches
  Baltic Coast, Germany 127, 182–3
  Barcelona, Spain 166
  Brittany, France 39, 42
  Camargue, France 114–15
  Costa Brava, Spain 169, 172–9
  County Antrim, Northern Ireland 267
  Grunewald, Germany 124
  the Hague, the Netherlands 48–9
  Northern France 26, 27, 29–30
  San Sebastián, Spain 60
  Scottish Islands, United Kingdom 274, 276, 280–1
  Tarragona, Spain 103
  Venice, Italy 245
beds and bedding, dog 19
Belgium
  dog culture 15
  Wallonia 35, 52, 78–85
    Dinant 78, 80–1
    dog rules 85
    food and drink 80–1, 82
    getting there and getting around 85
    La Roche-en-Ardenne 81–2
    Nisramont Lake 81
    where to sleep 83–4
boat trips
  Camargue, Southern France 110–17
  Costa Brava, Spain 175
  Dinant, Belgium 81
  Dresden, East Germany 134
  the Hague, the Netherlands 50
  Interlaken, Switzerland 214

Leipzig, Germany 131
Montreux, Switzerland 197
Pinhão, Spain 153
Potsdam, Germany 124
River Spree, Berlin, Germany 123
Schulenberg, Germany 93–4
Sept Isles, Brittany, France 40
Usedom, Germany 184
Venice, Italy 244–5

camping with dogs 20
caves
  Grottes de Han, Wallonia 82
  Sandhöhlen caves, Harz Mountains 90
  Vallèe Trogloditique Goupillières 73
Channel, crossing the English 17
Christmas markets 192–4, 196–7, 198, 208
coastal walks
  Brittany, France 39, 42
  Giant's Causeway, Northern Ireland 264
  The Hague, the Netherlands 48–9
  Northern France 29–30
  see also beaches
cold weather 200, 209, 218
culture, differences in dog 15
cycling 49, 116, 143–4, 228

driving abroad 18

etiquette, accommodation 19

ferry services 17
fleas and ticks 15–16
France
  the Alps 202–9
    dog rules 209
    food and drink 206, 207–8
    getting there and getting around 209
    Morzine 201, 204, 206, 219

    where to sleep 208–9
    winter sports 204, 206, 219
  Brittany 35, 38
    beaches 39, 42
    dog rules 44
    food and drink 43
    getting there and getting around 44
    Île Callot 39, 42
    Île de Batz 39
    Roscoff 41–2
    Sept Îles 40
    where to sleep 43–4
  Camargue 63, 110–17, 169, 178, 231
    Aigues-Mortes 113
    beaches 114–15
    boat hire 115–16
    Carnon 114
    dog rules 117
    food and drink 113, 115
    Frontignan 115
    Gallician 113
    La Grande-Motte 113–14
    Maguelone 115
    Palavas-les-Flots 114–15
  dog culture 15
  Loire Valley 45
    Touraine region 66–75
    Amboise 73
    dog-friendly châteaux 68–70
    dog-friendly wine and beer experiences 71–2, 73
    dog rules 75
    food and drink 71–2, 73
    getting there and getting around 75
    Île de la Métairie 73
    where to sleep 74–5
  Luberon Regional Park 222–30
    Apt 117, 222, 226
    Aureto 226
    Claparèdes plateau – the Lilac Ways 224

← Arty at Château du Clos Lucé

The Hague 48–50
Keukenhof tulip fields 51
where to sleep 51, 53
Northern Ireland 261
  County Antrim 264–71
    Ballycastle 267
    beaches 267
    dog rules 270
    food and drink 268
    getting there and getting around 270–1
    Giant's Causeway 264
    Glenariff Nature Reserve 267
    Portrush 267
    Rathlin Island 267
    where to sleep 268–9

packing for your dog 21
parks, gardens and woodlands
  Baltic Coast, Germany 184
  Berlin, Germany 123, 124
  Brittany, France 39, 42
  Calais, France 27
  Cheltenham, England 256
  the Dolomites, Italy 234–6
  Dresden, Germany 134
  Faia Brava nature reserve, Spain 154–5
  Glenariff Nature Reserve, Northern Ireland 267
  Grunewald forest, Germany 124
  the Hague, the Netherlands 50
  Lausanne, Switzerland 194
  Le Touquet, France 28–9
  Leipzig, Germany 131
  Luberon Regional Park, France 222–3
  Morzine, France 206–7
  Palamós, Spain 173
  Parc Güell, Barcelona, Spain 164–5
  Parque Natural da Serra de São Mamede, Portugal 142, 144, 146
  Potsdam, Germany 124
  Saxon-Switzerland National Park 135–7
  Tours, France 72–3
  Venice, Italy 244, 245–6
  Wallonia, Belgium 81
  WeltWald arboretum, Germany 93
  Westonbirt Arboretum, Cotswolds 254, 256
  see also hiking
pests 15–16
phrasebook 23
poo, picking up 22

Portugal 16
  Alentejo 142–9, 159
    Castelo de Vide 144
    dog culture 15
    dog rules 148–9
    food and drink 144, 146
    getting there and getting around 148–9
    Marvão 142–4
    Parque Natural da Serra de São Mamede 142–9
    where to sleep 146–8
  Angeiras beach 156

safety for dogs abroad
  cold weather 200, 209, 218
  hot weather 20, 22, 168, 179, 250
  pests 15–16
sandflies 16
Scottish Islands 261, 274
  beaches 274, 276, 279–81
  dog rules 282
  food and drink 276, 278, 281
  getting there and getting around 278, 281
  Orkney 279–81
  Shetland 275–6, 278–9
  Skara Brae 280
  where to sleep 278–9, 281–2
snowshoeing 204
Spain
  Barcelona 63, 105, 162–9
    beaches 166
    dog rules 168
    food and drink 164, 166
    Gaudí architecture 162, 164–5
    getting there and getting around 166–7
    overtourism 168
    Poble Espanyol open-air museum 165–6
    where to sleep 166–7
  Catalunya 102–7
    castells 100, 102, 103, 104, 107, 169
    dog rules 107
    food and drink 104–5
    getting there and getting around 107
    recommended accommodation 106
    Tarragona 100, 102–4, 169, 178
    Valls 104
    Vilafranca 104
  Costa Brava 169, 172–9
    beaches 172, 231

  Platja de la Ribera & Platja del Port de la Vall, El Port de la Selva 175
  Platja de la Rubina, Empuriabrava 175
  Platja de l'Estartit, L'Estartit 174
  Platja de Sant Antoni, Palamós 173
  Platja del Rec, L'Escala 174
  dog rules 179
  food and drink 176
  getting there and getting around 179
  Girona 175–6
  where to sleep 177
Douro Valley 152–9
  Casal de Loivos 152
  dog rules 158
  Douro Superior 154–5
  food and drink 152, 153–4, 156–7
  getting there and getting around 158
  Pinhão 153–4
  Porto 156, 157
  where to sleep 157–8
San Sebastián 56, 58–9, 117, 149, 178
  beaches 60
  dog rules 62
  getting around 62
  recommended accommodation 61–2
Spanish dog culture 15
steam trains and ships
  Baie de Somme Railway 31
  Dresden, East Germany 134
  Gloucestershire Warwickshire Steam Railway, England 256
  Harz Railway, Germany 90, 92
  Potsdam, Germany 124
Switzerland
  dog culture 15
  Grindelwald
    dog rules 218
    Eiger Express and Jungfrau Railway 212, 214
    First Cliff Walk and zipline 214
    food and drink 215
    getting there and getting around 218
    where to sleep 215, 217
  Interlaken 214
  Jungfrau 201, 212, 214
  Lake Geneva
    Christmas markets 192–4,

INDEX

196–7, 198, 208, 219
dog rules 200
food and drink 193–4, 196, 198
getting there and getting around 200
Lausanne 192, 193–4, 219
Montreux 192, 196–7, 219
where to sleep 198–9
Waldspitz 214
Wengen 214

ticks and fleas 15–16
toileting, dog 19, 20, 22
train travel 18
see also steam trains and ships

United Kingdom
 the Cotswolds 254–61, 271
  Burford 256–7
  Cheltenham 256
  Chipping Norton 257–8
  dog-friendly shopping 256–7
  dog rules 260
  food and drink 257–9
  getting there and getting around 260
  Tetbury 254–5
  where to sleep 259–60

walking tours
 Bad Grund, Germany 93
 Berlin, Germany 120
 Bolzano, Italy 237
 Boulogne-sur-Mer, France 28

Calais, France 27
Carnon, Camargue, France 114
Château de Lavaux-Sainte-Anne, Belgium 82
Explore Iberia, Spain 155
FarmEd, Daylesford, England 258
Girona, Costa Brava 176
Heringsdorf, Germany 182
Lausanne, Switzerland 194
Porto, Spain 156
Roscoff, France 41
San Sebastián, Spain 60
Tours, France 72
water, dog drinking 21
water sports 81, 114–15, 132
wildlife
 Alentejo, Portugal 142
 the Alps, France 204
 County Antrim, Northern Ireland 267
 Faia Brava nature reserve, Spain 154–5
 Harz Mountains, Germany 88
 and livestock protection 22
 Meijendel nature reserve, the Netherlands 49
 Scottish Islands, United Kingdom 274
 Sept Îles boat trip, Brittany 40
wine tasting and vineyards
 Bolzano, Italy 237
 Château de Bioul, Belgium 81
 the Dolomites, Italy 237
 Douro, Portugal 152, 153, 154, 156

Dresden, East Germany 134
Gallician Signature wine cooperative, France 113
Mont Rubí, Mastinell and Parés Baltà, Spain 105
Provence, France 226
Touraine, France 71–2
Vilafranca, Spain 104
winter sports 204, 206, 214

Photo Credits

All photos belong to the author with the exception of:

Adobe Stock: 35, 110–11, 213, 216, 218–19

Christian-Hüller, Courtesy of Leipzig Travel: 122
Back-Packer.org, Courtesy of Leipzig Travel: 123 (bottom)

JC Coutand, Courtesy of ADT Touraine: 72